Multiplication and Division Facts for the Whole-to-Part, Visual Learner:

AN ACTIVITY–BASED GUIDE TO DEVELOP FLUENCY WITH MATH FACTS

Christopher L. Woodin, Ed. M.
2013

Acknowledgement and Dedication

Writing a book is not a process that is done alone. Throughout the process of writing this book, my family and many individuals from the Landmark community have taken time out to help. I am grateful to Dan Ahearn who continually and convincingly conveyed a spirit of productivity, as well as the Ammerman family for their ongoing generosity and encouragement. I'd like to give a special thanks to Anna DiPerna who provided valuable editorial guidance, feedback and contributions, persistence, and patience throughout the writing process.

Many of the ideas and methodologies presented in this book diverge from convention. It is with similar intent that these innovative techniques empower creative students to emerge as hooves from the hoof prints of traditional instruction.

The information and educational interventions presented in this book are for classroom use and should not be construed as substitutions or replacements for evaluations and recommendations from physicians, psychologists, or neuropsychologists.

Copyright © 2013 Christopher L. Woodin and Landmark School Outreach Program

PO Box 227

Prides Crossing, MA 01965

landmarkoutreach.org

All rights reserved. Unless it is for classroom use with students, this book may not be reproduced, in whole or in part, including illustrations, figures, tables, and photographs in any form without written permission from the publishers.

ISBN 978-0-9713297-6-8

Printed in the United States of America.

To reference this publication, please use the following citation: Woodin, C. L. (2013). *Multiplication and division facts for the whole-to-part, visual learner: An activity-based guide to develop fluency with math facts.* Prides Crossing, MA: Landmark School Outreach Program.

Contents

5	Principles of Quality, Student-Centered Instruction
7	Overview
8	Math Facts are Necessary
9	Strategies for Teaching Multiplication and Division Facts
12	The Student Math Fact Notebook
13	Readiness Skills for Multidigit Number Processing
20	Order Of Fact Family Instruction
22	Facts That I Know Motivational Poster
23	Whole-to Part 2× Multiplication
28	Finger Stamping 2× Facts
37	Part-to Whole Practice for 2× Facts
43	Standardized Methodology to Introduce the Pattern-Based Fact Families
44	0 - 100 Chart
53	**Define Length, Width, and Area Using Multimodal Cues**
58	Multiplication Grid Area Model
64	Use Semantic Associations to Teach Fact-Based Word Problems
72	Solving Word Problems Involving Multiplication and Division Facts
79	Rehearsal Techniques and Activities to Teach Fact Families
80	Use Gross Motor Kinesthetic Practice to Drive Integrated Fact Production
86	Dry Erase Flash Card Fact Production Template
93	Accuracy Benchmark Pretests and Fluency Assessment Worksheets
100	Baseball Fact Game
104	The 5× Fact Family
110	Introduction to the 5× Whole-to-Part Multiplication Facts
143	The 10× Fact Family
174	The 1× and 0× Families
180	Introduction to Multidigit Multiplication
223	The 9 × Fact Family
257	The 3× Fact Family
283	The 6× Fact Family
302	The Perfect Squares
311	The 4× Fact Family
331	The 7× Fact Family
339	Ladder Charts: A Function of the Distributive Property and the Fibonacci Sequence
353	The 8× Fact Family
363	The 11x and 12x Facts
366	Appendix 1, Templates for Multidigit Multiplication
377	Appendix 2, Multiplication Grid (12 × 12)
378	Appendix 3, Instructional Video References with QR Codes
379	References

© 2013 C. Woodin & Landmark School

Principles of Quality, Student-Centered Instruction
LANDMARK'S SIX TEACHING PRINCIPLES™

The Landmark School was founded in 1971 to provide structured, success-oriented instruction to students with learning disabilities. For more than forty years, Landmark teachers have continually enhanced and refined teaching strategies to help students learn more effectively. All of the teaching methods have been developed, tested, and proven effective in Landmark classrooms. Landmark has shared its teaching strategies with public and private school teachers from all over the world through seminars, Landmark-sponsored graduate-level courses, national education conferences, and school workshops and partnerships. All students can and do learn from Landmark's structured and success-oriented instructional models. At the heart of Landmark's instructional strategies and programs are six teaching principles.

Provide Opportunities for Success

Providing students with opportunities for success is key. Failure and poor self-esteem often result when teachers challenge students beyond students' abilities. Landmark begins teaching students at their current levels of ability. This approach improves basic skills and enhances confidence. As Landmark teachers introduce each new skill, they provide basic examples and assignments to build confidence and keep students from becoming overwhelmed. As the information becomes more challenging, teachers assign students easier problems to supplement the more difficult ones. In this way, students who are having trouble with the material complete at least part of the assignment while they work at understanding and learning to apply new information. Teachers give themselves permission to provide students with whatever structure is necessary to help students be successful, such as study guides for tests, templates for writing, and guidelines for projects. Only with a solid foundation of basic skills and confidence can students make progress.

Use Multisensory Approaches

Multisensory teaching is effective for all students. In general, a multisensory approach involves presenting all information to students via four sensory modalities: visual, auditory, tactile, and kinesthetic.

- Visual presentation techniques include using graphic organizers for structuring writing and pictures for reinforcing instruction.
- Auditory presentation techniques include conducting thorough discussions and reading aloud.
- Tactile presentation techniques include using manipulatives that students can hold in their hands.
- Kinesthetic activities involve gross motor processing of material that is usually relegated to paper and pencil, allowing some students to learn without the encumbrances of visual-motor integration issues.

Overall, implementing a multisensory approach to teaching is not difficult; in fact, many teachers use such an approach naturally in their teaching. It is important, however, to be aware of these four sensory modes and to plan to integrate them every day.

Micro-Unit and Structure Tasks

Effective teaching involves breaking down information into its smallest units and providing clear guidelines for all assignments. This is especially important for students with learning disabilities.

"Micro-uniting" and structuring are elements of directive teaching, an approach Landmark consistently uses with students. Micro-uniting means analyzing the parts of a task or assignment and teaching those parts one step at a time. Teachers organize information so students can see and follow the steps clearly and sequentially. As students learn to micro-unit for themselves, they become less likely to give up on tasks that appear confusing or overwhelming. Consequently, these strategies enable students to proceed in a step-by-step, success-oriented way.

Your school's math department or the teacher's edition of your basal text likely has a scope and sequence chart or a set of long-range goals for your class or student. This hierarchic list of skills is usually too general for a diagnostic planning guide. Break down these goals into microunits and add the substrates to that hierarchic list. Then teach one microunit at a time until the student achieves mastery.

Avoid or adapt curricula that expose students to new concepts before they have achieved a complete understanding of preceding material. Many textbooks give a cursory introduction to a subject, provide minimal opportunities to assimilate it, and then abandon it until the next year, when it is studied at a higher level of complexity. Many students fail to make significant gains with this approach. The material is never mastered or retained long enough to serve as a foundation the following year.

Ensure Automatization through Practice and Review

Automatization is the process of learning and assimilating a task or skill so completely that it can be consistently completed with little or no conscious attention. Repetition and review (spiraling) are critical to achieving automatization. Sometimes students appear to understand a concept, only to forget it a day, week, or month later. It is not until students have automatized a skill that they can effectively remember and use it as a foundation for new tasks. Teachers must therefore provide ample opportunities for students to repeat and review learned material. For example, Landmark math homework is composed of previously learned skills for the student to practice. This approach provides students with an ongoing, consistent review of learned skills.

Provide Models

Providing models is simple, yet very important. It is one of the most effective teaching techniques. Models are concrete examples of a concept or procedure. Teachers first provide students with concrete models and then ask students to produce semiconcrete diagrams. Students then apply conceptual models to abstract procedures. Ultimately, the students should be able to reproduce the teacher's actions, producing concrete models to illustrate abstract procedures.

For example, the area of a 3 × 2 rectangle could be represented by 6 square tiles arranged in the shape of a rectangle on a desk (a concrete model). Students could then use the concrete model to draw a proportional diagram of the model (semiconcrete diagram). Finally, students would generate a standardized matrix diagram to represent the same information (see fig. 1):

FIGURE 1.

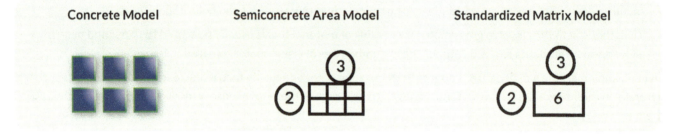

Include Students in the Learning Process

Students are not passive receptacles to fill with information. They come to class with their own frames of reference. Their unique experiences and knowledge affect them as learners and should be taken into account. Therefore, during every exercise, teachers accept student input as much as possible. Teachers justify assignments, accept suggestions, solicit ideas, and provide ample time for students to share ideas. Teachers include students in assessing their progress by reviewing test results, written reports, and educational plans. Creating and improvising opportunities to involve students in the learning process allows students to become aware of how they learn and why certain skills benefit them. As a result, students are motivated and more likely to apply those skills when working independently. In short, an included student becomes an invested student who is eager to learn.

OVERVIEW

Multiplication and Division Facts for the Whole-to-Part, Visual Learner
AN ACTIVITY-BASED GUIDE TO DEVELOPING FLUENCY WITH MATH FACTS

Students must know multiplication facts in order to multiply and divide multidigit numbers and to perform fraction operations. The application of this factual knowledge base demands that these facts be available in both multiplication and division format, and that these facts be organized in a relational context so that students may order and compare them. The purpose of this program is to provide students with a way to store, access, and communicate information about multiplication and division facts. The methodology presented supports various learning styles and culminates with students being able to learn, compare, and express math facts accurately and fluently.

Whole-to-Part Processing Models

It is easier to acknowledge the elements of a recognizable whole than it is to create a whole from a large number of discrete elements. A methodology based on this concept is powerful for all students—and for some, necessary. Whole-to-part processing models provide structure that can compensate for deficits in working memory, expressive language mechanisms, and executive function. Pictures or images of familiar objects present a great deal of information within a bundled package, or gestalt. These visual models are useful in that they provide learners with a means of retaining information long enough to name, organize, and describe the component parts within the context of the whole. For example, when assembling a toy, some people find it useful to ignore the part-to-whole written directions. Instead, they choose to look at the picture of the completed toy on the front of the box and manipulate the components until they have matched the picture. After the toy has been assembled, these people may use episodic memory to document the part-to-whole assembly process. Whole-to-part processing models are particularly effective for students with auditory working memory limitations.

Motor Memory

The most effective method of teaching number facts is to use as many modalities as possible. Motor memory is one of the strongest and most primal memory retrieval systems. Children develop and refine gross motor movement patterns at an early age. People use these learned motor patterns throughout life to walk while talking, ride a bike while looking in store windows, and sign their names in the dark. Motor memory is a powerful ally when children are learning to use graphic organizers that prompt the accurate expression of facts. This therapy is especially valuable to those students with language-based deficits.

Semantic Memory Associations

Efficient learning takes place when students link new information to related familiar information. When this occurs, students access the new information using existing contextual cues. Effective teaching links multiplication concepts and facts to students' existing knowledge base across a broad spectrum of modalities. Drawing on students' experiential knowledge can help them develop a robust understanding of multiplication and division facts and processes.

To develop facility with multiplication and division facts, students must develop meaningful associations between number facts and important events or objects in their lives. Number facts that are learned and practiced within the context of common applications become more useful. For example, teaching the 5× and 10× facts within the context of coin or minute values provides a vehicle for students to learn these facts in a relational context while also developing an important skill base with time and money. By establishing a strong conceptual base, students are able to learn, store, and retrieve information accurately and apply it efficiently to solve problems.

Math Facts Are Necessary

Learn the Basic Facts

A student with learning disabilities who can use and refine oral language can be taught to remember and recite the majority of the multiplication facts. Students who are fluent in their native oral language possess the necessary skills to form complete English sentences. Consequently, they can create and automatize complete mathematical sentences, such as 2 × 3 = 6. Almost all students can learn to recite common multiplication facts. As you teach, however, you must take care to ensure that students are developing a deep, relational understanding of accurate factual knowledge. Math facts are of limited value unless applied to a process or situation. Students should develop factual knowledge within the context of everyday life. Students should also be able to recognize factual knowledge as it is represented in various forms and modalities, readily accessing and applying factual knowledge to various situations.

Advocating the automatization of basic multiplication facts seems to emphasize a weakness rather than a cognition-based strength. Consider, however, the memorization of common sight words. When recognition of these words becomes automatic, reading fluency takes a quantum leap. Similarly, math literacy is so enhanced by automatization of multiplication and division facts that the end justifies the means.

Automatization of multiplication and division facts is a daunting challenge for some, yet indispensable for all. Students who fail to master the multiplication tables risk limiting their mathematical potential. Without a working understanding of these facts, students' ability to perform multidigit multiplication and division is compromised. Consequently, students lose firsthand experience with large numbers. Complex operations involving fractions and simple algebraic equations become overwhelming. Students take longer to understand and master higher-order operations because sequential steps are fragmented by intermittent searches for relevant math facts. Like a mason building a chimney without an accessible supply of bricks, students must descend and then rescale the ladder of math skills to retrieve each individual brick experience, which is inefficient and frustrating. Clearly, it is better to provide students with a full cache of readily available facts, just as one would supply the mason with a full tote of bricks. Even if a student needs to learn a somewhat elaborate strategy to compute a fact, he or she will eventually develop fluency through rehearsal. When these facts are not readily accessible, algorithms that should be fluid, thought provoking learning situations are interrupted and reduced to strings of isolated tasks that provide little understanding of the process being addressed.

Clearly, some students take longer than others to automatize facts. In most cases, students simply need sufficient exposure to the material through some form of rehearsal exercise. Many students attain reasonable proficiency through repeated oral or written drills and practice with the correct facts. For some students, however, more exposure to the same type of input is less effective. These students need to receive the input in different, more salient ways to process it in a useful and dynamic manner. They need to have instruction tailored to their strongest modality preferences in a manner that makes the best use of their abilities.

Providing students with a verbal answer, calculator, or multiplication table may be a way to arrive at a static solution, but these bypass strategies may do little to make headway toward fact learning. Providing students who have language-based learning disabilities (LBLD) with a multiplication product without having them explicitly pair and rehearse it with its determining two factors does little to reinforce the relationship between factors and product. Students learn multiplication facts more efficiently when they rehearse the facts in their entirety: 6 × 8 = 48. Students learn even more effectively when they are asked to reconfigure facts and express them in dynamic ways: 8 × 6 = 48 or 48 ÷ 6 = 8.

Teach Facts Efficiently

Some students have profound difficulty with automatization. Strive to provide a working understanding of the commutative property of multiplication (3 × 2 = 2 × 3) and memorization of the 1, 2, 5, 9, and 10 fact families. Automatizing these five fact families accounts for 75 of the 100 hundred squares on a 10 × 10 multiplication grid.

A working knowledge of these seventy-five basic facts enables students to devote time to learning higher-level processes while continuing to learn the twenty-five remaining facts.

Although total automatization of the entire multiplication grid is possible for all students, this fact is analogous to the notion that anyone could walk any distance given enough time and determination. At some point, intensive fact training must give way to the development of higher-level processes that apply these facts. Regardless, a slow automatization rate is not an excuse to abandon the fact-learning process. The benefits of a rich, automatic, dynamic fact base are worth a hard-fought battle.

Strategies for Teaching Multiplication and Division Facts

Instructional Videos are Available

Many of the activities and techniques presented in this book are presented in movie format for your convenience. They are located in Appendix 2 and they have URL links, as well as QR codes that can be scanned with a smart phone to activate these YouTube videos.

Pattern Recognition: Append Structure to the Guessing Game

Efficient learners make implicit generalizations on the basis of consistencies in spelling and language syntax patterns. They internalize and generalize these patterns to facilitate the spelling of similar unfamiliar words and the creation of novel sentences. Inconsistencies or nonroutine spelling patterns (sight words) necessitate slower, word-specific learning. Students must resort to less-efficient rote learning strategies to learn these words.

For example, Terri is a poor reader. She has not learned that a vowel is short (that is, does not say its own name) when sandwiched between two consonants (consonant-vowel-consonant). As a result, Terri correctly pronounces some familiar words that follow this pattern, but she misreads others. For example, she may misread "The dog and the cat sat on a hat by a log" as "The dog and the cat sat on a hate by a loge."

Robbie has difficulty remembering her multiplication facts. She has not learned that all multiples of 2 are even numbers—the products should always end with 0, 2, 4, 6, or 8. She responds with correct products for the facts that she is familiar with, yet fails to produce acceptable products for others:

$$2 \times 2 = 4, \quad 2 \times 3 = 6, \quad 2 \times 4 = 8, \quad 2 \times 7 = 17, \quad \text{and } 2 \times 9 = 21.$$

Notice that Robbie probably arrived at $2 \times 7 = 17$ through inaccurate counting or by perseverating on the 7 to such a degree that she included it in the product. She then found $2 \times 9 = 21$ by adding two more 2s. If she understood the pattern associated with the 2× fact family, she would have rejected the two erroneous responses.

Without explicit instruction and guidance, students with learning disabilities have difficulty making accurate generalizations and then recognizing and retaining these general patterns. Attempting to memorize isolated multiplication facts with no ordering structure is analogous to learning to spell all words as sight words. These students may see the elements in equations as discrete units instead of sentences that can be manipulated within constraints. When students lack pattern sense, spelling or producing a multiplication product becomes a guessing game that often results in failure. Students may not see the consistencies evident in each fact family and may therefore treat number facts as unrelated. Patterns must be identified and explained to these students so that they can begin to impose order on the way they view the language of mathematics. Once students see these patterns, the patterns must be reinforced until automatized.

Effective pattern recognition provides the student with a subset of possible answers. This subset shrinks as the student further internalizes other math facts and math patterns, much as developing linguistic awareness molds invented spelling in young learners. With a smaller subset of possible answers, a student becomes more likely to select the correct one. Errant guesses are replaced by systematic methods that enable thoughtful, and usually correct, responses.

Correct Paired Associations

Automatization is the process through which learned information becomes accessible from memory nearly instantly—recall requires minimal effort. Automatizing basic math facts involves the pairing of two distinct pieces of information in long-term memory so that the presentation of one piece (stimulus) immediately elicits the other (response). The pairing, such as a word and its definition or factors and their product, is achieved by repeatedly linking the pieces of information. The rate of automatization is affected by the frequency and consistency of the pairings. If the student does not rehearse the pairing enough, or if the integrity of the pairing is compromised through an association with errant information, the automatization process is hampered. Teachers must intervene to prevent students from rehearsing an incorrect pairing.

Consider the following example: After receiving poor directions to someone's house and taking a wrong turn, you discover your mistake, retrace your path, and reach your destination. The next time you drive to the same place, you make the wrong turn again, quickly realize your mistake, and retrace your route to arrive at the correct location. You were predisposed to take the errant turn because you rehearsed this pathway and partially automatized the route. Your body followed this route kinesthetically. You made associations along the route, linking, for example, visual landmarks and auditory stimuli from a construction site. You may even have developed semantic associations between street names and points on the route.

Let's say you took a wrong left turn onto Campbell Avenue, and remembered that Bob Campbell sat on your left in high school chemistry class. That association may be triggered the next time you reach the intersection with Campbell and may influence your decision to take the same wrong turn again! All of these impressions compete with your ability to make the correct turn.

Such is the case with the partial automatization of errant math facts. Errant facts interfere with the learning process in that they make the student choose between competing possible responses rather than expressing a complete fact in a fluent manner. This is especially true if a student is learning facts through rote memorization, because the student will lack the ability to analyze the appropriateness of a response.

To achieve effective automatization, teachers should provide students with a way to produce accurate facts, and then have students work on expressing the facts in an increasingly efficient manner. The most effective processing strategy demonstrates an accurate paradigm that explains the nature of multiplication. Teachers should exploit the consistencies inherent in the mathematics language to explain the multiplication and division facts and should never sacrifice accuracy in the name of producing a rapid response.

Flash Cards

Traditionally, flash cards have been used to teach facts through drills that encourage a student to identify a product on the basis of its two factors (for example, $6 \times 4 =$). The student is expected to produce the product from memory, a process that represents a part-to-whole approach to learning. If the student says the wrong product or fails to respond, the answer is provided, and the student then reviews and practices the fact.

The whole-to-part flash cards presented in this book are similar in that they provide students with two elements of a multiplication or division fact, prompting students to produce the rest of the fact. The flash cards differ, however, in that they usually provide the product and a factor that defines the fact as belonging to a specific fact family. The cards also provide additional cues to the missing factor. These cues are specific to each fact family.

Having the product available provides students with a way to activate their knowledge base about the product so that they may employ semantic and visual strategies to respond to the card. The specific cues provide a means for the student to process and name the missing factor and then use it to recite an entire fact sentence. For example, the traditional flashcard (such as $2 \times 3 =$) may result in the student skip counting (2... 4... 6). In contrast, the whole-to-part fact flash cards afford additional benefits and empowers students to employ higher-order thinking skills to solve the problem.

The diagram below presents the product, 6, in conjunction with a related factor, 2. The product of 6 may elicit the familiar image of a rectangular six-pack of soda. The availability of this image provides the structure necessary to elicit the width of the rectangle, 3. Although the flash card presents numbers in an arrangement customarily expressed as a division fact, the student is encouraged to apply the missing factor to express a number of related fact sentences:

FIGURE 2.

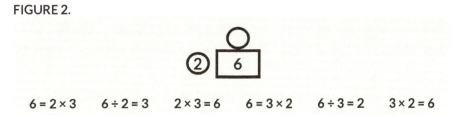

$6 = 2 \times 3$ $6 \div 2 = 3$ $2 \times 3 = 6$ $6 = 3 \times 2$ $6 \div 3 = 2$ $3 \times 2 = 6$

Efficient Fact Learning

Fluency Involves Accuracy and Efficiency

Fluency is achieved through the accurate repetition of knowledge, in this case number sentences that express math facts. It is very important that a student drill for fluency only after he or she can produce a math fact accurately. The student should never be placed in a situation that forces him or her to guess and produce a fact error. Verbalizing inaccurate fact sentences compromises the learning process and leads to frustration. Students should always have the option of referring to the correct answer and reading it, using a learned strategy to create the answer, or saying "pass" and having the correct answer supplied before expressing the entire fact sentence. A great deal of time in math class is spent developing strategies that promote awareness of patterns relating to fact families and empower students to construct accurate fact sentences. Progress in efficiency cannot be achieved without accuracy.

Provide Time for Verbal Expression

Many students with LBLD need ample time to formulate and express their responses. Learned strategies that help such students may involve visualizing a graphic organizer or referring to a pattern inherent in the fact family. This active reasoning demands processing time. Allow students to make a response or say, "pass" before you attempt to cue or prompt a response. A student may take as long as fifteen seconds to formulate a response. Try to be patient, and do not reveal your impatience or frustration—it will only add to the student's anxiety. Time a fifteen-second period of silence prior to working with the student. These pauses may seem to take an eternity, but if you allow students time to process in a thoughtful manner, they will eventually produce accurate and increasingly efficient responses. When given time to process responses, students will have the opportunity to integrate the efficient expression of math facts with the visual, kinesthetic, or semantic (meaning-based) patterns that have been associated with that fact family.

Use Rhythmic and Tonal Patterns

There is evidence to support the notion that some individuals benefit from associating multiplication facts with a musical theme (Gfeller 1986). After learning a repetitive rhythmic melody, students can learn lyrics to the tune that express multiplication facts. Students can sing such songs repeatedly in a consistent fashion to cement the memory of facts. In effect, a relatively unknown code, the lyrics containing facts, is superimposed over a known code, the tune. This rehearsal technique appears to help some individuals in the rote learning of facts.

Be aware, however, that this approach does not develop a conceptual understanding of multiplication and may lead to students depending on the mnemonic to produce the facts. Students that learn to chant the rhyme "Six times six is thirty-six" will not necessarily be able to recognize the related division fact ($36 \div 6 = 6$). Sometimes, students cannot recite a fact without rehearsing the melody. Facts that are memorized through the practice of rote rehearsal may be learned in this very specific, instrumental way. Another possible result is the creation of an errant fact, similar to the way the letters L, M, N, O may be heard and misconstrued as the nonexistent letter "ellehmenoh" in the alphabet song.

To avoid such pitfalls, be sure to check that students have retained information outside of the melodic or rhythmic context and apply a consistent visual structure to all fact learning to facilitate a systematic way of archiving, comparing, and retrieving these facts.

Integration of Multiplication and Division Facts

Have students practice multiplication facts in conjunction with their division counterparts. Initially, however, exclude division when first introducing the 2× facts. Introduce division after students are able to formulate 2× facts from whole to part prompts. Learning facts in a relational context that prompts the student to recognize and express facts in both multiplication and division formats is very important. Facts, with the exception of perfect squares, may be expressed with four fact sentences—two multiplication and two division. The entire fact family can be modeled with a rectangular matrix diagram that dovetails visually with the area model of multiplication, as well as traditional division notation (see fig. 3).

Gaining exposure to the dynamic expression of fact knowledge allows students to develop necessary flexibility with their knowledge base. Creating these related math sentences from a completed diagram provides students a relatively error-free opportunity to practice. It also involves processing the three fact elements rather than merely repeating them. Time spent holding fact information in short-term memory while formulating the related facts may facilitate transfer of the fact to long-term memory.

An initial strategy to facilitate this integration involves the alteration of traditional multiplication syntax (number and word order). To use this strategy, prompt students to produce a multiplication sentence by first giving them the product (see fig. 3). This approach serves to activate an image of the fact as a whole, while also triggering related background semantic knowledge.

For instance, say, "Picture a six-pack of cans. How are the cans arranged?" The student should respond, "6 = 2 × 3." Altering the multiplication syntax fosters the integration of multiplication and division facts by activating the three elements of each fact simultaneously in students' processing, leading students to articulate and store the fact family as a complete unit.

FIGURE 3.

Concrete Model	Area Model	Rectangular Matrix Diagram	Division Notation	Related Facts
				Initially:
				6 = 2 x 3
				6 = 3 x 2
				6 ÷ 2 = 3
				6 ÷ 3 = 2
				Then...
				2 x 3 = 6
				3 x 2 = 6
				6 ÷ 2 = 3
				6 ÷ 3 = 2

The Student Fact Notebook

Store student work in a systematic manner by creating a Fact Notebook for each student. Use a three ring binder with a one inch spine to archive worksheets and track progress. The notebook should be organized into sections. Use reinforced insertable dividers with colored transparent tabs to separate each section. Index each section with a divider that has a colored tab that corresponds to the theme color for each family.

The first section (clear tab) should include the large progress-tracking **Facts That I Know** "thermometer" found on page 22, the **0-100 Chart** from page 44, and the **Multiplication Grid** from page 52. The following sections will be partitioned according to the sequence of fact families that are presented in the text: 2×-yellow, 5×-red, 10×-orange, and so forth. Start each section with the divisibility poster, and end each section with fact fluency sheets.

Readiness Skills for Multidigit Number Processing

Before a child can read a book, he or she must acquire certain readiness skills, such as a sense of oral language and an understanding of how to orient a book. Just as there are readiness skills for the task of reading books, there are similar readiness skills for the arduous processes of multidigit computation.

Group Theory, Cardinality, and Number Sense

Before they can accurately manipulate groups of items, students must become aware that these groups exist in everyday life. Students need exposure to the process of organizing and compartmentalizing similar items in groups of discernible sizes. Students must then develop an understanding of the relationships between the quantities of items in these groups and the total number of items. Students can then move on to expressing these relationships as number facts.

Students must be led to append numbers to quantities they routinely encounter—for example, the number of ears on a rabbit, wheels on a tricycle, paws on a cat, toes on a foot, and so on. Once a student knows these quantities, he or she can begin to see things in terms of finite groups instead of loosely defined quantities, such as "a lot". These finite groups establish a critical knowledge bank from which the student can make comparisons to similar groups of items.

Additionally, the concept of multiplication demands the acknowledgement of sets of elements, all of which contain the same number of elements duplicated a number of times (×). Some students need direct instruction to acknowledge, label, and quantify grouped objects that are already present within their experiential world.

The examples that follow provide lasting, durable images that you may use later to give semantically meaningful examples of multiplication, division, and the encoding of fractions. Instruction should include the pairing of a common object with its enumerated attributes (parts).

EXAMPLE

bikes: 2 tires	triangles: 3 sides	cows: 4 hooves	hand: 5 fingers
people: 2 eyes	tricycles: 3 wheels	cars: 4 tires	foot: 5 toes
rabbits: 2 ears	days: 3 meals	square: 4 sides	starfish: 5 legs

In mathematics, the cardinality of a set is a measure of the number of elements of the set. Rather than trying to establish cardinality by counting objects from part to whole in a linear fashion, consider the benefit realized by counting the elements of a recognized set from whole to part. For instance, envision counting a handful of cereal piece by piece to determine the quantity—"one, two, three, four, five," and so on—versus looking at a starfish and counting its five legs. Which process does a better job of establishing a cardinal understanding of the number 5? Whole-to-part processing models provide the ability to integrate parts within the context of a whole number to establish cardinality.

These whole-to-part models provide necessary durable semantic examples of nouns paired with their attributes, but it is difficult to compare the relative quantities of attributes between different facts. It is hard to establish a relative comparison between starfish legs and tricycle wheels. For this reason, although semantic whole-to-part relationships can be used to introduce cardinality, other standardized models must be implemented to promote a relational understanding of fact information.

Many students develop a dependence on sequential or part-to-whole counting strategies to perform addition. Students are typically taught to use a counting strategy to add single-digit numbers. Many children implicitly pick up patterns and consequently learn addition facts through familiarity. Some do not, even when provided with endless repetition. These students benefit from differentiated instruction that allows them to quantify and compare relative quantities in a whole-to-part manner.

The part-to-whole counting method is similar to sounding out a word phonetically. It is an effective, and perhaps initially necessary, strategy for students at lower levels. Yet, consider the efficiency of recognizing syllables or entire words on sight, rather than synthesizing words from individual sounds. It is inefficient merely to become a proficient counter. Just as learning-disabled students strive to recognize patterns among familiar words on sight, they must be taught to recognize and envision patterns among numbers.

Consistent graphic organizers that relate quantities to both 5 and 10 provide the structure necessary to establish one-to-one correspondences between numbers and discernible quantities and help students develop a relational understanding of the numbers 1 through 10. These visual models also provide a way to extend this knowledge to the base-ten system and multidigit computations. Number sense is developed through the process of assigning values to groups of objects and then making comparisons between these groups. Consider the following patterns that relate to the gestalts of 5 and 10.

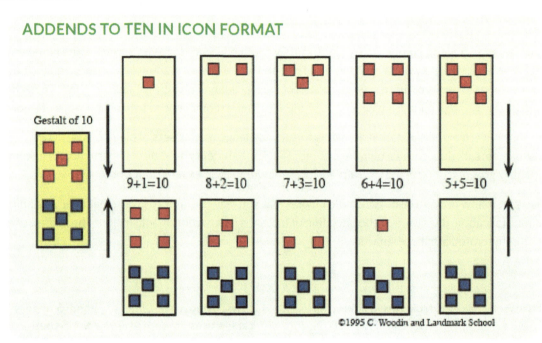

Visual Clustering

Children's exposure to number-related dot patterns (patterns on dice, playing cards, and dominoes) has diminished as pastimes that feature cards and dice have been replaced by electronic games and television. Students should be provided with opportunities to develop their ability to "see" numbers as recognizable clusters instead of collections of discrete elements to be counted.

The nonverbal visual channel may prove to be a relatively strong modality for some students. Displaying Arabic numerals in conjunction with familiar dot patterns helps strengthen the relationship between an Arabic numeral (2) and a concrete quantity (••). When visual representations (∷ = : + :) are paired with facts expressed in Arabic numerals (4 = 2 + 2), the accompanying clusters of corresponding dots help to reinforce the facts in a visual yet nonverbal manner. This method of presentation is a boon to students who have difficulty processing auditory information. The icons allow visual processing to occur. Then, after students have processed the number relationship, they may label it and name it as a number fact.

EXAMPLE

The side of a dice showing six dots clearly depicts two subordinate groups of three (∷∷) within the gestalt of the quantity six (6 = 3 × 2). This number fact exemplifies the visual symmetry inherent in the even multiplication fact families, in which the same numbers of dots occur in each row. These iconic relationships may be further developed using the activities presented later in this book.

It is very important to play games that use objects that display familiar (canonical) patterns: dice, playing cards, and dominoes. Time spent in the classroom or during recess teaching students games involving these items is compounded when students can play these games at home. Two effective games are cribbage and bones. Cribbage is a sufficiently popular game to make an explanation of the rules unnecessary here. Bones, on the other hand, is a wonderful game that requires six dice, pencil and paper, and two to six players.

GAME

Bones

Bones is a dice game that allows students to develop visual memory, practice place value, and internalize the regrouping process. When playing the game in math class, do not permit students to write down scores that need to be added. Instead, have students retain and add the numbers mentally. Thinking in terms of place value will help students substantially, encouraging them to use their place value knowledge. This is not an original game—it has existed for years under several names like Zilch or Farkle! *This game can be played with two or more players.*

Materials:
- six dice (per group of players)
- pencil and paper to record totaled scores

Goal
The goal of the game is to be the first player to earn more than 5,000 points.

How to Earn Points:
When a player rolls the dice, different numbers are worth different amounts of points.

- A 1 is worth 100 points.
- A 5 is worth 50 points.
- A 2, 3, 4, or 6 is not worth any points unless the number comes up on three dice in the same turn (three of a kind).
- When a player rolls three of a kind, he or she multiplies the number rolled by 100. For example, three 2s would be worth 200 points (100 × 2 = 200). An additional (fourth) 2 would not be worth additional points.
- Rolling a straight with all six dice (1, 2, 3, 4, 5, 6) is worth 1,000 points.
- Rolling six dice in one toss that are all worth points (a combination of 5s, 1s, and/or 3 of a kind) is worth 1,000 points.

Overview:
During his or her turn, a player rolls the dice a number of times to accumulate the most points possible. As a player rolls numbers that earn points, he or she puts those particular dice aside, taking them out of play. These points are not secure until the player chooses to stop his or her turn and register the points with the scorekeeper. The player may choose to continue rolling remaining dice as long as each roll contains a scoring die or dice (1, 5, three of a kind). If a player chooses to roll and gets no points in the roll, he or she has rolled "bones." Rolling bones ends the turn, and all the points the player put aside during that turn are lost. A player may choose to stop rolling at any point to avoid bones and earn the points from dice that were put aside. At the end of a turn, the player must tell the scorekeeper how many points he or she rolled (so the scorekeeper isn't the only mathematician).

When a player surpasses 5,000 points on a complete turn, each other player has one complete turn to beat that score. If no player can beat that score, the player who surpassed 5,000 points wins and the game ends.

Example Play:
- To determine the starting player, each player rolls a die. The player who rolls the highest number goes first. Play continues clockwise.
- Player One rolls all six dice. He or she rolls a 1, 2, 3, 5, 5, and 6. The 1 and the two 5s are worth points if the player chooses to put them aside. The player chooses to put the 1 aside to count as 100 points. Note that the player does not need to put aside *all* scoring dice. In order to continue, however, at least one die must be put aside. Here, although the 5s could count as 50 points each, the player chooses to keep the dice in play in an attempt to earn more points.
- Player One rolls the five remaining dice. If at least one of these dice scores, he or she may continue to roll. Player One rolls a 3, 4, 4, 4, and 6 and chooses to put

aside the three 4s as 400 points. At this time, Player One has 500 points and decides not to roll the two remaining dice (to avoid rolling bones, which would eliminate all the points scored on the turn).

- Player One says the point total out loud ("I have 500 points"), and the scorekeeper records it. All players should be performing the calculations mentally to check Player One's addition. If a player miscalculates, the classmates should politely help!
- Play continues with each other player rolling and putting aside dice that score points. Each turn stops when a player chooses to register points or when he or she rolls bones.

Note: Once a die is put aside, its points are set. For example, if in three consecutive rolls a player puts aside a 5 each time (for a total of 150 points), he or she cannot later consider those three 5s three of a kind for 500 points.

- As rounds of play continue, players must add new points earned to the recorded points *without* the aid of pencil and paper. A player may look at the recorded score on the scorekeeper's sheet, but must do the addition computation mentally. The player says the new total out loud and the scorekeeper writes it down. Again, all students should be doing the mental calculations in order to check the math of other players.

Encourage students to think of the numbers as hundreds when the values become larger. For example, "900 + 300 = 1200" becomes "nine hundreds plus three hundreds equals twelve hundreds." Also, students may find it helpful to use the dice themselves to assist with adding. For example, in 850 + 450, have the student place the dice with the 5 (50 points) on top of the 850 on the scoring sheet and say, "900." The student will now have nine hundreds plus four hundreds, to equal thirteen hundreds.

Special Situations

- If three 1s are rolled, a player may choose to count them as 100 points three times, equaling 300 points, or as three of a kind, equaling 100 points (1 × 100 = 100). Counting three 1s as 100 points might be a useful strategy if the player doesn't want to pass the 5,000 threshold because he or she wants another full turn. (Another full turn might allow the player to earn far more than 5,000 points, making it very unlikely that another player could catch up.)
- If a player rolls a 1,000-point combination (a straight of six dice or all six dice earning points), he or she can put the points aside and continue rolling. That is, the player can end his or her turn and register the 1,000 points, or continue rolling the dice to earn more points, with the 1,000 points at risk should the player roll bones.

Ending the Game

Once a player surpasses 5,000 points, each other player has one turn to try to beat that total score. The highest total score wins!

Place Value

Students have limited success with mathematics involving large numbers until they gain an accurate understanding of place value. Understanding of place value in the base-ten system can be developed using concrete models. Base-ten blocks and similar commercial materials provide a means to demonstrate this process visually. Having students add 10 and then 11 to a number without paper is a good way to provide insight and instill familiarity with the base-ten system. Students quickly discover that it is easier to add 11 to a number by increasing the digit in the ones place by 1 and then increasing the digit in the tens place by 1 than to count upward 11 times from the number. Similarly, it is very easy to add 9 to a given number by first increasing the digit in the tens place by 1 and then counting back by 1 from the ones place.

Estimation skills should be tied directly to multidigit computations to instill a better understanding of large numbers. For example, before asking a student to perform a multidigit computation, provide a rationale for performing the task and ask for an approximate answer. Then examine the actual answer for acceptability in terms of the situation being modeled. Compare the answer to the initial estimate. If the student produces an estimate that is vastly different from the correct answer, provide a strategy to produce a better estimate. For instance, if a student is asked to estimate the difference between 600 and 401, and he or she responds with an estimate of 9, show the student that the difference between the digits in the hundreds place is most important to an accurate estimation.

To solidify the student's understanding, illustrate the point with base-ten blocks. Create each number (600 and 401) using the blocks, and place the blocks so that their place values align vertically. Have the student imagine the blocks to be quantities of chocolate. Ask the student to identify which of the types of blocks represents the largest amount of chocolate. It should be abundantly clear that the two hundreds (or flats) would yield the largest quantity; therefore, 200 would be a better estimate.

The game Big Number is an entertaining way for students to practice reading and writing multidigit numbers while developing place value, estimation, and comparison skills. Big number is a very easy game to prepare for and play. Students must use their knowledge of place value to construct the largest number possible from a series of digits. Base-ten Ball is another interactive way to practice place value, and may be adapted for practicing a variety of mathematical skills.

BIG NUMBER GAME

Start by telling the students how many digits there will be in the final number. Instruct them to draw a corresponding number of horizontal blanks on their paper, as if they were about to play a game of hangman. Tell them that you will be calling out digits from zero to nine, but you will never call the same digit twice in the same game. Students must try to place the digits in a way that will create the largest number. Call the digits out one at a time. After you call a digit, each student writes that digit in one of the spaces on his or her paper. Make sure that all the students record the digit in one of their available spaces before you call the next digit. Record the digits on the chalkboard as you call them out.

After all the spaces are filled, have students help you create the largest number possible from the available digits. Then have them estimate how close their number is to the largest possible number. Next, each student should find the actual difference between their number and the largest number, and compare that result to their estimate. The winner of the round is the student in the group who has the largest number and can correctly read it aloud. The winner gets to call out the next round of numbers.

There are several variations on this same idea. Decimal Big Number follows the same set of rules, but a decimal point is placed between two of the spaces. Fraction Big Number has spaces in the numerator and the denominator, and students must use division to convert the fraction into a decimal to determine a winner. Small Number is yet another option.

BASE (TEN) BALL

Place value may be practiced using a ball with the numerals 1 through 9 written on it. The ball is tossed to a student who catches it and reports the first number that he or she sees. The student then performs a predetermined operation, such as adding 10 to that number. Initially it may be helpful to demonstrate by holding a base-ten stick (or rod) to the left of the ball (in the tens place). This demonstrates the addition of 10 without the need to count or disturb the ones place. This exercise makes a great icebreaker activity and can be adapted to a large number of situations.

Base Ten Ball - teen numbers

Handwriting Skills

Before addressing multidigit algorithms, it is important to deal with the prerequisite skills of numeral formation and spacing. Deficiencies in fine motor skills, visual-motor integration (VMI), and spatial perception skills may manifest themselves in poor numeral formations. Individual numerals might be illegible, or numerals within the same number may vary drastically in size. Disorganized placement on the page may also occur.

These issues have an impact even at the level of single-step arithmetic because students are unable to decode and rehearse their written text. In addition, teachers who are unable to decode written text may tend to consider it wrong, even if the child produced an accurate answer at the verbal level. These issues need to be addressed as soon as possible. Such students receive negative feedback for correct responses and risk developing math anxiety.

Horizontal Alignment of Numbers

Legibility and spacing issues must be addressed at the single-step (number fact) level. At this time, the student's writing demands numeral legibility and, to a lesser degree, appropriate spacing between numbers. When the student starts to perform such procedures as multidigit addition, subtraction, and multiplication, linear alignment relative to place value places additional demands on spacing and consistent formation of written numerals.

Students with difficulty in this area should receive training in single numeral formation, as well as in the proper production of spaced digits within numbers. This training is similar to that used to improve handwriting with letters and words. Any student having trouble producing legible numerals is surely experiencing the same difficulty with letter formations. Use the same strategies that are currently working to improve letter and word formations, or try some of the activities outlined here.

Have the student trace and then copy numerals, multidigit numbers, and number sentences (2 + 3 = 5). Use commercial handwriting paper, which has solid top and bottom horizontal lines and dashed midlines.

Tactile paper is available with raised horizontal lines that constrain the pencil point. These lines help limit the height of numerals to a consistent vertical standard. You can draw light vertical lines on this paper to create a grounding point for the student to initiate numeral formations. Tell the student to start forming the numeral only when he or she has placed the pencil point on the intersection of a bottom line and a vertical line. This exercise helps students who have spatial perception difficulties. It also provides a focus point for those students who easily go off task. Students must be able to form legible horizontal number strings before they are introduced to multidigit computation.

DO NOT USE GRAPH PAPER

Graph paper may seem like a welcome vehicle for creating correct numeral placement; however, it actually offers limited success. Students who you think would gain the most from it frequently have the worst spatial perception abilities. Graph paper imposes too much visual structure, which may overwhelm students' visual (perceptual) abilities.

Students with poor spatial perception abilities tend to put few constraints on where they place numerals. More often than not, these students ignore the gridlines on graph paper and continue to misalign numerals. When they are ready to add subproducts, they tend to rely on the grid to determine digit alignment below instead of relying on the place value of their sloppy numerals. Students add numbers that appear to be in a column of squares, irrespective of whether the numerals are the first, second, or third digit in each string. In a sense, graph paper enhances the possibility of error rather than minimizing it. Additionally, the gridlines on the periphery of the problem can provide added visual distraction.

Instead of graph paper, provide students with vertical lines. Vertical lines help students align digits vertically, yet force students to accept the onus of creating a multidigit number for each subproduct instead of merely attempting to fill in discrete holes in the graph paper grid. Vertical lines tend to provide just enough of a reference point for students, without setting a level of structure that is too demanding for students' abilities.

An alternative two-step approach may be necessary for students with exceptionally poor handwriting skills. Create handwriting paper by turning primary (wide ruled) lined writing paper ninety degrees so that the blue lines are vertical. Initially emphasize the horizontal spacing of digits by using the now horizontal red margin as a grounding bottom line. Have the student start each numeral on the intersection of the red line and each blue line. The horizontal spacing is critical to the proper alignment of place value.

Another advantage that lined paper (in landscape format showing vertical lines) has over graph paper is that it allows the students initially to write numbers of varied height, placing emphasis on grounding the written output to the horizontal, red bottom line and maintaining consistent horizontal spacing. Graph paper imposes consistent horizontal lines that will be violated—the student will write over them or, if constrained by this vertical structure, create malformed numerals. Again, the horizontal spacing is critical to the proper alignment of place value.

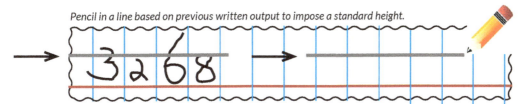

Pencil in a line based on previous written output to impose a standard height.

As the student learns to establish acceptable horizontal spacing with a written line of numerals, start penciling a second line, parallel to the red line to help develop consistent vertical height. First, using the student's work, pencil in a line that touches the tops of their most appropriate-sized numerals. Using that vertical distance as a guide, impose a lightly penciled line on subsequent handwriting assignments. This provides a realistic, student-specific starting point. Over time, begin to draw these parallel lines closer to one another until the student is writing numerals at an acceptable height. Then, encourage the student to maintain that height. Continue to pay close attention to the horizontal spacing of numbers, as this is crucial for place value alignment within multidigit computations.

Numeral and Number Formation

Provide students gross motor tactile and kinesthetic practice with number formation through activities that allow students to use larger muscle groups to form numbers. Such activities allow them to practice motor skills in a novel way. If a student makes handwriting errors when using a pencil, then he or she will have practiced making errors alongside correct formations. As a result, the student's output could be based on accurate or inaccurate memories. Activities that incorporate gross motor skills remove ambiguity. Novel exercises involving gross motor production provide students with a clean slate devoid of learned errors.

Gross motor work involves creating enlarged number formations. Have students write numbers with their index finger in a tub of sand, on an interactive whiteboard, or with finger paint on easel paper. Students can also form numbers on a new carpet remnant or with chalk on the blackboard. Another option is to have students "write" numbers by shining a flashlight beam on a wall. All of these conditions allow the instructor to monitor the formation of students' writing.

Gross motor practice provides the teacher with an opportunity to intervene during numeral production. The teacher may help guide the student's hand while the number is being formed, rather than correcting an error after it has occurred. When left-handed students write with a pencil, they cover their output with their writing hand as they move it to the right. As a result, the student, as well as the teacher, is unaware of the quality of the output until the student has moved the hand out of the way. At this point, it is too late to intervene. The mistake has been made—and practiced. This error will be added to the student's motor memory and could serve as an errant model for future writing.

Vertical Alignment Within Multidigit Addition and Subtraction Computations

Multidigit computation introduces additional vertical alignment constraints. Students who are hamstrung by their inability to align numerals in a vertical format make computational errors due to resulting issues with place value. Training students in vertical alignment is best addressed when adding or subtracting numbers. Accurate and legible number encoding is a necessary subskill within the context of multiplication and division procedures. This important skill may be overlooked if the student is restricted to consumable workbooks that emphasize filling in blanks rather than constructing and performing written computations.

Number and problem copying from a book, the chalkboard, or oral dictation should be a regular occurrence. Students who need assistance with vertical alignment of numbers may benefit from the drawn vertical line formats used in many of the templates that occur throughout this book. Students can also be prompted to create their own template by turning lined paper ninety degrees to create a vertical line format instead of a horizontal one. Small journal books are useful in this regard. Have students open the journal book with the spine in a horizontal position. Use this book to perform daily warm-ups that include number dictation and practice with learned problem types.

If the student needs help apportioning space on the page for each problem, fold the book to produce four sections. Direct the student to produce two problems per section, numbering each problem immediately before performing it. You may help number each problem to scaffold this organization. When students have demonstrated proficiency with the aforementioned requisite skills, it is time to introduce multiplication.

Order Of Fact Family Instruction

Rather than proceeding in a sequential manner through the multiplication tables (0×, 1×, 2×, and so on), introduce fact families in the order outlined below. This progression provides a developmentally appropriate sequence that starts with facts that can be presented with familiar concrete materials, examples and manipulatives. Facts introduced later in this progression build on this knowledge base. Emphasis should be placed on functional fluency through the 9× family, which comprises 75% of the facts on a 10 x 10 grid. The 11× and 12× facts are included at the end of the book.

2× Facts:
    a) Teach whole-to-part multiplication using an axis of symmetry to partition a whole into halves.
    b) Teach part-to-whole multiplication facts using semantic cues and contexts.
    c) Teach the divisibility rule with the 0–100 chart. Integrate learned multiplication facts with division.

5× Facts:
    a) Teach the divisibility rule with the 0–100 chart.
    b) Introduce clock-based minute products in a relational context through kinesthetic activities.
    c) Integrate clock-based products with multiplication and division syntax.
    d) Integrate these facts with the area model and the semantic context of nickels.

10× Facts:
    a) Teach the divisibility rule with the 0–100 chart, and extend the fact family semantically to dimes.
    b) Teach multiplication and division facts using base-ten sticks (or rods) and a matrix model.

Rule-Based 1× and 0× Facts:
Teach the multiplication and division facts concurrently using semantic cues.

- Expand factual knowledge to magnitudes of 10.
- Introduce the multiplication of single-digit numbers by multidigit numbers using first composite area models and then tabular arrays.

9× Facts:
Teach the divisibility rule with the 0–100 chart. Teach whole to part, and then part to whole.

3× Facts:
Teach the divisibility rule with the 0–100 chart. Teach the facts using divisibility cues and patterns.

6× Facts:
Teach the divisibility rule with the 0–100 chart.

Perfect Squares:
Teach the facts using a visual strategy based on a 10 × 10 area model.

4× Facts:
Teach the divisibility rule, and then the relation to the 2× family.

7× Facts:
Teach the facts using the distributive property.

8× Facts:
All these facts have been introduced through fact families previously learned. Review these facts through the use of the commutative property ($8 \times 5 = 40 = 5 \times 8$)

Begin with Cadenced Facts: 2×, 5×, 10×, 1×

These facts are the most important and most frequently required facts. They are called cadenced facts as the products may be skip counted with a metered beat in the manner of a drum cadence. These four fact families comprise 64 percent of the 100 multiplication facts. They are necessary for performing multidigit computation, telling time, developing an understanding of base ten relationships, and simplifying fractions. They also lend themselves to many semantic associations that may be modeled and expressed through word problems.

Skip counting helps familiarize the student with the products; however, it is not a reliable or efficient means to produce facts. The process of defining factors of products by skip counting may place overwhelming demands on students' auditory processing abilities. Students often miscount the number of beats of the cadence or arrive at the correct product without ever rehearsing the entire fact sentence. As a result, they become rigidly dependent on this counting strategy and fail to make progress toward recognizing and retrieving the entire multiplication fact sentence or its division correlate.

Time spent producing the cadenced facts in an effortless, fluent manner has a marked impact on math learning. These are the fact families that students must drill and practice regularly to develop fluency. Time spent at school or home working on these fact families will have a great positive impact on a student.

Learning first the related facts of the most predictable fact families provides a way for students to learn many facts belonging to less predictable fact families. For instance, learning $2 \times 7 = 14$ within the context of the 2× family will also teach the student $7 \times 2 = 14$. As students assimilate facts, they become familiar with an ever-increasing portion of the multiplication chart.

In terms of the 100 basic facts (1 × 1 through 10 × 10), an efficient presentation yields the following progress:

- After learning the 2× family, students have learned nineteen facts; eighty-one facts remain unfamiliar.
- After learning the 5× family, students have learned seventeen additional facts (36 percent); sixty-four facts remain.
- After learning the 10× family, students have learned fifteen additional facts (51 percent); forty-nine facts remain.

Over halfway!

- After learning the 1× family, students have learned thirteen additional facts (64 percent); thirty-six facts remain.
- After learning the 9× family, students have learned eleven additional facts (75 percent); twenty-five facts remain.

At this point, students have learned 75 percent of the multiplication facts. These facts are high-frequency facts that will be used in the production of multidigit, whole-number computations and the manipulation of fractions. Fluency with these high-frequency facts has an impact on math discourse similar to the way familiarity with common sight words (such as *is*, *the*, and *why*) promotes efficient and accurate reading and written expression.

- After learning the 3× family, students have learned nine additional facts (84 percent); sixteen facts remain.
- After learning the 6× family, students have learned seven additional facts (91 percent); eight facts remain.

Almost there!

- After learning the perfect squares, students have learned three additional facts (94 percent); six facts remain.
- After learning the 4× family, students have learned four additional facts (98 percent); two facts remain.
- After learning the last two facts — $7 \times 8 = 56 = 8 \times 7$ — students have learned 100 percent of the facts.

Facts That I Know!

Name: _____

Color sections of this chart after you master each fact family. Keep this at the front of a **"Fact Notebook"** made from a three ring binder. Archive all completed fact worksheets in this notebook in sections organized by fact family.

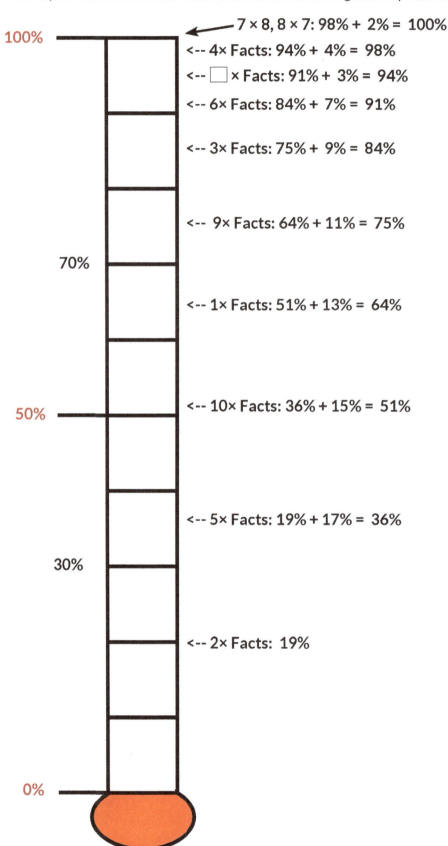

- 7 × 8, 8 × 7: 98% + 2% = 100%
- <-- 4× Facts: 94% + 4% = 98%
- <-- ☐ × Facts: 91% + 3% = 94%
- <-- 6× Facts: 84% + 7% = 91%
- <-- 3× Facts: 75% + 9% = 84%
- <-- 9× Facts: 64% + 11% = 75%
- <-- 1× Facts: 51% + 13% = 64%
- <-- 10× Facts: 36% + 15% = 51%
- <-- 5× Facts: 19% + 17% = 36%
- <-- 2× Facts: 19%

22 © 2013 C. Woodin & Landmark School

Whole-to-Part Multiplication

The teaching of multiplication fact families should begin with the 2× family. The 1× and 0× families have more predictable answers; however, it is difficult to illustrate the 0× family with the area model of multiplication, and it is difficult to distinguish the 1× family from counting. Students are able to learn these rule-driven families by definition soon after mastering the cadenced facts.

There are several student-friendly aspects of the 2× family:

- The 2× facts apply to many familiar semantic associations.
- Visual images that may be divided in half along an axis of symmetry enable whole-to-part processing of the 2× facts.
- The 2× facts have an easily discernible pattern and cadence.
- Products of the 2× facts can be checked with an easily learned divisibility rule.
- Fewer manipulatives are required to create relatively small, familiar products from the 2× facts.

Part-to-Whole Strategies Fail to Establish Effective Multiplication Models

Some students have a difficult time developing multiplication fact sentences from part-to-whole processing. Skip counting to a cadence—"two, four six, eight"—or skip counting groups of items of the same quantity are examples of building a product from its parts. Though students may be able to skip count, they are unable to use this strategy to learn fact sentences efficiently. They may produce correct multiples of 2, but they are not able to keep track of the number of skips. As a result, they fail to create an entire fact sentence. For example, when using a skip counting strategy to solve a written problem, such as 4 × 2 = __, or a manipulative-based problem, such as determining the total when given four groups of two paper clips, a student might skip count "two, four, six, eight." The student would reach the correct answer of eight, but would likely do so without linking the product to the initial prompt. The visual prompt of four groups of paper clips would fail to create an image of 8, and it would not produce a meaningful semantic relationship. The student would have no reason to group the paper clips in pairs. As a result, the student would neither establish nor remember a fact sentence.

Use Familiar Visual and Semantic Associations of Gestalts to Drive Facts

The 2× facts are easily learned and easily practiced. The products represent quantities of elements that are small enough for students to recognize visually and acknowledged semantically. However, these facts should initially be presented in a whole-to-part manner. Whole-to-part models provide all of the quantitative information in a math fact, as well as the structure necessary to visualize and then compose the fact in its entirety.

Common, familiar objects may be used as visual models or manipulatives to represent facts in a whole-to-part manner. To present the 2× visually, produce a durable image of a whole that is comprised of two identical, identifiable halves. These halves should be groups of familiar subordinate attributes of the whole.

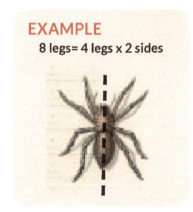

EXAMPLE
8 legs= 4 legs x 2 sides

© 2013 C. Woodin & Landmark School

fluency pictures
Spider, cans

A spider's legs, for example, may be used to illustrate a 2× fact. The image of the spider serves to produce a durable semantic and visual graphic organizer of the number 8. The spider has eight legs. When divided on its axis of symmetry, it has four legs on each side. The use of this visually familiar object facilitates the student's ability to link the new concept of multiplication to his or her background knowledge. To present the fact in a way that corresponds to the image, alter the traditional syntax of multiplication so that the student produces a fact sentence that starts with the product (8 = 4 × 2). When the student first verbalizes the product (8), he or she is prompted to activate background knowledge related to 8 to help generate the fact sentence. It is easier to acknowledge the elements of the recognizable whole than it is to assemble a large number of discrete elements. This methodology is powerful, though its scope is limited by the student's ability to recognize and visualize objects with many subordinate attributes.

Whole-to-part models are useful in that they provide a means to map out and then describe a solution process. A durable image of a spider may be used to scaffold the production of a multiplication sentence. The spider has eight legs. When partitioned along its axis of symmetry, it has four legs, two times: 8 = 4 × 2 and 4 × 2 = 8.

Activate Retrieval Mechanisms with Semantic-Based Cueing

Effective, integrated fact retrieval is a function of effective fact storage. Many dyslexic students are capable of remembering vast amounts of semantic-based information. These students score high on the Similarities subtest of the Wechsler Intelligence Scale for Children (WISC.) They have the ability to remember and express a great deal of information about high-interest subjects (i.e., describing an animal in detail that they have learned about from television). In contrast, dyslexic students lack the ability to remember or express information that does not have a contextual basis. For instance, they find it difficult to remember their zip codes or phone numbers. These students usually have relatively low scores on the Coding and Digit Span subtests of the WISC. They benefit greatly from instruction that requires them to apply their semantic processing abilities to activate and hold information in their short-term memory while they develop the language skills necessary to relate and express the information accurately.

EXAMPLE

For example, to teach 8 = 4 × 2 using semantic-based cueing, make a model of a spider with your hands. Place your hands on a desk, palms down. While looking at the backs of your hands, hook your thumbs together and wiggle your outstretched fingers to approximate a spider. Ask a student to do the same.

Wiggle eight fingers. Say, "Eight equals."
Have the student mimic the gesture and repeat, "Eight equals."

Wiggle the four fingers on your right hand, and make a fist with your left.
- Prompt, "How many legs on each side?"
- The student should mimic the gesture and say, "Four."

Wiggle the four fingers on your left hand, and make a fist with your right, then alternate the gesture by wiggling the right fingers and making a fist with the left.
- Prompt, "How many *times* does a spider have four legs?"
- The student should mimic the gesture and say, "Two times."

Provide the student with additional phonemic prompts if necessary.
Repeat the drill several times, having the student mimic the gestures. Each time, however, hold off providing a verbal prompt. Instead, provide a phonemic cue. For instance, now, to begin the drill, wiggle all eight fingers, but do not prompt, "How many fingers?" Instead, provide wait time based on the student's processing speed. After waiting 5-15 seconds, you should say, "Eigh...". This initial phoneme should be enough to prompt the student to say, "Eight." The goal is to have the student say the entire, uninterrupted fact sentence, "Eight equals four, times two." Respond to this sentence by writing 8 = 4 × 2, and 4 × 2 = 8. Verbalize each number and symbol as you write them. Subsequently, ask the student to read each sentence as you point to each number and symbol in turn.

Pair 2× Multiplication Facts with Highly Salient Whole-to-Part Visual and Semantic Representations

Use the Oral Recitation Template for Whole-to-Part 2× Facts to help reinforce 2× multiplication facts with pictures. The pictures on the template show animals and objects that should be familiar to most students. The pictures show whole items that have been divided into two equal halves by an axis of symmetry. Each half contains the same number of attributes. Each picture functions to manage these two groups of attributes so that the student may simultaneously perceive the whole ("all the parts") in conjunction with the pair of partitioned attributes. This whole-to-part "chunking" lessens the burden on working memory and facilitates the expression of each fact.

Pictures

	All the parts		# on each side		# sides
OBJECT: ATTRIBUTE					
Person: eyes	2	=	1	×	2
Fox: paws	4	=	2	×	2
Ant: legs	6	=	3	×	2
Spider: legs	8	=	4	×	2
Gloves: fingers	10	=	5	×	2
Carton: eggs	12	=	6	×	2

Product "All the parts"

Initially, recite a multiplication fact that relates to one of the pictures—for example, "Six equals three times two." Ask students to point to the picture that best represents the fact sentence. Choose a student who (correctly) points to the ant, and have him or her describe the picture as it relates to the fact.

Initially, the students' descriptions will need to be facilitated with leading questions. An example of this cueing follows.

© 2013 C. Woodin & Landmark School

EXAMPLE

Before beginning, remind the students that they are not writing anything on the Oral Recitation Page.

Say, "Six equals three times two. Point to the picture that describes this fact."
The student points to the correct picture.

Say, "Yes, you are pointing to the correct picture. What did you select?"
The student replies, "An ant."

Ask, "How many legs are on the ant?"
The student replies, "Six." Write 6 = on the board.

Ask, "How many legs are on a side?"

The student replies, "Three."

Add 3 to the incomplete fact sentence 6 = .

Ask, "How many sides?"

The student replies, "Two."

Saying "Times two," add × 2 to complete the fact sentence 6 = 3.

Say, "See whether you can describe the whole **picture** as I point to each part of the fact."

As you point to each part of the fact, the student identifies it: "Six legs... equals... three legs... times two." (He may also note that six legs equals 3 two times.)

As repetition makes them more familiar with the act of labeling each picture's object and pair of attributes, students will need less cueing to describe each fact sentence. At this point, you can ask the students to produce a multiplication fact using only the picture as a prompt. See the example below.

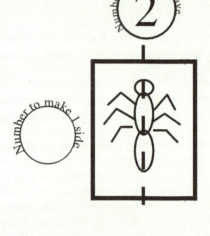

EXAMPLE

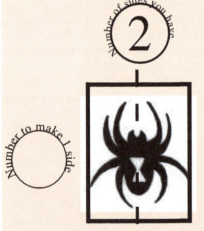

Say, "Look at the animal with eight legs. Hold up fingers to match the number of legs on each side." Point to a student holding up four fingers and say, "Make a fact. Start with the number eight."

Write 8 = on the board.

The student should respond, "Eight equals four times two."

If the student pauses after saying "eight equals," tap the student's four fingers to cue the next number in the fact sentence.

Oral Recitation Page for 2× Facts

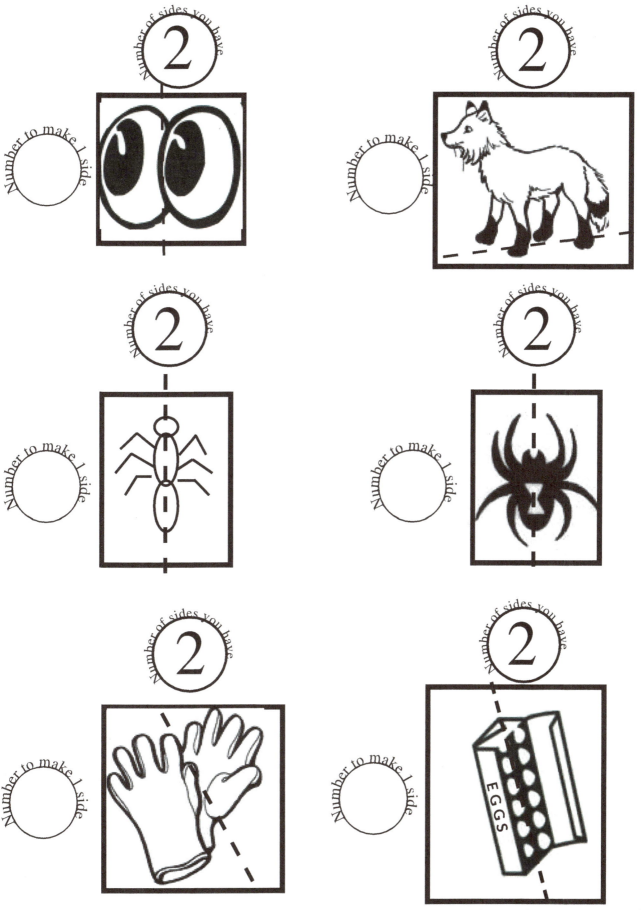

Finger Stamping Template

Another effective way to practice 2× facts is to generate them by stamping finger patterns on the template provided. Write the number of fingers to be stamped in the top circle. The student then holds out that number of fingers, dips them in paint, and stamps this quantity onto the template "two times." The student should first stamp above the grey line and then duplicate the pattern by stamping below the line.

Have students use their right hands to produce patterns of the 2× facts using one, two, three, and four fingers. Have students dip the fingers of their right hand in red paint, and then stamp the pattern twice on the red portion of the template. To form patterns with the right hand, use the following fingers:

- One - index finger,
- Two - index and middle,
- Three - thumb, index and middle - in a triangle as shown in the following example.
- Four - thumb, index, middle, ring in a square pattern.

EXAMPLE

- To stamp 3 two times (2 × 3 = 6), dip three fingers on the right hand in red paint.
- Stamp three red fingers on the right (red) side of the Finger Stamping Template two times (once above the grey line, once below) to make six red fingerprints.
- The six red dots can be smeared into an Arabic numeral 6 when done.

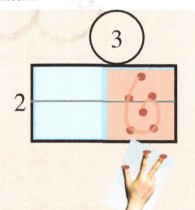

To stamp numbers 5 and larger two times, the fingers of the left hand will be needed. Dip all of the left-hand fingers in blue paint, and then extend additional right (red) fingers necessary to match the number.

EXAMPLE

- To stamp 5 two times (5 × 2 = 10), extend all left-hand fingers and dip them in blue paint.
- Stamp five blue fingers on the left (blue) side of the Finger Stamping Template two times (above and below the grey line) to make ten blue fingerprints

EXAMPLE

- To stamp 8 two times, extend all left-hand fingers and three right-hand fingers.
- Dip the left hand in blue, and at the same time dip the right hand in red.
- Stamp both hands two times on the Finger Stamping Template to make sixteen fingerprints.
- Looking at the prints, call attention to fact that 8 two times results in one (blue) 10 and six (red) 1s.
- (8 × 2 = 16)

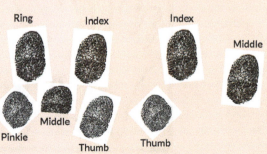

28 © 2013 C. Woodin & Landmark School

Finger Stamping Template

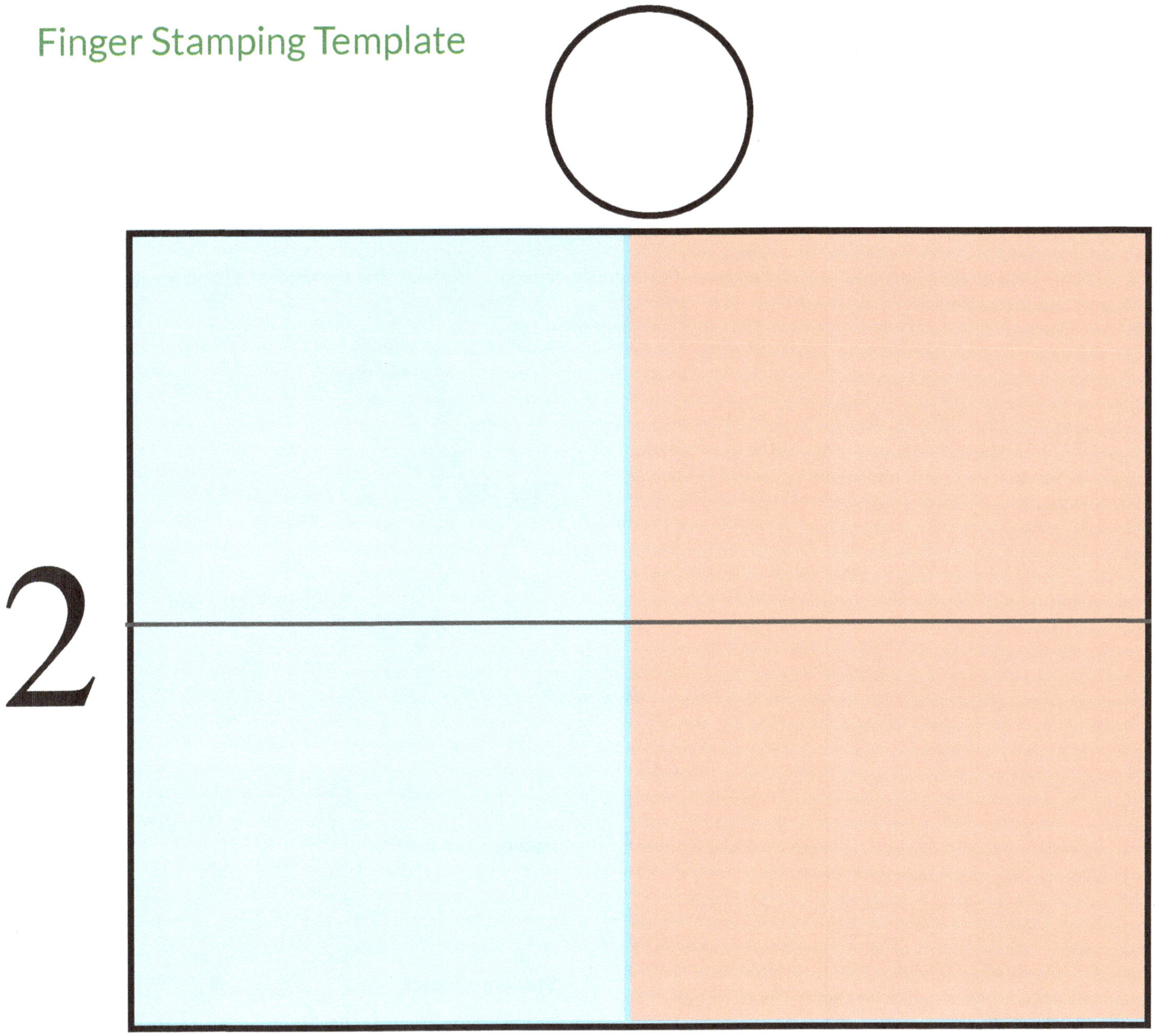

2

Diagram

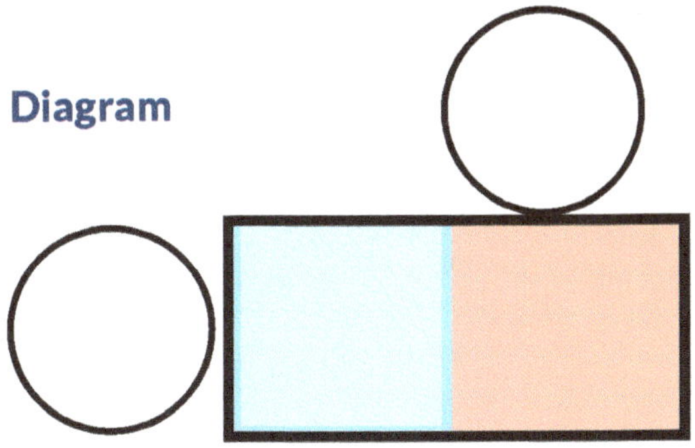

Facts:

_____ _____

_____ _____

© 2013 C. Woodin & Landmark School

Use Hands to Model 2× Facts and Place Value

The following exercises will represent 2x facts and place value within the student's primary reference frame. These activities provide the student with an internal place-value template to help him or her encode the digits in their proper order (14, not 41).

> **EXAMPLE**
>
> Have a student hold out his or her left hand with the fingers extended. Make sure that the student's hand is within his or her visual field.
>
> - Say, "You are showing me five fingers, one time."
> - Model the correct action by mirroring the student, extending your *right* hand as you face the student.
> - High-five the student to make a "clap."
> - Say, "This is five two times, or one ten."
> - Ask the student to keep his or her left fingers extended.
>
>
>
> - Say, "Now show me seven fingers by sticking out two more fingers on your right hand."
> - When the student shows seven fingers, say, "You are showing me seven one time."
> - Face the student, and model the action by mirroring the student. Extend five fingers on your right hand, as well two fingers on your left hand.
> - Touch the student's hands. Clap the "ten".
> - Say, "This is fourteen. It is seven two times. Two times seven is fourteen.".
>
>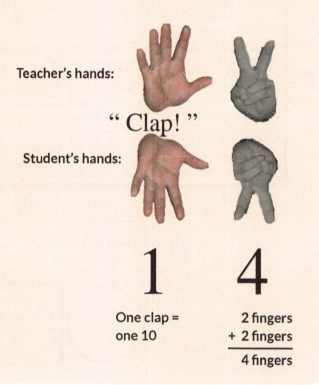

2 × FINGER REFLECTION GAME

To start the game in the ready position, stand with all five fingers on your right hand extended. This hand should hang at belt level. Students will be producing mirror images of the teacher's hands/finger patterns. The student should assume a similar posture, with the fingers of his or her left hand extended and by his or her side.

- Call out a number from five to nine. This is the signal to display the correct number of fingers as quickly as possible. You and the student should display the given number of fingers, pointing your hands at each other.
- The pairs of hands will create a 2× fact that should be verbalized by the person who drew his or her hands first. The other person should state a related fact.

For example, if you call out "Seven," both you and the student draw seven fingers as pictured previously. Move toward each other, clap your five-fingered hands, and identify the number of additional fingers that will comprise the digit in the ones place of the product (in this case, 2 + 2, or 4).

If the student gets his or her seven fingers extended first, have him or her verbalize the 2× fact: "Fourteen equals two times seven," or "Seven times two equals fourteen." You then verbalize a different form of the same multiplication fact.

Please note that when the teacher's and student's hands are united, only the student will see the one group of ten fingers and four ones (14) in their correct right/left orientation. The teacher will see a mirrored image with the tens on the right.

Follow up this exercise with the related flash cards.

Use Icons of Quantity to Model 2× Facts and Place Value

As discussed earlier, iconic formations of dots are a helpful way for students to develop their ability to "see" numbers as recognizable clusters instead of collections of discrete elements to be counted. The nonverbal visual channel may be a relatively strong modality for some students. Woodin Icon patterns can provide a useful, visual way to practice 2× facts.

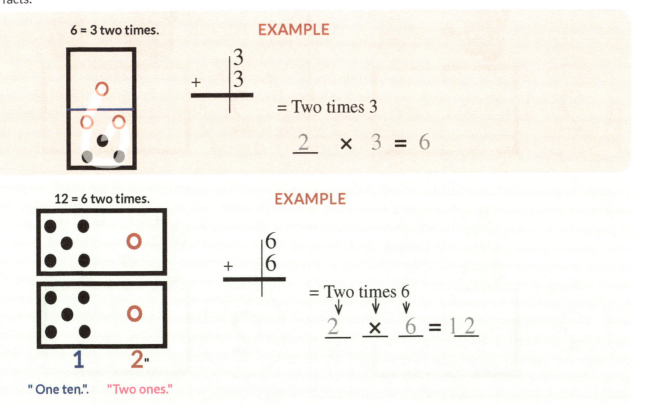

© 2013 C. Woodin & Landmark School

2× Facts:
Cut out these flash cards along the dotted lines. Mirror the fingers to produce two times the quantity of fingers, then verbalize the related facts.

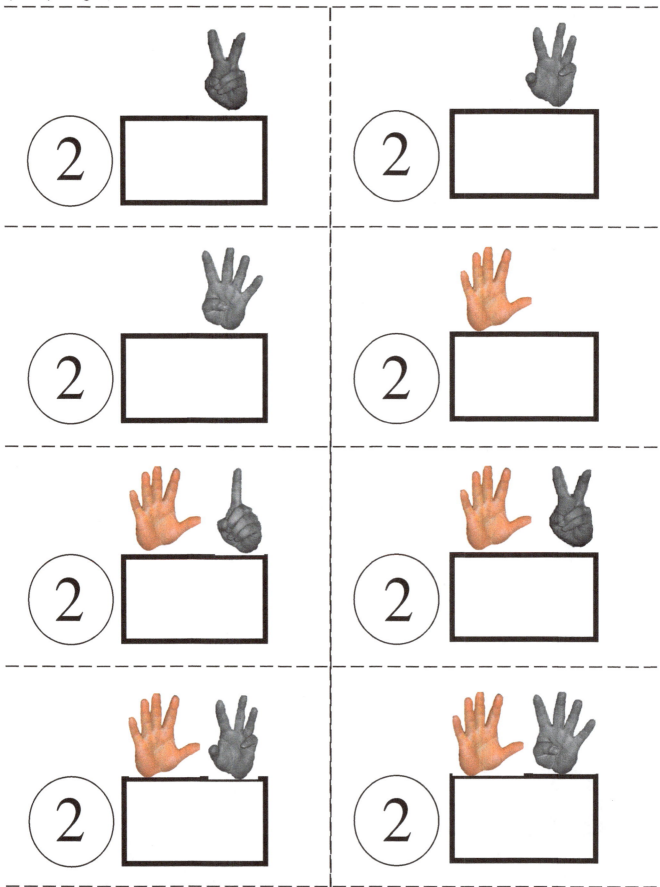

2× Practice with Icons

Name _____
Date _____
Day _____

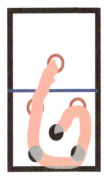

6 = 3 two times.

Add 3 two times.

$$+\begin{array}{r}3\\3\\\hline\end{array}$$

= Two times 3
↓   ↓   ↓
_2_ × _3_ = ___

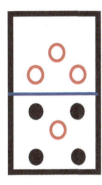

Add 4 two times.

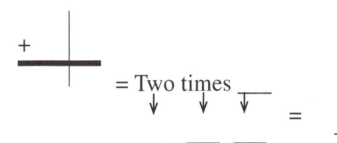

= Two times ___
↓   ↓   ↓
___ ___ ___ = ___

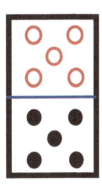

Add 5 two times.

+ ___|___

= Two times ___
↓   ↓   ↓
___ ___ ___ = ___

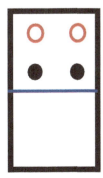

Add 2 two times.

+ ___|___

= Two times ___
↓   ↓   ↓
___ ___ ___ = ___

© 2013 C. Woodin & Landmark School

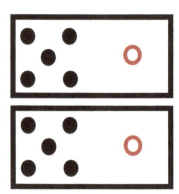

Add 6 two times.

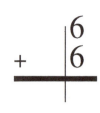

= Two times 6
 ↓   ↓   ↓

___ ___ ___ = ___

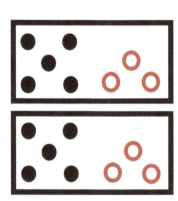

Add 8 two times.

+ |
―――

= Two times ___
   ↓   ↓   ↓

___ ___ ___ = ___

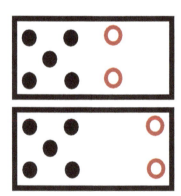

Add 7 two times.

+ |
―――

= Two times ___
   ↓   ↓   ↓

___ ___ ___ = ___

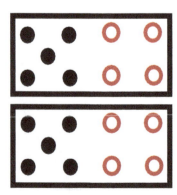

Add 9 two times.

+ |
―――

= Two times ___
   ↓   ↓   ↓

___ ___ ___ = ___

Multiplying by 2 Using Icons of Quantity

Name _____
Date _____
Day _____

Diagram the dot patterns: **Diagram, two times**

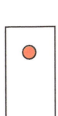 → 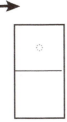   →

_2_ = _1_ × _2_

 →    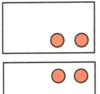 →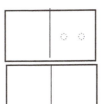

____ = __ × __

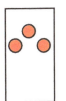 → 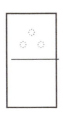   →

____ = __ × __

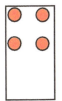 → 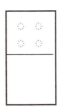   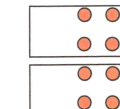 →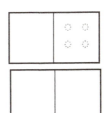

____ = __ × __

© 2013 C. Woodin & Landmark School

Multiplying by 2 Using Icons of Quantity

Name
Date
Day

Diagram the X and dot patterns: **Diagram, two times**

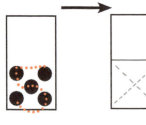 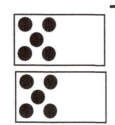 

Write the 2x fact.

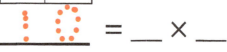

_____ = ___ × ___

  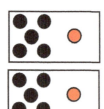 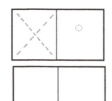

_____ = ___ × ___

  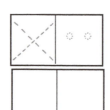

_____ = ___ × ___

  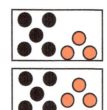 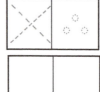

_____ = ___ × ___

 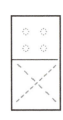 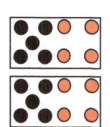 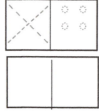

_____ = ___ × ___

Part-to-Whole Practice for 2x Facts

Similar to the previous whole-to-part Oral Recitation page, the following page is used for oral rehearsal of 2× facts. However, the following Oral Recitation page does not utilize whole-to-part symmetrical relationships, but rather part-to-whole familiar, semantic representations. For example, ten is represented by a dime, five is represented by a hand, and four is represented by a table.

Initially recite a multiplication fact that relates to one of the pictures—for example, "Eighteen players on two baseball teams." Ask students to point to the picture that best represents the description. Choose a student who (correctly) points to the baseball fields, and have him or her verbalize the fact as it relates to the picture. For example, the student might say, "Eighteen equals nine times two." Follow this activity with practice using part-to-whole flash cards. Initially these activities are driven by the teacher, but after the concept has been introduced they can be used between students or with parent involvement.

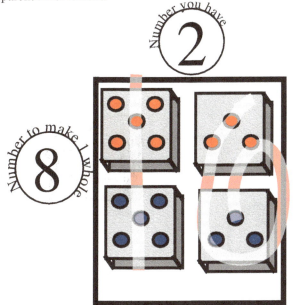

Note that these Iconic placement of dots make it possible to superimpose Arabic numerals.

Have students trace over the dot patterns with a fingertip to form these numerals.

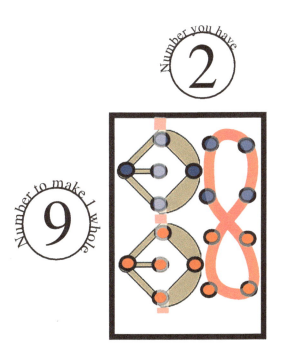

Although the positions of the 9 players are somewhat skewed, this representation enables the student to see two "teams" of 9 baseball players.

© 2013 C. Woodin & Landmark School

Oral Recitation Page for 2x Facts
- **The teacher describes a fact on this page.**
- **Students point to it, then verbalize it.**

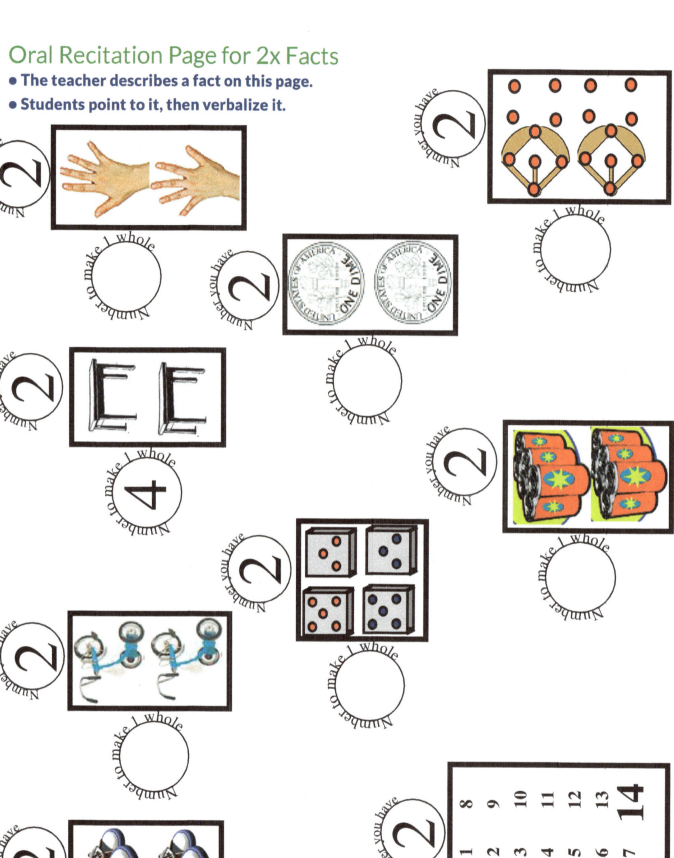
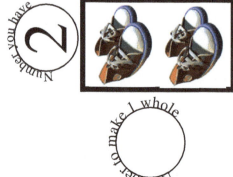
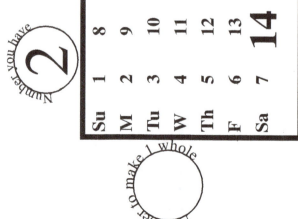

Number to make 1 whole ○ *Number you have* ②
10 fingers on 2 Hands
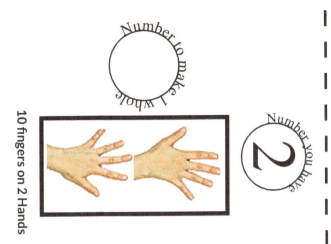

Number to make 1 whole ○ *Number you have* ②
4 sneakers in 2 pairs
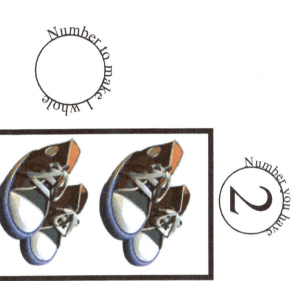

Part-to-Whole Flash Cards

- **Paste this sheet to the front of the following page.**
- **Cut out the glued cards to make five flash cards.**

Number to make 1 whole ○ *Number you have* ②
6 wheels on 2 tricycles
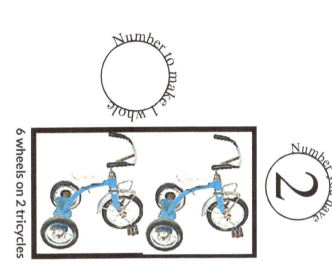

Number to make 1 whole ○ *Number you have* ②
12 cans in two 6-packs
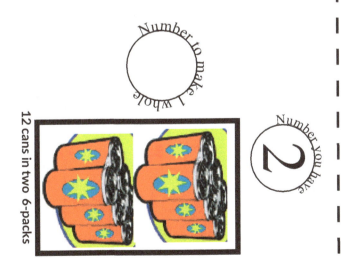

Number to make 1 whole ○ *Number you have* ②
8 legs on 2 tables.
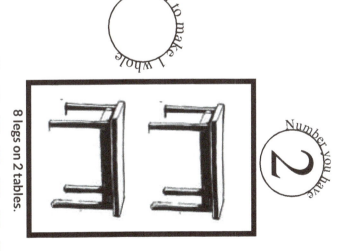

© 2013 C. Woodin & Landmark School

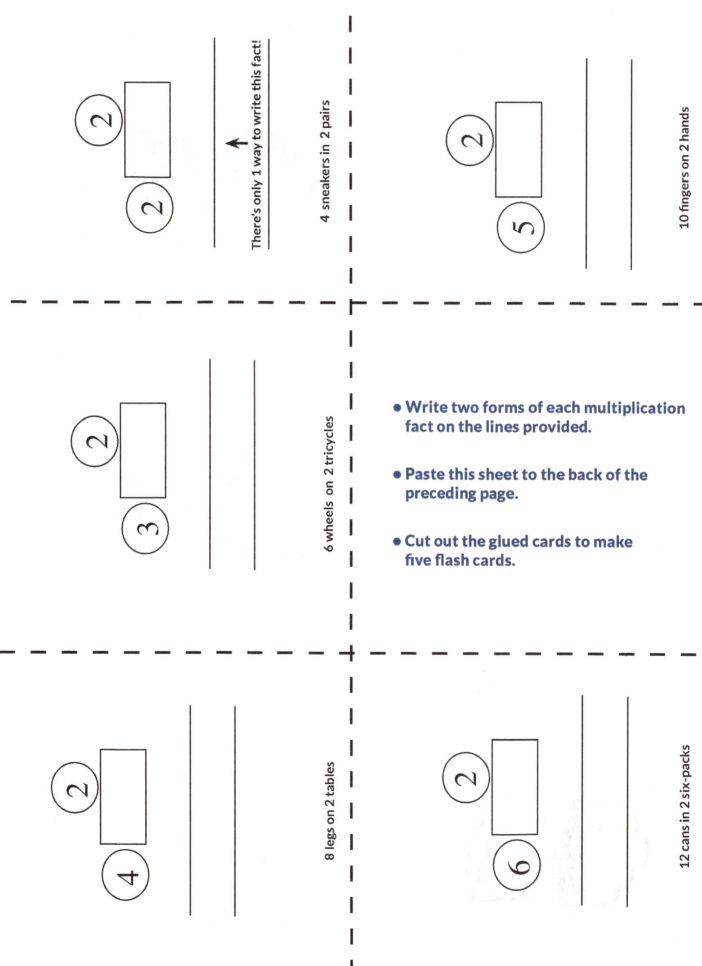

- **Paste this sheet to the front of the following page.**
- **Cut out the glued cards to make four flash cards.**

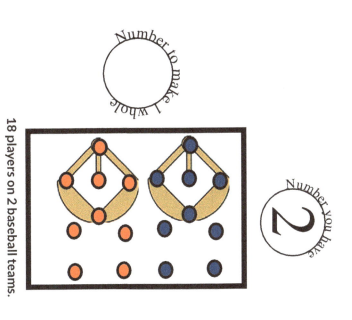

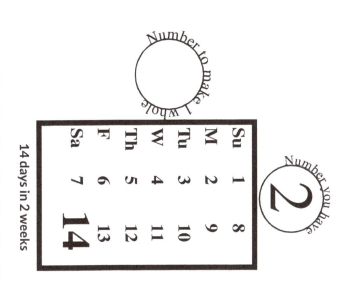

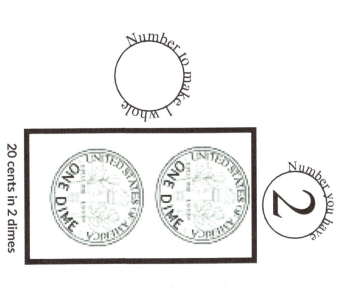

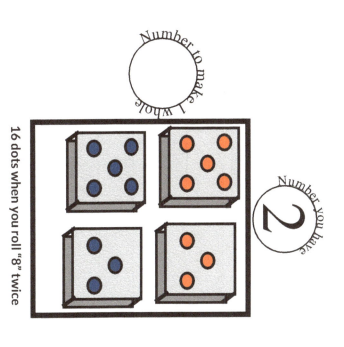

© 2013 C. Woodin & Landmark School

- **Write two forms of each multiplication fact on the lines provided.**
- **Paste this sheet to the back of the preceding page.**
- **Cut out the glued cards to make four flash cards.**

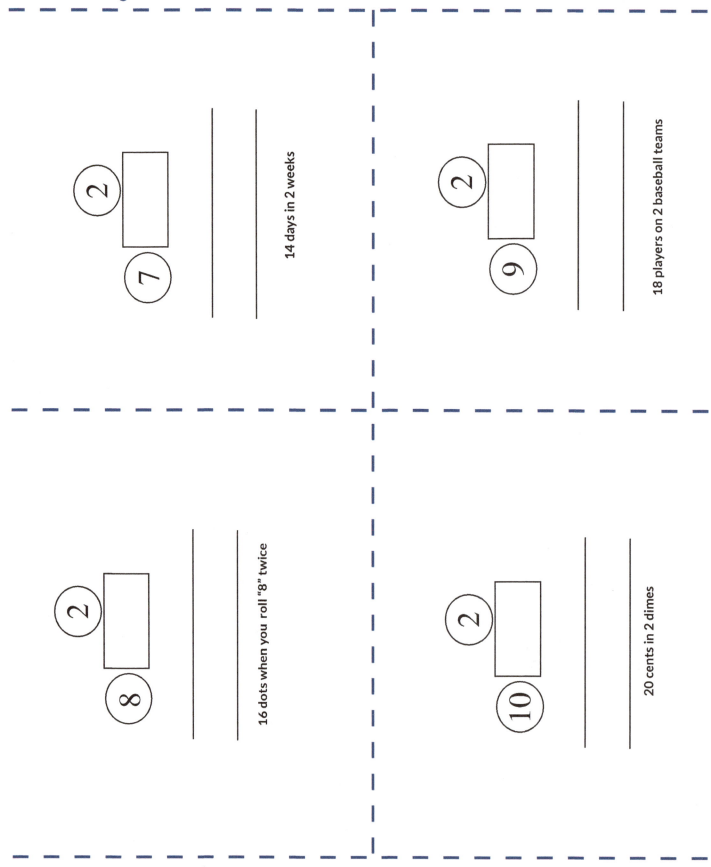

Standardized Methodology to Introduce the Pattern-Based Fact Families: (2×, 5×, 10×, 1×, 0×, 9×, 3×, 6×, 4×)

As explained earlier, students with learning disabilities have difficulty making accurate generalizations and then recognizing and retaining these general patterns without explicit instruction and guidance. Attempting to memorize isolated multiplication facts with no ordering structure is, for these students, analogous to learning to spell all words as sight words. These students need to have the patterns explained so that they can begin to impose order on the way they view the language of mathematics. Once students see these patterns, the patterns need to be reinforced until automatized. With the exception of the 2× family, students will first engage with the pattern-based fact families by discovering the divisibility rules of the fact family.

Introduce Fact Families with Divisibility Rules by Exploring Patterns on the 0–100 Chart

The 2×, 10×, 5×, and 1× fact families have products that are easily recognizable. Divisibility rules have been developed to define the products. These rules are helpful in that they provide an efficient means to recognize and accept, or exclude and reject, a product from each family.

Prior to having students practice a multiplication fact family, it is helpful to review the accompanying divisibility rule. The rule will help students to narrow the products to a pool of acceptable answers. Highlighting each fact family on a 0–100 chart (next page) provides an opportunity for the student to see these patterns.

Work on one fact family at a time, and wait until students achieve fluency with that family before moving on to the next. Prior to working on a specific fact family, highlight the multiples. Examine the pattern with students. Cadenced facts are represented on the 0–100 chart as columns. Guide the students to detect the pattern and then develop the divisibility rule for the family.

Time spent developing these divisibility rules will have a great benefit later. These rules may be used to check multidigit multiplication products, simplify fractions, and factor numbers. Time should be spent developing students' understanding of these rules in conjunction with each multiplication fact family. To ensure that students internalize these rules beyond their factual repertoire, ask them to create a three-digit number that conforms to a divisibility rule and explain why it fits the rule. For example, ask, "What is a three-digit multiple of two?" A student could respond, "One hundred eight is a multiple because there is a zero, two, four, six, or eight in the ones place." Then ask students to provide an example of a three-digit number that does not conform to the divisibility rule. Also, use a divisibility rule to check a product. Ask, "Does two times seventeen equal thirty-four or thirty-five?" The student might respond, "Two times seventeen cannot equal thirty-five because the ones place does not have a zero, two, four, six, or eight." Eventually, students will be able to state the rule more simply: "The product is not an even number."

ACTIVITY

The activity that follows models how to introduce the 2× family in a part-to-whole manner using visual patterns and divisibility rules.

Ask students to color all of the 2× fact products yellow.

Students may start this process by skip counting, but they should soon see the pattern of the multiples and alter their coloring strategy. Make sure that students start with the number 2!

- Pattern: The 2× products will emerge as five (vertical) columns of yellow.
- Collaboratively generate the divisibility rule and then have each student write individually on a 2× Divisibility Rule Sheet:

A number is divisible by 2 if it has 0, 2, 4, 6, or 8 in the ones place.

Students keep completed Divisibility Rule Sheets for 2× facts in their binders for reference. Students should each have a fact binder to archive their completed fact work. Use index tabs to separate the work done for each fact family. Start each of these sections with the Divisibility Rule Sheet for that fact family. In addition, post the rule Poster in a visible place in the classroom.

Divisibility Rule Chart

© 2013 C. Woodin & Landmark School

0 – 100 Chart

Upon starting a new fact family, highlight the multiples to reveal a pattern.

2× = Yellow **5× = Red** **10× = Orange** **9× = Dark Blue** **3× = Light Blue** **6× = Green**

Name _____

0	1	2	3	4	5	6	7	8	9
10	11	12	13	14	15	16	17	18	19
20	21	22	23	24	25	26	27	28	29
30	31	32	33	34	35	36	37	38	39
40	41	42	43	44	45	46	47	48	49
50	51	52	53	54	55	56	57	58	59
60	61	62	63	64	65	66	67	68	69
70	71	72	73	74	75	76	77	78	79
80	81	82	83	84	85	86	87	88	89
90	91	92	93	94	95	96	97	98	99
100									

© 2013 C. Woodin & Landmark School

Divisibility Rule Poster

DIVISIBLE BY 2

A number is **divisible by 2** if it has 0, 2, 4, 6, or 8 in the ones place. It is an even number.

Examples: 2<u>0</u>   14<u>2</u>   7<u>4</u>   30<u>6</u>   111<u>8</u>

If a number is a **multiple** of 2, it will end in 0, 2, 4, 6, or 8.

Some multiples of 2:   1<u>8</u>   4<u>0</u>   5<u>6</u>   10<u>2</u>   23<u>4</u>

2 is a **factor** of any number that ends in 0, 2, 4, 6, or 8.

Multiple		Factors
20	=	2 × 10
66	=	2 × 33
18	=	2 × 9
424	=	2 × 212

Divisibility Rule Sheet
Fill in the divisibility rules as you learn them.

Name
Date
Day

A number is **divisible by 2** if …

_____

_____

EXAMPLES:

USE THIS DIVISIBILITY POSTER TO START SECTION #1 OF YOUR FACT NOTEBOOK

GAME

Divisibility Rule Game Similar to Musical Chairs

After students identify multiples of 2 on the 0–100 chart by shading them yellow, establish and post the Divisibility Rule Poster: *A number is divisible by 2 if it has a 0, 2, 4, 6, or 8 in the ones place. Multiples of 2 are even numbers.*

- Give each student four index cards and a Magic Marker or crayon.
- Ask students to say out loud a three-digit number that is a multiple of 2 (358, 554, 990, and so on). After you have validated each answer, students may write the numbers on a card.
- Repeat until each student has labeled two cards with valid multiples of two. **358** **554**
- Ask students to say out loud a three-digit number that is a not a multiple of 2 (253, 657, 995, and so on). After you have validated their answers, students may write the numbers on a card.
- Each student should label two cards with numbers that are not multiples of two. **253** **657**
- Have the students take turns providing pairs of cards: one card that is a multiple of 2 and one that is not a multiple of 2. Ask each student in turn to explain why each number is or is not a multiple of 2.
- Place the pairs of cards side by side on the floor to make two concentric circles that are about one foot apart. Place multiples and nonmultiples in a random or alternating pattern. These circles of cards will be "stepping stones" for the students to follow. As a student walks on the path, each step should provide a choice to walk on a multiple or a nonmultiple.
- Instruct students to step only on multiples of 2 as they walk around the circle.
- Tell students to stand still on a card that is multiple of 2. Students should all be facing the same direction (so they can walk clockwise.)
- Ask each student in turn to explain why the number he or she is standing on is a multiple of 2.
- Ask everyone to take a step forward to the next multiple, then the next, and then say stop.
- Ask each student in turn to explain why the number he or she is standing on is a multiple of 2.

* *If a student is not on a multiple of 2, he or she must make the correction (move to the correct card).*

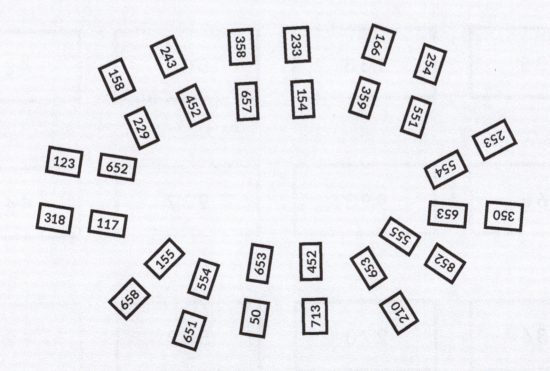

© 2013 C. Woodin & Landmark School

Use Divisibility Rules to Identify Multiples of 2

Name _____
Date _____
Day _____

These are car license plates. Multiples of 2 have 0, 2, 4, 6, or 8 in the ones place.

- Color multiples of 2 yellow.
- Draw an X over numbers not divisible by 2.

135	450	138	449
430	163	431	944
465	133	648	149
835	138	503	439
768	993	937	441
836	278	588	922

Use Divisibility Rules to Identify Multiples of 2

Multiples of 2 have 0, 2, 4, 6, or 8 in the ones place.

- Color multiples of 2 with yellow.
- Draw an X over numbers not divisible by 2.

Teachers: customize this template by filling in blanks with appropriate values.

Transfer the Multiples of 2 to the Multiplication Grid

After students have discovered the divisibility rule for 2 by highlighting the multiples of 2 on the 0-100 chart and have practiced applying the rule, have them highlight in yellow the 2× row and column of the 10×10 Multiplication Grid.

After students highlight the row and column, have them write the products in pencil. When a student is able to produce a fact with accuracy and fluency, he or she may be write over the products in ink. This practice can be applied to all the fact families on the multiplication grid. When the 2× facts have been learned, have the student use a yellow crayon to color the bottom 19% of the *Facts That I Know* graphic from page 22, which should be stored at the front of their Fact Notebook binder. Inking in the multiplication grid and coloring the *Facts That I Know* "thermometer" in this manner provides a great deal of motivation for the student and justifies the suggested order of fact instruction.

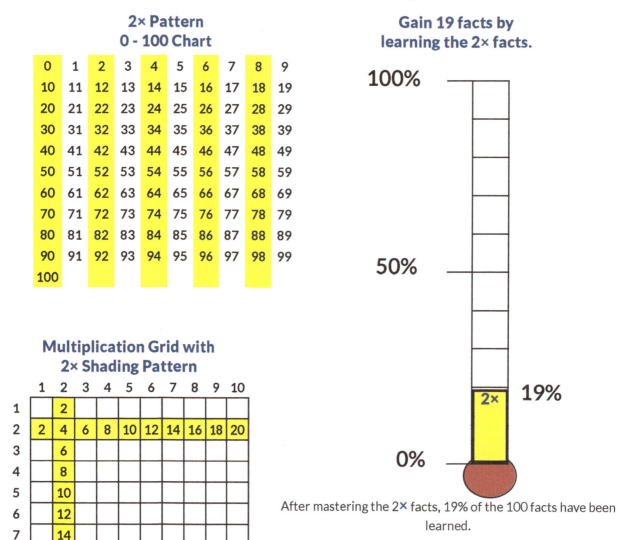

After mastering the 2× facts, 19% of the 100 facts have been learned.

Have the student use a yellow crayon to color this portion of the *Facts That I Know* organizer found on page 22. This big thermometer will get colored in as the facts get mastered. This progress chart should occupy the first page of a three ring **Fact Notebook** binder for each student.

Fill the notebook with completed fact worksheets that are organized by fact family to create an archive of familiar work that may be referenced for future review.

10 × 10 Multiplication Grid Example

Students will highlight the 2× row and column yellow. They will then pencil in this fact family and learn these multiplication facts. This grid should be stored in the front of the student's three ring Fact Notebook. After learning the 2× facts, they will write over the products in ink. Later, students will use the same multiplication grid to learn other fact families.

Specific colors will be used to highlight fact families.

2× = Yellow,   5× = Red,   10× = Orange,   1× = Grey,   9× = Dark Blue,   3× = Light Blue,   6× = Green

	1	2	3	4	5	6	7	8	9	10
1		2								
2	2	4	6	8	10	12	14	16	18	20
3		6								
4		8								
5		10								
6		12								
7		14								
8		16								
9		18								
10		20								

© 2013 C. Woodin & Landmark School

10 × 10 Multiplication Grid

After discovering a pattern on the 0 - 100 chart, highlight the rows and columns in the same color (below). This grid should be stored in the front of your three ring **Fact Notebook**. It will be completed as each fact family is learned. Write the multiples you are studying in pencil. Before moving to the next fact family, ink them in.

Name
Date
Day

2× = Yellow,   5× = Red,   10× = Orange,   1× = Grey,   9× = Dark Blue,   3× = Light Blue,   6× = Green

	1	2	3	4	5	6	7	8	9	10
1										
2										
3										
4										
5										
6										
7										
8										
9										
10										

© 2013 C. Woodin & Landmark School

Define Length, Width, and Area Using Multimodal Cues

The backbone of a multiplication and division fact problem is the matrix diagram, which is based on an area model defined by the length and width of a rectangle. Establish these dimensions with gross-motor, gestural cues.

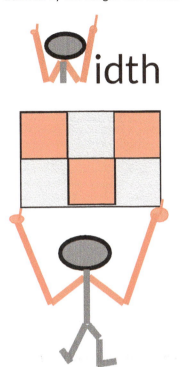

WIDTH

Create a large sheet of paper with 6 squares in a checkerboard pattern. Grab it by the bottom corners and hold it over your head. Ask the students to hold a sheet of paper the same way.

Define the width as the distance between the top or bottom corners.

Say, "Copy me. Grab the corners of the bottom edge of a sheet of paper. Hold it up high. The distance between your hands is called the width."

Ask, "What letter is formed by our arms?" "**W!**"

Say, "Even though width is a difficult word to read, you can recognize it because it begins with W. When you grab the width, you make a "W" with your arms."

Grab the top corners of the paper and hold it over your head to show that the top edge is also the width.

Say, "Grab the top edge of the sheet of paper."
Say, "The distance between the top corners is also called the **width**."

LENGTH

Tape the sheet of paper to the wall and point to both the top and bottom left corners like the man in the diagram at the right.

Define the length as the distance between the left or right corners.

Say, "I am pointing to the **length**."

Say, "The distance between the top and bottom corners is the **length**."

Say, "Look at the letter formed by each of my arms"

Ask, "What letter is formed by each arm?" "**L!**"

Ask, "Can a volunteer come up and point to the rectangle's length?"

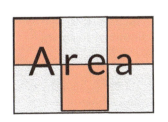

AREA

Use the same sheet of paper that has been taped to the wall to clarify area.

Define area as the number of squares inside of a figure.

Say, "The **area** is described as the number of squares inside the shape."
Ask, "How many squares are inside of the rectangle?"
Prompt the students to answer by pointing to the inside of the rectangle:
Say, "There are six squares in the area."

© 2013 C. Woodin & Landmark School

Determine Area from a Length and Width Description

DEFINE AREA WITH LENGTH AND WIDTH

Use the template on the following page to have students generate a rectangular area using two index cards.

Students create a rectangle by masking the checkerboard pattern on their paper with two index cards as shown below. Cue that the "*" star should always be visible.

Step 1) Place one index card over the checkerboard so that it is aligned with the left edge and the "*".

Say, "The checkerboard is 6 units wide."

Say, "Slide your card right 6 units."

Step 2) Place a second index card over the checkerboard so that it is aligned with the top edge and the "*".

Say, "The checkerboard is 2 units long."

Say, "Slide your card down 2 units."

Step 3) The two index cards now mask the checkerboard to make a smaller rectangle with an area of 12 squares.

Ask, "How many squares are in the area?"

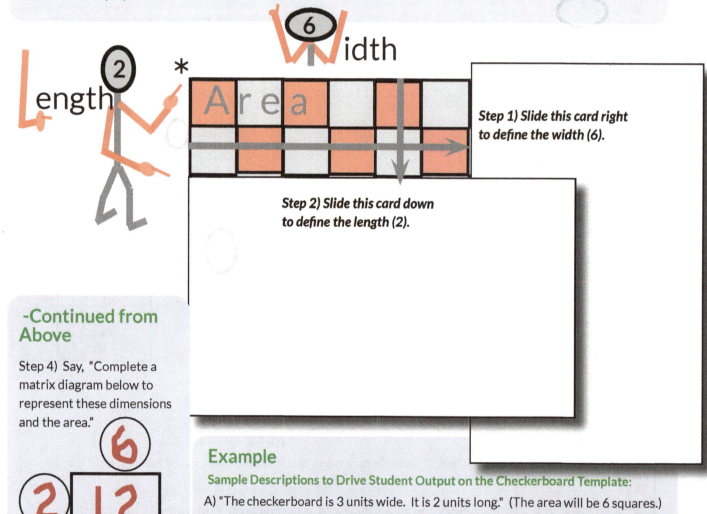

-Continued from Above

Step 4) Say, "Complete a matrix diagram below to represent these dimensions and the area."

Example

Sample Descriptions to Drive Student Output on the Checkerboard Template:

A) "The checkerboard is 3 units wide. It is 2 units long." (The area will be 6 squares.)

B) "The checkerboard is 2 units wide. It is 3 units long." (The area will be 6 squares.)

C) "The rug is 5 units wide. It is 2 units long." (The area will be 10 squares.)

D) "The rug is 3 units wide. It is 5 units long." (The area will be 15 squares.)

E) "The card is 2 units wide. It is 4 units long." (The area will be 8 squares.)

Determine Area from a Length and Width Description

The teacher will describe the width and length of the checkerboard rectangle. Use your two index cards to make the rectangle described by your teacher.

Complete a matrix diagram below by labeling the dimensions and the area.

Teachers: customize this template by dictating width values of 1-11, and length values 1-5.

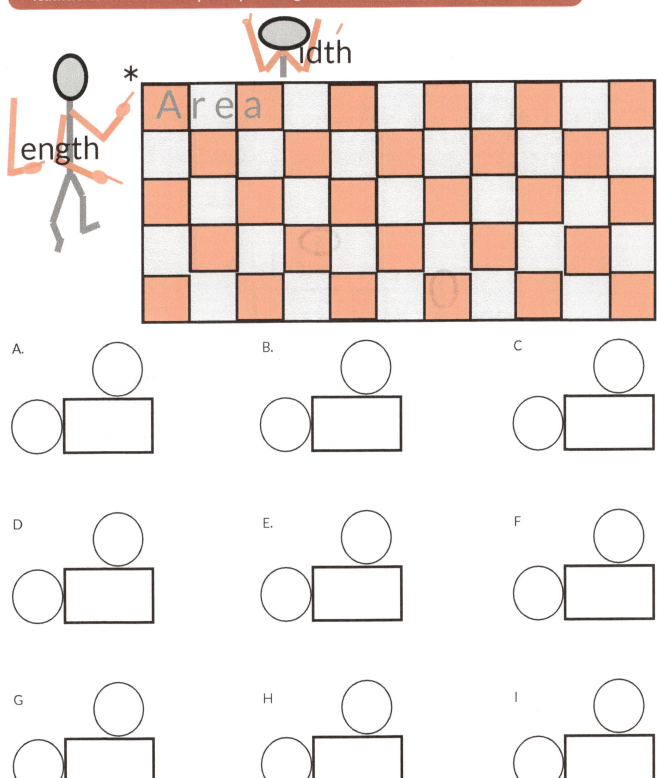

A.

B.

C.

D.

E.

F.

G.

H.

I.

© 2013 C. Woodin & Landmark School   55

Teacher's Instructions: Determine Width From a Length and Area Description

This activity will model the division process.
The teacher will describe the area and length of the checkerboard.
The divisor is represented by the length, and the area represents the dividend.
The resulting quotient will be the width.
Students create the rectangle by masking the checkerboard pattern with two index cards as shown below.
Cue that the "*" star should always be visible.

Example,
Step 1) Place an index card over the checkerboard so that it is aligned with the top edge and the "*."
Say, "The checkerboard is 2 units long."
Say, "Slide your card down 2 units."
Step 2) Place a second index card over the checkerboard so that it is aligned with the left edge and the "*."
Say, "The checkerboard has an area of 8 squares."
Say, "Slide your card to the right until there are 8 squares visible in the area."
Step 3) Ask, "What is the width of the checkerboard?" Answer, "The width is 4 units."

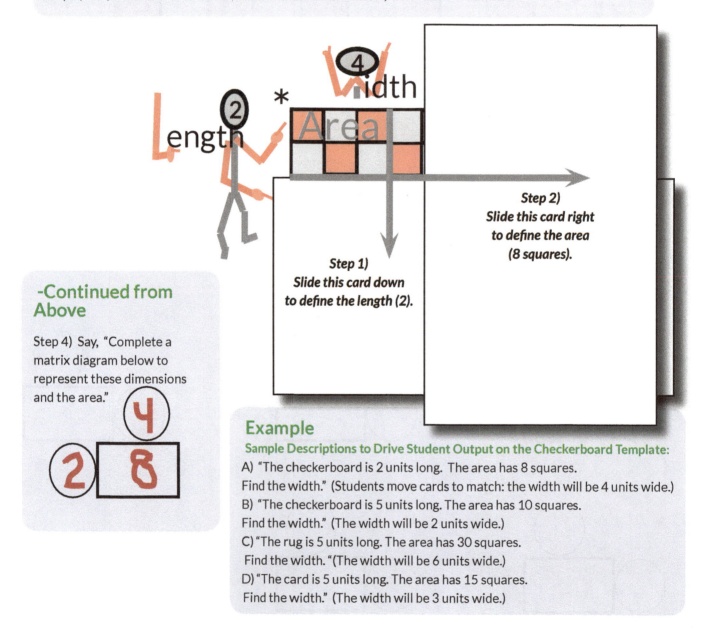

Step 2) Slide this card right to define the area (8 squares).

Step 1) Slide this card down to define the length (2).

-Continued from Above

Step 4) Say, "Complete a matrix diagram below to represent these dimensions and the area."

Example
Sample Descriptions to Drive Student Output on the Checkerboard Template:
A) "The checkerboard is 2 units long. The area has 8 squares.
Find the width." (Students move cards to match: the width will be 4 units wide.)
B) "The checkerboard is 5 units long. The area has 10 squares.
Find the width." (The width will be 2 units wide.)
C) "The rug is 5 units long. The area has 30 squares.
Find the width. "(The width will be 6 units wide.)
D) "The card is 5 units long. The area has 15 squares.
Find the width." (The width will be 3 units wide.)

© 2013 C. Woodin & Landmark School

Determine Width From a Length and Area Description

The teacher will describe the length and area of the checkerboard rectangle. Use your two index cards to make the rectangle described by your teacher. Complete a matrix diagram below by labeling the dimensions and the area.

Teachers: customize this template by dictating length values 1-5, and areas <55 that are multiples of the length.

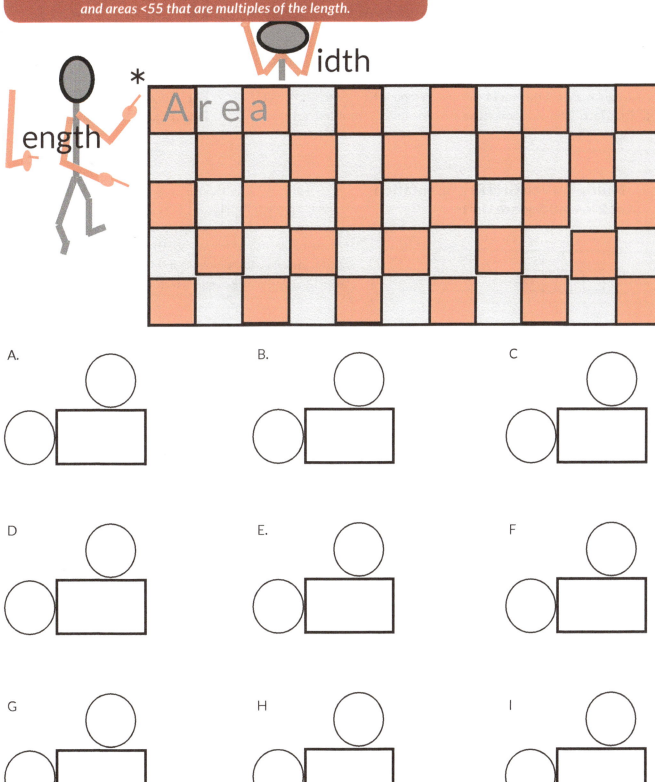

© 2013 C. Woodin & Landmark School

Multiplication Grid Area Model

The multiplication table can be used like a geoboard to show area. A geoboard is a mathematical manipulative often used to explore basic concepts in plane geometry, such as perimeter or area. A geoboard consists of a physical board covered in an array of nails—usually in a symmetrical 5 × 5 square—that serve as pegs. Students can place rubber bands around the pegs to model various geometric concepts or to solve other mathematical puzzles.

To use a multiplication grid like a geoboard, mask the right side and bottom of the multiplication grid with two pieces of paper. This will define a rectangular area of the chart that will correspond to a multiplication or division fact. This is an opportune time to introduce division facts.

Geoboard Representation of 2 × 4 = 8 Square Units

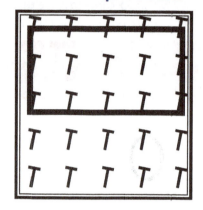

Multiplication Grid Representation of 2 × 4 = 8 Square Units

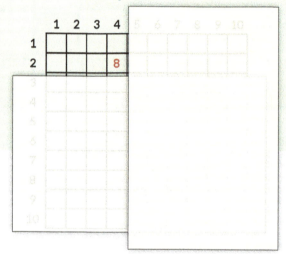

The 2 × 4 grid on the left shows an area of 8 square units. This grid would prompt the student to say, "Eight equals two times four, or eight divided by two equals four." When you use a geoboard, start using terminology that relates to the concept of area (length and width). Note that the grid shown also relates to the rectangular matrix diagram pictured below.

Students should verbalize and/or write each fact in its entirety so that they store the fact as an intact verbal string. Use visual cues from the masking process to prompt verbal responses. Use verbal cues to prompt the student to complete a matrix diagram for each fact (see the following page). This cross-modal processing fosters integration between the auditory, fine motor, and visual processing systems.

Avoid asking the student to trace or copy diagrams or parrot fact — activities that require minimal novel processing. Active processing, the act of building structure, serves to prolong the amount of time that the fact is held in short-term memory, facilitating the long-term retention of the fact.

Rectangular Matrix Diagram   **Related Facts**

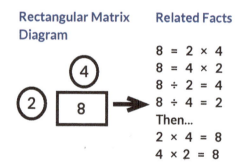

If you'd prefer to use an actual geoboard, you will likely need to make your own because most geoboards are too small to model multiplication facts through 10 × 10. Make a geoboard by pasting grid paper with one-inch squares onto a piece of plywood that is half an inch thick and one foot square. Drive 121 (eleven rows of eleven) brads or nails into the interior intersections of the grid lines. Number each row and column to create a geoboard that replicates a 10 × 10 multiplication grid. Use circular strips cut from nylon stockings rather than rubber bands to eliminate noisy (strummed), and ballistic (shot across the room) manipulatives.

Word Problems Related to Area: 2× Facts

Masking a multiplication grid can be a helpful strategy for students to use when solving word problems related to area.

As you read a problem aloud, students will mask the multiplication grid with two index cards to frame the rectangle described by the word problem. They use the grid to find the answer, then transfer the information to the diagram and label the answer with the appropriate units.

Use the following worksheet series to explore the terms and concepts relating to linear dimensions and area.

- The area is represented by the space inside the rectangle of the matrix diagram.
- The terms length and width height are interchangeable, though initially define width as the horizontal dimension, as in previous exercises.
- Area is labeled using square units. Prompt this label by referring to the number of squares inside the rectangle on the multiplication table that has been framed with the index cards.
- Take time to describe the language relating to dimensions. The nouns that are used to describe a dimension are significantly different from the adjectives used to describe them. e.g., width: wide, length: long, height: tall.
- Division concepts are introduced through these activities- though division terminology is not yet expressed.

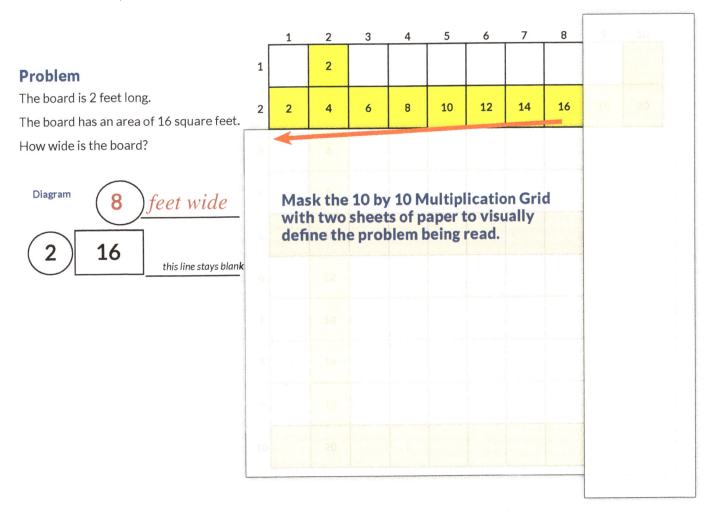

Problem
The board is 2 feet long.
The board has an area of 16 square feet.
How wide is the board?

© 2013 C. Woodin & Landmark School

Word Problems Related to Area: 2× Facts

- Mask the multiplication grid with two index cards to frame the rectangle described by the word problem.
- Use the grid to find the answer.
- Transfer the information to the diagram and label the answer with the appropriate units.

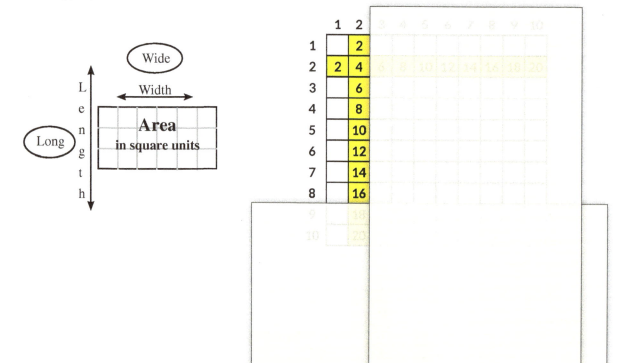

Problem #1

The board is 8 feet long.

The board has an area of 16 square feet.

How wide is the board?

Diagram

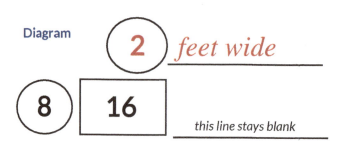

Problem #2

The door is 2 feet wide.

It is 8 feet long.

What is the area of the door?

Diagram

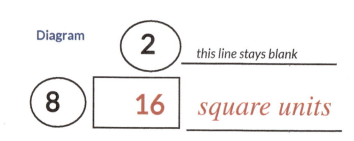

60   © 2013 C. Woodin & Landmark School

Word Problems Related to Area: 2× Facts

- Mask the multiplication grid with two index cards to frame the rectangle described by the word problem.
- Use the grid to find the answer.
- Transfer the information to the diagram and label the answer with the appropriate units.

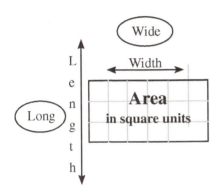

	1	2	3	4	5	6	7	8	9	10
1		2								
2	2	4	6	8	10	12	14	16	18	20
3		6								
4		8								
5		10								
6		12								
7		14								
8		16								
9		18								
10		20								

Problem #1
The board is 8 feet long.
The board has an area of 16 square feet.
How wide is the board?

Diagram

Problem #2
The rectangular rug is 2 feet long.
The area of the rug is 16 square feet.
How wide is the rug?

Diagram

Problem #3
The garden has an area of 12 square feet.
The garden is 2 feet long.
How wide is the garden?

Diagram

Problem #4
The door is 2 feet wide.
It is 9 feet long.
What is the area of the door?

Diagram

© 2013 C. Woodin & Landmark School

Word Problems Related to Area: 2× Facts

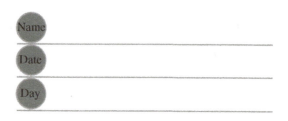

- Mask the multiplication grid with two index cards to frame the rectangle described by the word problem.
- Use the grid to find the answer.
- Transfer the information to the diagram and label the answer with the appropriate units.

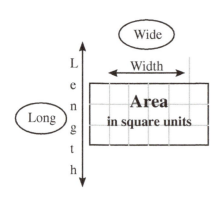

	1	2	3	4	5	6	7	8	9	10
1		2								
2	2	4	6	8	10	12	14	16	18	20
3		6								
4		8								
5		10								
6		12								
7		14								
8		16								
9		18								
10		20								

Problem #1

The board is 7 inches long.

The board has an area of 14 square inches.

How wide is the board?

Diagram

Problem #2

The rectangular bookmark is 2 inches long.

The area of the bookmark is 10 square inches.

How wide is the bookmark?

Diagram

Problem #3

The card has an area of 8 square inches.

The card is 2 inches long.

How wide is the card?

Diagram

Problem #4

The table is 2 feet wide.

It is 8 feet long.

What is the area of the table?

Diagram

62 © 2013 C. Woodin & Landmark School

Word Problems Related to Area: 2× Facts

- Mask the multiplication grid with two index cards to frame the rectangle described by the word problem.
- Use the grid to find the answer.
- Transfer the information to the diagram and label the answer with the appropriate units.

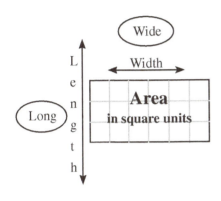

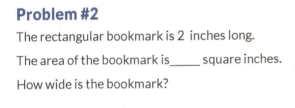

Problem #1

The board is 2 inches long.

The board has an area of _____ square inches.

How wide is the board?

Diagram

Problem #2

The rectangular bookmark is 2 inches long.

The area of the bookmark is _____ square inches.

How wide is the bookmark?

Diagram

Problem #3

The card has an area of _____ square inches.

The card is 2 inches long.

How wide is the card?

Diagram

Problem #4

The strip of paper is 2 inches wide.

It is _____ inches long.

What is the area of the paper?

Diagram

© 2013 C. Woodin & Landmark School

Use Semantic Associations to Teach Fact-Based Word Problems

While teaching specific fact families, generate examples of fact-related nouns in conjunction with their specific attributes. For example, generate examples of whole things that customarily have two identical attributes. When practicing the 2× family with students, use the nouns that have been introduced earlier with 2× flash cards.

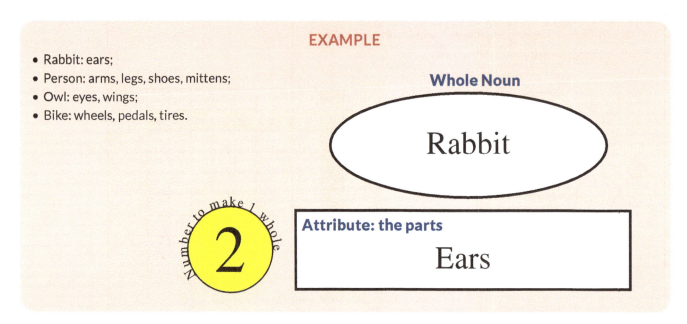

Use the standardized matrix diagram as a graphic organizer to relate the whole noun to its specific attributes. The most salient and recognizable pairings involve things that students interact with frequently. Activities using these semantic based relationships are most productive when performed with the 2×, 5×, and 10× grids, as there are many familiar examples available to use.

The templates that follow show the most common noun-attribute pairings. As students study the 2× facts, start using these associated nouns in your descriptions of the multiplication facts. Generate examples with your students, and have students complete the Reference Bank for the 2× Fact Family. Say, "Think of things that always come in twos. For example, a face has two eyes. Cookies can be grouped in twos, but they can also come in other amounts. Can you think of examples of things that always come in twos?" You will use this prompt as you introduce other fact families as well.

When you introduce a new fact family, start a new reference bank that features fact-specific noun pairings that relate to the fact family. Start with familiar pairings that strengthen the concept that multiplication is a process that describes a specific group or noun that is duplicated or repeated a number of times. When a group is defined by a specific noun, it is clear that the number of attributes is the quantity that will be repeated. For example, when a group is defined as a rabbit with two ears, it is clear that the number 2 will be repeated as many times as there are rabbits. The fact 2 × 3 can then be defined as three rabbits. Students are able to grasp a stable expression of the grouped quantity and differentiate it from the factor that replicates it. Without this distinction, some students forget the number that is to be repeated and vacillate between the grouped quantity and factor, adding groups of different quantities (for example, processing 2 × 3 as 2 + 3 + 3).

It can be helpful to use concrete presentations, or pictures, to generate and reinforce these word pairings.

Later you will use these fact-specific noun pairings within the context of word problems. Activities based on these pairings are described on the following pages.

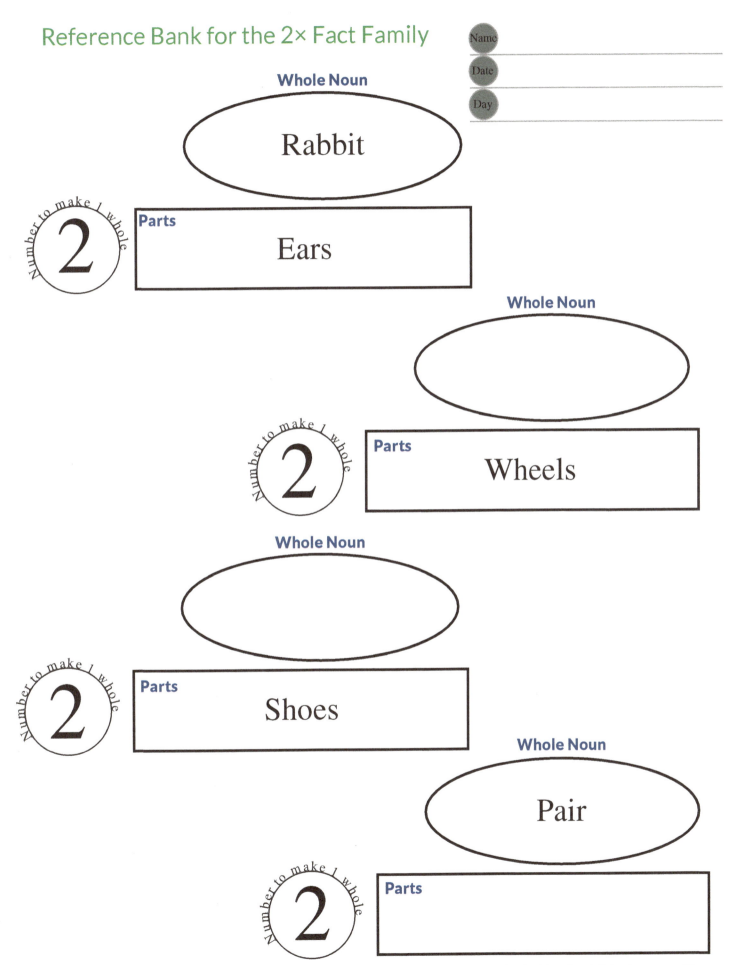

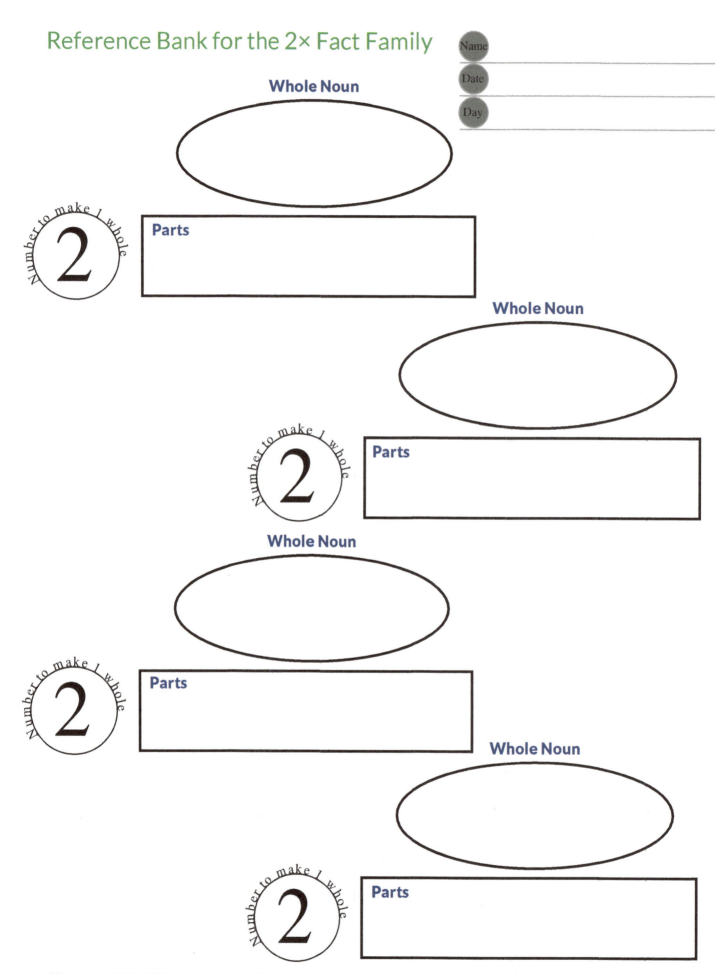

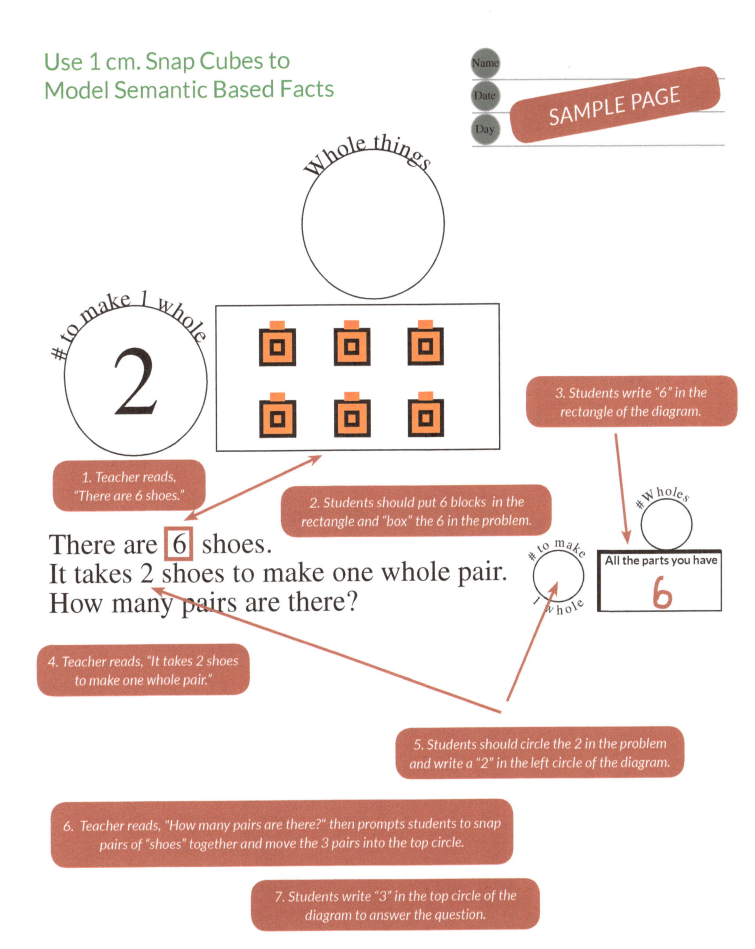

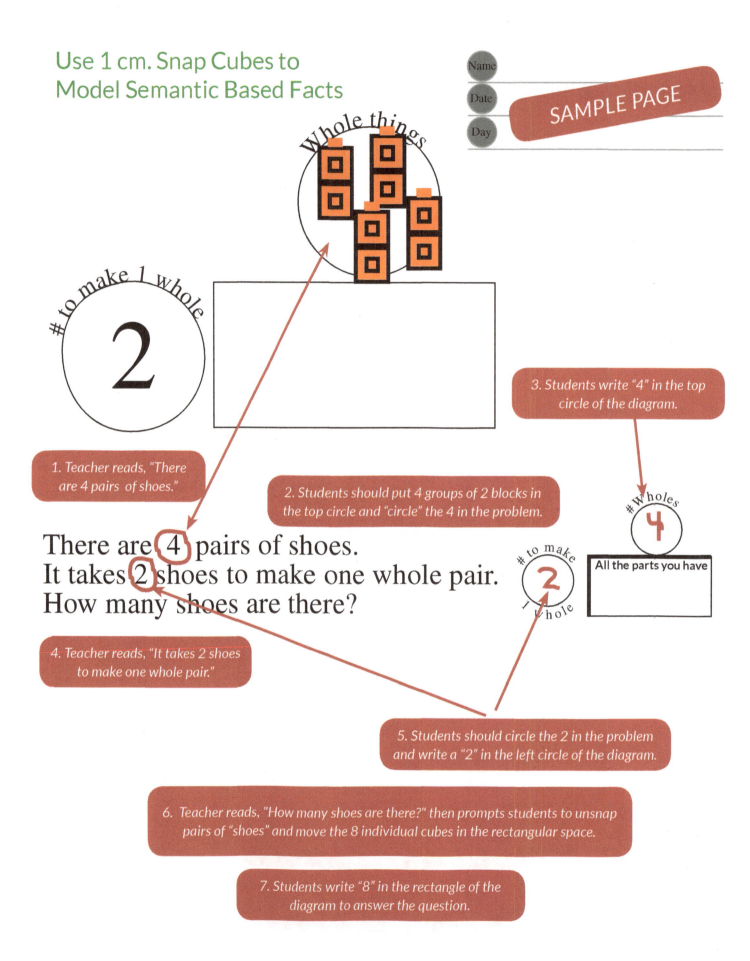

Use 1 cm. Snap Cubes to
Model Semantic Based Facts

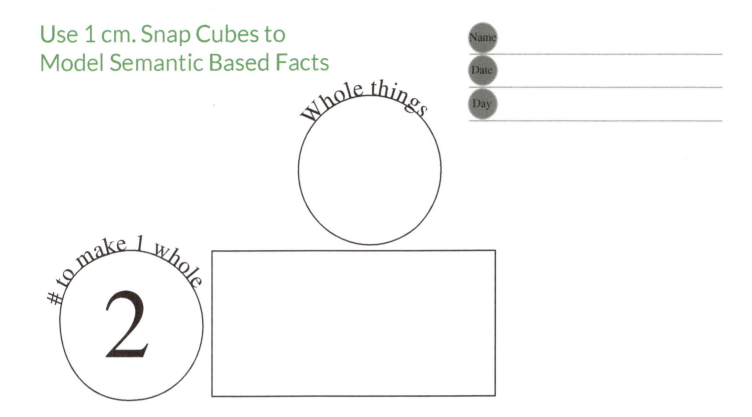

There are 6 shoes.
It takes 2 shoes to make one whole pair.
How many pairs are there?

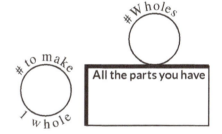

There are 4 whole pairs of shoes.
It takes 2 shoes to make one whole pair.
How many shoes are there?

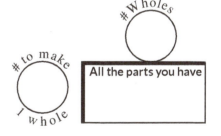

There are 4 shoes.
It takes 2 shoes to make one whole pair.
How many pairs of shoes are there?

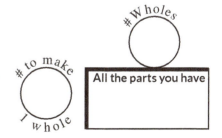

© 2013 C. Woodin & Landmark School

Use 1 cm. Snap Cubes to Model Semantic Based Facts

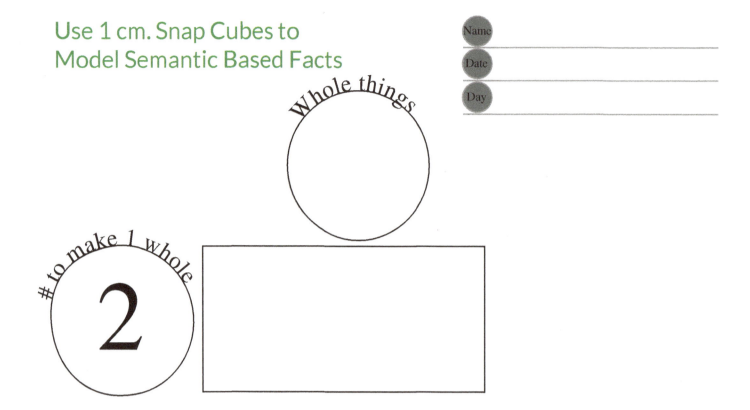

There are 6 wings.
It takes 2 wings to make one bird.
How many birds are there?

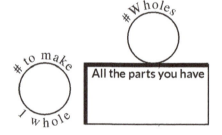

There are 4 birds.
It takes 2 wings to make one bird.
How many wings are there?

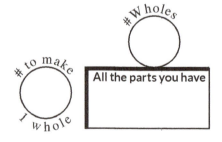

There are 10 wings.
It takes 2 wings to make one bird.
How many birds are there?

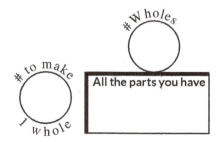

Use 1 cm. Snap Cubes to Model Semantic Based Facts - Template

Teachers: *customize this template by filling in blanks.*

Name _____
Date _____
Day _____

Whole things

 # to make 1 Whole: 2

There are ___ _____s.
It takes 2 _____s to make one _____.
How many _____s are there?

 # Wholes
 # to make 1 whole
All the parts you have

There are __ _____s.
It takes 2 _____s to make one_____.
How many _____ are there?

 # Wholes
 # to make 1 whole
All the parts you have

There are ___ _____s.
It takes 2 _____ to make one _____.
How many_____s are there?

 # Wholes
 # to make 1 whole
All the parts you have

© 2013 C. Woodin & Landmark School

Solving Word Problems Involving Multiplication and Division Facts

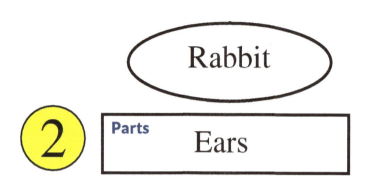

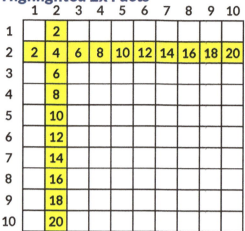

Now that students have gained familiarity with the area model and have manipulated concrete representations of semantic based problems, they are ready to transition to visually similar, more abstract models. Have students refer to their reference banks of completed noun-attribute pairings and the multiplication grids that have been filled in for the fact family. Read aloud a word problem that involves a noun-attribute pairing that has already been identified. Reread the problem, one phrase at a time. As you read each phrase of the problem, direct students to cover the multiplication grid with pieces of paper to define a rectangular area on the grid. This rectangle corresponds to a matrix diagram and prompts the multiplication or division fact necessary to solve the word problem. **Division is used when the story problem provides the total quantity of associated attributes, or ["all the parts"]. This quantity is represented visually as the rectangular area of squares within the multiplication grid.** Students then need to determine the quantity of parts necessary to make a whole or the number of whole things. Depending on the problem, one of these pieces of information will be given, and should go in the left circle (i.e., whole nouns will no longer always be at the top). All problems will generate a value in the left circle.

EXAMPLE

A) Read the entire problem: "All rabbits have two ears. Fred can see eight ears. How many rabbits are there?"

B) Next, repeat the first phrase: "All rabbits have two ears." Prompt that it takes two to make a whole.

C) Read the second phrase. Prompt that there are 8 parts. "Find these eight square parts."

D) Prompt the students to complete the matrix diagram with the missing information using the masked fact table and label the answer (in this case the quotient of four *rabbits*).

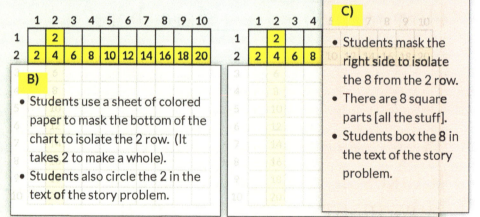

- Students use a sheet of colored paper to mask the bottom of the chart to isolate the 2 row. (It takes 2 to make a whole).
- Students also circle the 2 in the text of the story problem.

- Students mask the right side to isolate the 8 from the 2 row.
- There are 8 square parts [all the stuff].
- Students box the 8 in the text of the story problem.

Rectangular Matrix Diagram

This process of identifying the elements of a word problem as it is read aloud allows students to execute a problem-solving strategy without the need for a written output step. Placing each bit of information within the context of the rectangular matrix diagram immediately after hearing it mitigates demands on auditory working memory. This process will later be extended to problems involving larger numbers that are beyond students' factual repertoire.

Solving 2× Word Problems

- Using two sheets of paper, mask the multiplication table to isolate the information that is provided in the word problem.
- Use the table to find the answer.
- Transfer the information to the diagram and label the answer.

Problem #1

All rabbits have 2 ears.
Fred can see 8 rabbit ears.
How many rabbits are there?

Problem #2

There are 8 bikes.
All bikes have 2 wheels.
How many wheels are there?

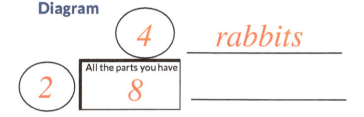

See the previous page to see the masked multiplication table.

Problem #3

Shoes come in pairs of 2.
There are 7 pairs of shoes.
How many shoes are there?

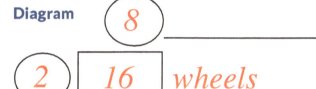

Problem #4

There are 10 bikes.
All bikes have 2 wheels.
How many wheels are there?

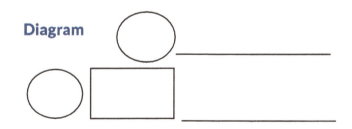

Problem #5

All rabbits have 2 ears.
Fred can see 9 rabbits.
How many ears are there?

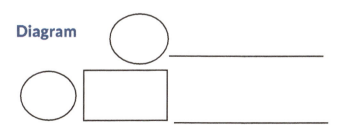

Solving 2× Word Problems

- Using two sheets of paper, mask the multiplication table to isolate the information that is provided in the word problem.
- Use the table to find the answer.
- Transfer the information to the diagram and label the answer.

Problem #1
All rabbits have 2 ears.
Fred can see 8 rabbit ears.
How many rabbits are there?

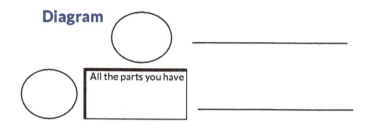

Problem #2
There are 8 bikes.
All bikes have 2 wheels.
How many wheels are there?

Problem #3
Shoes come in pairs of 2.
There are 7 pairs of shoes.
How many shoes are there?

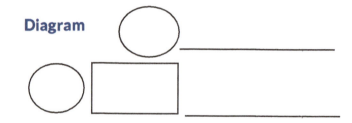

Problem #4
There are 10 bikes.
All bikes have 2 wheels.
How many wheels are there?

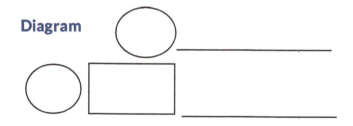

Problem #5
All rabbits have 2 ears.
Fred can see 9 rabbits.
How many ears are there?

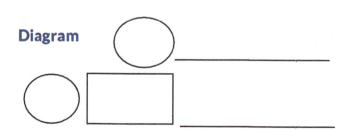

Semantic-Based 2× Multiplication Facts and Matrix Diagrams

- Circle the number of whole things.
- Circle the number of parts needed to make one whole.
- Box the number that represents all of the parts.
- Complete the diagram and write two related facts.

Fill in the diagram:

Tricycles have ③ wheels.
If there are ② tricycles, there are [6] wheels.

Facts: ② × ③ = [6]
         3 × 2 = 6

Tables have 4 legs.
If there are 2 tables, there are 8 legs.

Facts: _____
_____

Shoes come in pairs of 2.
If there are 2 pairs, there are 4 shoes.

Facts: _____
_____

Hands have 5 fingers.
If there are 2 hands, there are 10 fingers.

Facts: _____
_____

Dimes are worth 10 cents each.
If there are 2 dimes, they are worth 20 cents.

Facts: _____
_____

© 2013 C. Woodin & Landmark School   75

Semantic-Based 2× Multiplication Facts and Matrix Diagrams

- Circle the number of whole things.
- Circle the number of parts needed to make one whole.
- Box the number that represents all of the parts.
- Complete the diagram and write two related facts.

Fill in the diagram:

Facts: ②×④ = 8

Tables have ④ legs.
If there are ② tables, there are 8 legs.

Weeks all have 7 days.
If there are 2 weeks, there are 14 days.

Facts: _____

Spiders have 8 legs each.
If there are 2 spiders, there are 16 legs.

Facts: _____

Six-packs of soda have 6 cans.
If there are 2 six-packs, there are 12 cans.

Facts: _____

Baseball teams play 9 players at a time.
If there are 2 teams, there are 18 players.

Facts: _____

Teachers: customize this template by filling in blanks with appropriate values.

Semantic-Based 2× Multiplication Facts and Matrix Diagrams Template

- Circle the number of whole things.
- Circle the number of parts needed to make one whole.
- Box the number that represents all of the parts.
- Complete the diagram and write two related facts.

Fill in the diagram:

Problem #1: Facts:

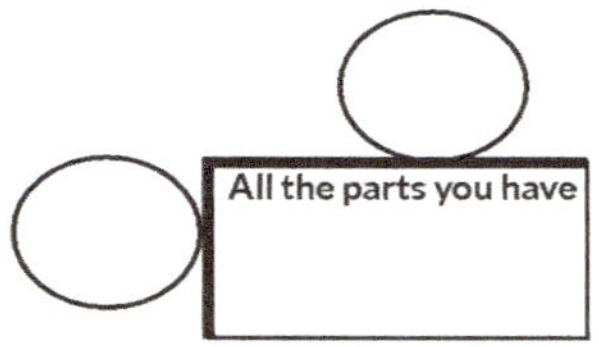

Problem #2: Facts:

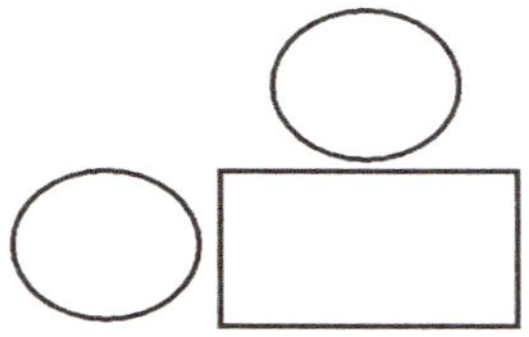

Problem #3: Facts:

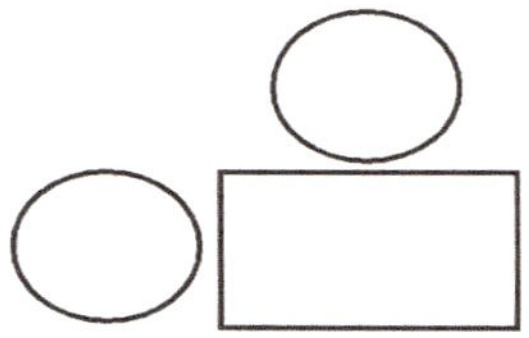

Problem #4: Facts:

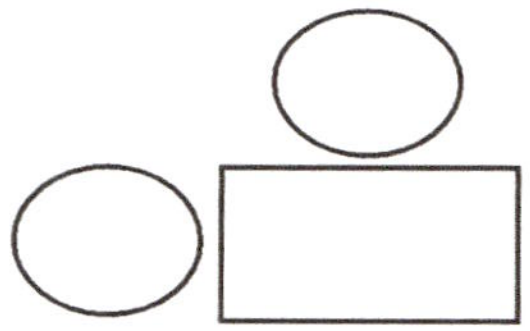

Problem #5: Facts:

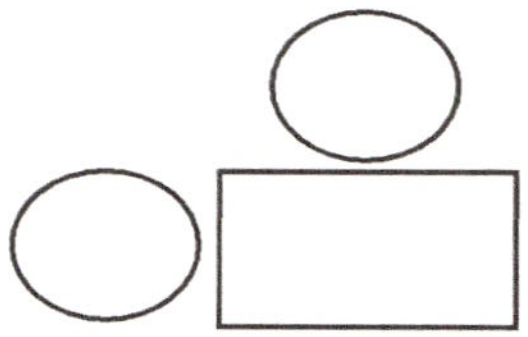

© 2013 C. Woodin & Landmark School   77

Semantic-Based 2× Word Problems

- Circle the number of whole things.
- Circle the number of parts needed to make one whole.
- Box the number that represents all of the parts.
- Complete the diagram to find the answer to the question.

Fill in the diagram and label the answer:

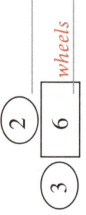

Tricycles have ③ wheels.
If there are ② tricycles, how many wheels are there?

Facts: ○ × ○ = ☐

Tables have 4 legs.
If there are 2 tables, how many legs are there?

Facts: _____

Shoes come in pairs of 2.
If there are 2 pairs, how many shoes are there?

Facts: _____

Hands have 5 fingers.
If there are 2 hands, how many fingers are there?

Facts: _____

Dimes are worth 10 cents each.
If there are 2 dimes, how many cents are there?

Facts: _____

78 © 2013 C. Woodin & Landmark School

Rehearsal Techniques and Activities to Teach Fact Families

Once students become familiar with the 2× family, they can practice the facts using games and activities. These activities can be used to reinforce all the fact families, but should be used only after students have received adequate instruction and practice with a given family. Incorrect answers that occur as a result of insufficient guided practice and explicit instruction disrupt the integrity of stored fact knowledge.

Make sure that students have the ability to look up each correct math fact if necessary. Students should never be forced to guess an answer. If a student seems unsure of a fact, prompt the student to wait and think, look up the fact, or say "pass" to have the answer supplied by you, the teacher. For example, if the student "passes", you may say, "Six times two is twelve. Give me a related fact. Start with two." The student should then supply the fact, saying it in its entirety.

FACT TWISTER

This activity reinforces number facts as well as directionality. Students can do this activity individually or in small groups. Write the products of the fact family you are addressing on (rectangular) index cards. Arrange the cards on the floor in front of students. In a class, each student should have their own set of cards spread out around them. Instruct students to answer your fact questions by touching the correct card with the appendage you name.

Example
TEACHER: Put your right foot on the product of two times five.

When students correctly perform the task, signal success by asking for the parroted fact, 2 × 5 = 10; the commuted multiplication fact, 5 × 2 = 10; or one of the two related division facts, 10 ÷ 5 = 2 or 10 ÷ 2 = 5.

FACT BALL

After practicing a multiplication fact family by using flash cards or through another production task, play a game of fact ball. Write numbers on a soft, light ball such as a tennis ball. Toss the ball to a student. The student should use the first number that he or she sees on the ball to begin a fact sentence. Initially, write only those factors that are most familiar—perhaps 1, 2, 5, and 10. Add more factors as the students gain confidence with harder facts.

Example

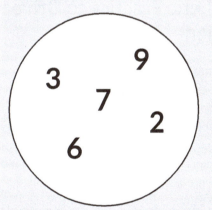

Toss the ball to a student who catches it with one hand. Have the student read the first number he sees—six, for example.

Say, "Say a two times sentence starting with six."

The student says, "Six times two is twelve."

Prompt the student to respond with a related fact: "Yes, and two times...."

The student says, "Two times six is twelve."

You may also choose to model one of the two related division facts: 12 ÷ 2 = 6 or 12 ÷ 6 = 2. The student then tosses or rolls the ball to you, and the roles are reversed. You may also have them toss the ball to another student.

CONSTANT TIME DELAY

The constant time delay therapy is useful when increasing the rate of fluency with familiar facts. It is a very useful strategy to use with children who have expressive language deficits. Students must have the ability to produce the correct fact from a prompt. This process involves showing the student a flash card or diagram or giving a verbal prompt of a portion of a fact sentence. Instruct the students to produce the answer to the fact sentence nonverbally (e.g., holding up fingers or pointing to an answer). After all students have expressed an answer, tell them that you are going to choose one student to recite the entire fact verbally when you clap your hands. Point to a student who has expressed the correct answer. Wait an additional four to six seconds, and then clap your hands to signal the student to recite the complete multiplication sentence. The imposed delay encourages the student to repeatedly recite the fact internally. Research has shown that this procedure facilitates long-term retention of facts in some children (Williams and Collins 1994).

EXAMPLE

Draw a matrix diagram on the board as shown:

Say, "Hold up the correct number of fingers to complete this fact."

Students hold up fingers to represent the answer (hopefully, each student holds up six fingers).

Select a student who is correctly holding up six fingers.

Wait four to six seconds, and then clap to prompt the student to respond.

The selected student says, "Six times two is twelve."

Use Gross Motor Kinesthetic Practice to Drive Integrated Fact Production

The term gross motor refers to movements that require the large muscle groups involved in basic posture and locomotion. Gross motor movements are acquired in a typical developmental progression: rolling over, sitting, creeping, cruising, and walking. Motivation is provided by a child's natural curiosity to explore. Refinement of these skills is necessary to combat the effects of gravity and avoid painful falls. Fine motor skills develop as a matter of course as children learn to grasp, point, control the mouth and tongue to formulate speech sounds, draw, and write. Both fine and gross motor skills are refined through practice, though gross motor skills may be practiced more frequently as a child struggles to exist in his or her environment.

Children with neurological problems, developmental delays, or disabilities that affect motor planning and articulation may have underdeveloped or ineffective gross and/or fine motor skills. However, it is usually easier to affect a change in gross motor expression if an effective therapy is used. Gross motor and kinesthetic exercises may be used to link motor planning with visual and auditory information while modeling fine motor production that can be refined at a later time. The expansive and general movements associated with gross motor output are forgiving in that minor inconsistencies are of little consequence. Also, there is a greater likelihood that these large motor actions will be perceived, acknowledged, or modified as a feedback loop becomes available. Often, children do not watch or see what they are writing as they are writing it. They see the (malformed or sloppy) written output on the page after there is no longer a chance of modifying its production.

Gross Motor Practice

Pretend that you are going to write on a large chalkboard that is at arm's length. Write a large number 5 (two feet tall) on this imaginary chalkboard. Notice how your eyes track your hand as it moves. When your eyes track your hand, a feedback loop is created. You are fostering visual-motor integration (VMI)—in this case, ocular motor movement and visual processing.

As a contrast, write the number 5 on lined paper. Note that your eyes do not move to match your fine motor pencil movements. In some cases, especially with left-handed students, there is very little eye contact with what is being, and has been, written. There is little or no visual feedback for the fine motor skills employed during written production.

To create another feedback loop, add a verbal description to correspond to the production of the large 5: "I start at the upper right. After that, I move left, then down, right and down, and left and down. I end by curving up." This verbal description could then be used to drive fine motor production with a pencil on paper.

Delays or impediments in fine motor processing are often evidenced by relatively low scores on the Processing Speed Index of the WISC. These students may have fine motor planning issues that may impact their handwriting output or fine motor problems associated with their verbal articulation. Their slow production rate, exacerbated perhaps by inefficient sensory-motor or visual feedback loops, prevents them from refining their rate or quality of production. Gross motor kinesthetic practice may have an immediate positive effect on such students' abilities to integrate visual and auditory processing with motor planning and production.

Athletes, capable of tremendous hand-eye coordination and feats of gross motor coordination, may struggle with fine motor planning and VMI. These individuals find it difficult to learn and refine handwriting skills. Multidigit computation can be very frustrating for them because they find it difficult to align digits correctly and conform to the spatial demands of these problems. Sometimes their production rate is slow in relation to their verbal processing abilities. This disparity between processing systems inhibits the systems' integration. It causes frustration because the individual's written output can't keep up with his or her inner voice. Teachers who are unaware of this issue may view a student's lack of production as laziness. Additional slower or louder verbal cues will not help the situation. Fine motor tracing will not be effective either because the student will not develop the fine motor planning skills necessary to improve.

Students benefit from activities that allow them to use gross motor kinesthetic processing in conjunction with visual cues and verbal descriptions. The picture to the left shows a girl jumping on elements of a large matrix diagram as she verbalizes a description of the process: "Eight divided by two is four." Using her body as a cursor, or "giant pencil," she is able to process the information in a multisensory manner. Her gross motor production serves as a metronome, keeping visual and auditory processing integrated with her motor planning. She generates different sentences on the basis of the first number that she is asked to stand on.

These whole-body gross motor exercises are later scaled down and refined. Eventually the student will verbalize fact sentences from a large matrix diagram that has been written on the board, touching each successive element with an outstretched hand while stating the fact. Further refinement involves downsizing the activity to tapping a pencil on a diagram the size of an index card. This exercise forces the integration of multiple modalities and serves to introduce the student to the motoric production steps of the long division algorithm. Students that practice these exercises develop the motor planning skills necessary to perform this potentially frustrating computation.

When executing whole-body gross motor exercises, students operate in their primary frame of reference: forward, backward, right, or left. The center point is implied, as it is the core of a student's own body. These movements must be consistent so that students may later externalize them to pencil and paper. When writing on paper, the center must be transferred from the core of the subject's body to a point that has been "decentralized" or externalized to the paper. The ability to decentralize one's reference frame is developmental in nature. Some students that can establish right and left directionality from their primary reference frame have difficulty performing this task with pencil and paper: they can point to the right or left when asked but have difficulty pointing to the right or left of a point drawn on a piece of paper. Letter and number transpositions (for example, 13 for 31), or reversals (for example, E for 3) may result from this inability to accurately express the visual-spatial information to an externalized reference frame.

The series of illustrations in Diagram M on page 84 illustrate the dynamic use of the matrix diagram combined with gross motor kinesthetic processing. To start this exercise, use sidewalk chalk to draw a completed matrix diagram on an area of blacktop outside. If it is sunny outside, orient the diagram so that the sun is at the top of the diagram as pictured in the illustrations. Ask the participating student to face the sun throughout the exercise. The sun's warmth on the student's face will provide a nonverbal cue to help the student maintain a constant orientation, which will provide a stable reference frame for the various movements.

If it is cold out or rainy outside, you may do this exercise inside by writing on a carpet with plain chalk. Don't worry—you can vacuum out the chalk. Take the place of the sun by standing above the quotient, facing the diagram. The student should face you throughout the exercise.

Ask the student to start on one of the three positions of the diagram. In the first illustration in the series, the student stands on the 2 of the diagram. For the student to make an accurate fact sentence, he or she must jump to the number 3 in the quotient position, and then down to the 6. The student should verbalize the numbers as his or her feet make contact with them: "Two times [hop] 3 [hop] equals six." If you need to provide directional cues, give them in the context of the student taking the place of a pencil and "writing" on the diagram. For instance, if the student hesitates when standing on the 3, cue him or her to hop down, not back. These descriptions of motor action should be consistent when later applied to the fine motor skill of writing with a pencil.

After the student has articulated the multiplication fact sentence (2 × 3 = 6), he or she is poised to start the next fact sentence: 6 ÷ 2 = 3.

The student must hop left, and then up and to the right, ending on the 3, to generate the division fact sentence. Starting from the 3, the student can perform the third and final sentence: 3 × 2 = 6. By performing these movements, the student learns three associated facts as a dynamic unit. The student should then move to a similar diagram that has the same product (6), but for which the two factors, 2 and 3, have been transposed. Using this second diagram, the student will develop further flexibility with the 2 multiplication facts (2 × 3 = 6 and 3 × 2 = 6) while adding 6 ÷ 3 = 2 to his or her repertoire of fact families.

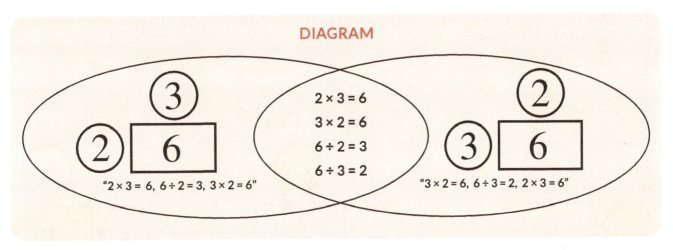

This activity has a great impact on the student's fluency rate and develops flexibility with syntax and factual knowledge within the context of dynamic units. It also serves to provide a useful introduction to the process of long division. The internalized gross motor movements serve to prompt the division steps. This is of great benefit to those students who have deficits in working auditory memory (that is, difficulty remembering and sequencing the numerous verbal directions provided through traditional instruction).

This gross motor activity may be extended to drive students' production of story problems. Using the same diagram, students are asked to describe the three numbers on the diagram as quantities of semantically related items. Instead of merely creating the fact sentence 2 × 3 = 6, the student is asked to compose a story problem while jumping on the numbers. For example, while on the 2, the student may say, "There are two tricycles." The student hops to 3 and says, "Each tricycle has three wheels." Now the student must formulate a question relating to the 6: "How many wheels are there?" The student hops to the 6 and says, "There are six wheels." The student is now poised to create a related division story problem that uses the same three numbers but asks a question about the quotient, 3.

This activity is further explained in the following *Whole Body Gross Motor Kinesthetic Multiplication and Division Word Problem Activity* section.

Diagram M: Whole Body Gross Motor Kinesthetic Multiplication and Division Fact Practice

Develop fluency by verbalizing two multiplication and one division fact using the three elements of the matrix fact diagram.

- Draw one diagram on the pavement or a carpet runner using sidewalk chalk.
- Have the student maintain a consistent reference frame (face the same direction) throughout the exercise.
* If this is done outside, draw the diagram so that the student will be facing the sun as he or she reads it.
- The student should hop from one element to the next, verbalizing each element in synchrony.
- Three facts will be produced: 1) A,B,C; "2 × 3 = 6," 2) A,B,C; "6 ÷ 2 = 3," 3) A,B,C; "3 × 2 = 6."
- Later, swap the circled values of a diagram to show how an additional (fourth) division fact can be expressed with the same two factors and multiple.

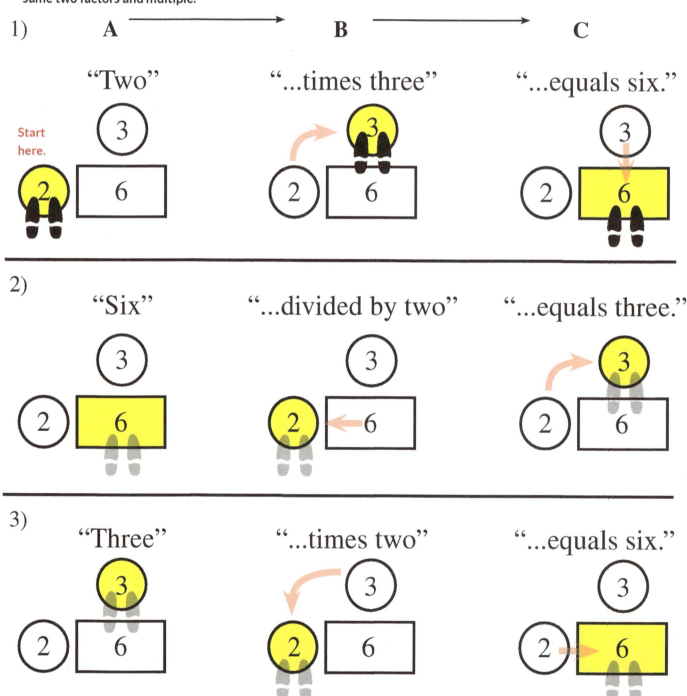

© 2013 C. Woodin & Landmark School

Diagrams that Generate Multiplication and Division Facts

- Complete the diagrams.
- After they are checked, write four related multiplication and division sentences for each diagram.

Dry Erase Flash Card Fact Production Template

Laminate this page, or put it inside a plastic sheet protector. Have each student put their name on it and store it in their Fact Notebook. Students will reuse this page for practicing all the fact families.

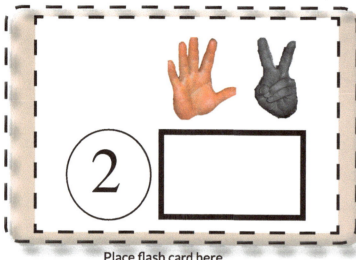

Place flash card here.

Complete this diagram to match the flash card.

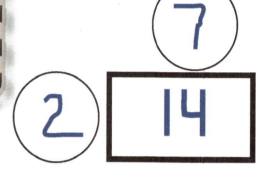

Write related multiplication and division facts below with a dry erase marker:

$2 \times 7 = 14$

$7 \times 2 = 14$

$14 \div 7 = 2$

$14 \div 2 = 7$

This sheet can be used many ways.

1) Ask students to all select the same flash card to drive fact production.

e.g., Say, "Find your 2 × 7 flash card and put it on the big rectangle at the top of the page."

Say, "Complete the fact diagram and write two multiplication and two division facts."

2) Give each student a different flash card. Choose the card based on the need of each student.

3) Use this template as a consumable paper worksheet. Place a flash card on the rectangle, then make a photocopy for each student. to complete with a pencil.

4) Have these sheets available to students while they are doing independent work. If a student asks, "What's 2 × 7?"

...Well, you get the idea!

Dry Erase Flash Card Fact Production Template

 Name

Laminate this page, or put it inside a plastic sheet protector.
Keep it in the front section of the Fact Notebook.
Reuse this page for practicing all the fact families.

Write with a dry-erase marker.

Complete this diagram to match the flash card.

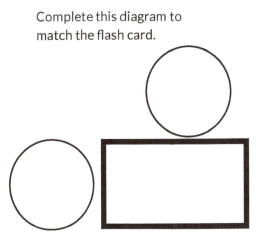

Write related multiplication and division facts below:

© 2013 C. Woodin & Landmark School

Create Dynamic Story Problems

In the text:
- Circle the number of whole things, circle the number of parts needed to make one whole, or box the number that represents all of the parts.
- Write a question using the two statements provided.
- Answer the question.

Name: *Stu Dent*
Date: *Nov.*
Day: *Tuesday*

5 rabbits (oval)
2 (oval) | **10 ears** (box)

○ There are (5) rabbits.
○ Rabbits have (2) ears.

Write a question using the two statements provided.

[?] *How may rabbit ears are there?*

Write the answer.

☐ *There are [10] rabbit ears.*

☐ There are [10] rabbit ears.
○ Rabbits have (2) ears.

Write a question using the two statements provided.

(?) *How many rabbits are there?*

Write the answer.

○ *There are (5) rabbits.*

☐ There are 10 rabbit ears.
○ There are 5 rabbits.

Write a question using the two statements provided.

(?) _____

Write the answer.

○ _____

88 © 2013 C. Woodin & Landmark School

Create Dynamic Story Problems

In the text:
- Circle the number of whole things, circle the number of parts needed to make one whole, or box the number that represents all of the parts.
- Write a question using the two statements provided.
- Answer the question.

Name ___
Date ___
Day ___

(5 rabbits)

(2)   [10 ears]

○ There are 5 rabbits. ___
○ Rabbits have 2 ears. ___

Write a question using the two statements provided.

[?] ___

Write the answer.

[ ] ___

[ ] There are 10 rabbit ears. ___
○ Rabbits have 2 ears. ___

Write a question using the two statements provided.

(?) ___

Write the answer.

○ ___

[ ] There are 10 rabbit ears. ___
○ There are 5 rabbits. ___

Write a question using the two statements provided.

(?) ___

Write the answer.

○ ___

© 2013 C. Woodin & Landmark School   89

Create Dynamic Story Problems

In the text:
- Circle the number of whole things, circle the number of parts needed to make one whole, or box the number that represents all of the parts.
- Write a question using the two statements provided.
- Answer the question.

Name _____
Date _____
Day _____

(3 bikes)   (2)   [6 wheels]

○ There are 3 bikes. _____
○ Bikes have 2 wheels. _____

Write a question using the two statements provided.

[?] _____

Write the answer.

☐ _____

☐ There are 6 wheels. _____
○ Bikes have 2 wheels. _____

Write a question using the two statements provided.

(?) _____

Write the answer.

○ _____

☐ There are 6 wheels. _____
○ There are 3 bikes. _____

Write a question using the two statements provided.

(?) _____

Write the answer.

○ _____

90   © 2013 C. Woodin & Landmark School

Create Dynamic Story Problems

In the text:
- Circle the number of whole things, circle the number of parts needed to make one whole, or box the number that represents all of the parts.
- Write a question using the two statements provided.
- Answer the question.

Name _____
Date _____
Day _____

Teachers: customize this template by filling in blanks with appropriate values.

○ _____
○ _____

Write a question using the two statements provided.

[?] _____

Write the answer.

□ _____

□ _____
○ _____

Write a question using the two statements provided.

(?) _____

Write the answer.

○ _____

□ _____
○ _____

Write a question using the two statements provided.

(?) _____

Write the answer.

○ _____

© 2013 C. Woodin & Landmark School

Whole Body Gross Motor Kinesthetic Multiplication and Division Word Problem Activity

Develop language skills relating to word problems by kinesthetically interacting with three statements that correspond to the three elements of the now familiar matrix fact diagram. Draw a large diagram on the pavement with sidewalk chalk like you did to practice multiplication and division fact expression. Extend this activity to a semantic context by adding a noun that relates to the whole and a related attribute from the students' Reference Bank for the 2x fact family.

- Draw one diagram on the pavement or a carpet runner using sidewalk chalk.
- Have the student maintain a consistent reference frame (face the same direction) throughout the exercise.
* If this is done outside, draw the diagram so that the student will be facing the sun as he or she reads it.
- The student should hop from the first element to the second, verbalizing each related phrase in synchrony.
- After hopping on and verbalizing the first two phrases, prompt the student to ask a question that relates to these elements and can be answered with the third element.

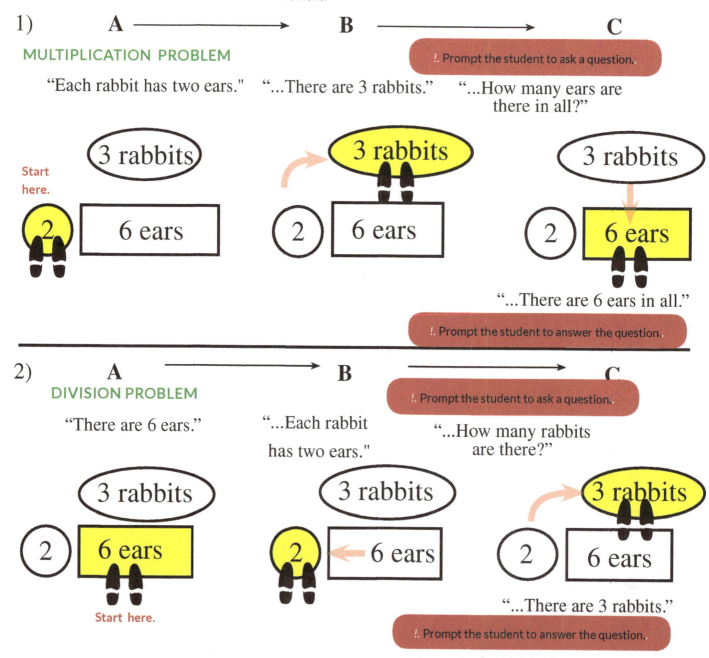

1) **MULTIPLICATION PROBLEM**

   A → B → C

   "Each rabbit has two ears."   "...There are 3 rabbits."   "...How many ears are there in all?"

   ! Prompt the student to ask a question.

   "...There are 6 ears in all."

   ! Prompt the student to answer the question.

2) **DIVISION PROBLEM**

   A → B → C

   "There are 6 ears."   "...Each rabbit has two ears."   "...How many rabbits are there?"

   ! Prompt the student to ask a question.

   "...There are 3 rabbits."

   ! Prompt the student to answer the question.

Accuracy Benchmark Pretests and Fluency Assessment Worksheets

This program was created as a means to develop fact fluency. The Accuracy Benchmark Pretests and timed Fluency Assessment worksheets should not be used as a fact-learning system. These assessment devices provide a way to assess and increase the speed with which a student can access and produce an accurate fact, and express that factual knowledge within the context of fact sentences. The impetus behind this program is to develop accurate fact retrieval on an independent basis, then (and only then) express this knowledge using written language with increasing efficiency.

Accuracy should never be sacrificed in an effort to increase the rate of expression. Every time a student responds to a stimulus with an errant response, (e.g., "2 × 7 = 17") that response is, to some degree, learned. This adds to confusion, and as a result, corrupts and slows the fact learning process. For the same reasons that a teacher should not work on reading fluency with material beyond the decoding skills of a student, math fluency drills should only be used to increase a student's skills with familiar facts.

Many students with language-based language disabilities have difficulty efficiently naming things from a visual presentation. This is evidenced by poor scores on naming (R.A.N., R.A.S., Boston Naming Test, etc.). Though naming speed may improve over time, this trait tends to be an enduring one for dyslexic students. Their ability to produce an oral or written label for a visual prompt will always tend to be relatively inefficient. These students will also be inefficient at fact fluency worksheets and exercises when they are asked to look at a partial math fact, then produce an accurate label in a rapid drill format.

These students should not be given tests that have them produce as many facts as possible in a prescribed amount of time. This methodology precludes some students from the production of many facts and places the student in a failure setting from the start. Instead, stress accuracy.

Use the Accuracy Benchmark Pretest to allow a student to demonstrate the ability to produce correct matrix diagrams for each fact of a fact family. These diagrams are presented in a whole-to-part manner (division) format that provides the product and one factor. After the students have completed the diagrams, walk around and check accuracy or correct collaboratively. Note students who are not getting them correct. After the making notes, this is a great time to play a game that features oral recitation of the specific facts such **as Fact Ball** or question and answer using constant time delay. When the game is over, have the students produce one entire multiplication fact and one division fact for each of the 10 diagrams on the twenty lines provided. The students should write each fact as a linear sentence. Again, stress accuracy and disregard the speed component of fluency at this point.

After all students are able to produce an Accuracy Benchmark Pretest with 100% accuracy, it is time to work on efficiency. Use the timed Fluency Assessment to document the efficiency of written fact expression. As before, stress accuracy over speed. The diagrams on this test feature part-to-whole organization. The student must first produce the product from the two factors provided. This initial step serves to measure accuracy and fact retrieval efficiency with a minimal demand on fine motor output. When finished, encourage the student to proofread by checking all of the products with the fact family's divisibility rule. After given this opportunity to proofread, correct any products if necessary. The second wave of output asks the student to produce two complete written fact sentences using correct numbers, operators (×, ÷, =) and syntax. These additional processing and production demands provide a way to codify a student's ability (or inability) to process and express written language. Archive completed tests along with other worksheets in the student's three ring Fact Notebook to keep a record of ongoing fact fluency. Consider a student to be functionally fluent **if he or she can complete all of the Fluency Assessment Worksheet diagrams accurately in under 1 minute, then write the 20 related fact sentences with 100% accuracy in under three minutes**. At this point the student may move to the next fact family; however, continue to administer fluency tests to concurrently review familiar facts while learning new fact families. Archive these additional Fluency Assessment Worksheets in the Fact Notebook, filed with the associated fact family. Strive for the student to achieve a personal best on each successive administration.

Administration of the Accuracy Benchmark Pretest and Fluency Assessment Worksheets.

1:1 Administration by a Teacher / Tutor

- First, have the student complete all of the diagrams. Note the time that it takes to complete the ten diagrams (if indicated). Students may initially make mistakes. Review the diagrams, and note the number correct in the space provided: N/10. Then, ask the student to make necessary changes to make all diagrams accurate before using them to generate fact sentences.

- Next, ask the student to write one multiplication fact and one division fact for each of the 10 diagrams. Note the accuracy (number correct / 20) as well as the amount of time taken to produce the twenty facts (if indicated).

Errors include the expression of inaccurate factors or products, inaccurate operational symbols (e.g., substituting "+" for "×"), illegible writing, and use of incorrect syntax (e.g., improper order of numbers or operational signs within sentences).

Group Administration

Option 1, Teacher Administered Tests

- First, have the students complete all of the diagrams. Note the time that it takes to complete the ten diagrams (if indicated). This may take the form of asking students to put their pencils on their desks after completing the diagrams, then noting the students that finish **before 30 seconds, before 1 minute, or after 1 minute.**

- Write the correct diagrams on the chalkboard. Have the students erase errors, then use colored pencil to make necessary changes to their diagrams. Students should record the number correct in the space provided.

- Next, ask the students to write one multiplication fact and one division fact for each of the 10 diagrams. Note the time needed (if indicated). This may take the form of asking students to put their pencils on their desks after completing the sentences, then noting the students that finish **before 2 minutes, before 3 minutes, or after 3 minutes.** Collect and score the accuracy of the sentences. Record the accuracy (number correct / 20) as well as the amount of time taken to produce the twenty facts.

Option 2, Teacher Directed Tests With Self-Timing

Provide each student with a stopwatch. Administer the test by starting the timed events. Each student starts the stopwatch at your command, does the assigned task, stops the watch when finished and records his or her time. Another option involves having a stopwatch application running on the Smartboard for the students to look at.

Additional Fluency Practice

The Vertical Fact Practice worksheet provides another way to test and develop a student's rate of fact production. It also serves to introduce the student to another traditional production format. Some students will have initial difficulty as they transition to this new template. Vertical problems place additional demands on visual tracking as students must scan and acquire symbols in a novel way. They may scan left to right as if they are reading, then must track left and down as if acquiring the next line of written text in a book. Some students have a great deal of difficulty learning and performing this ocular-motor scanning task. There are also additional visual motor demands as the product should be encoded with reference to the columnar arrangement of the problem as dictated by it's place value. Archive completed tests along with other worksheets in the student's fact notebook to keep a record of ongoing fact fluency.

Time to Get a Head Start on the Fives!

While students are practicing the 2× multiplication facts to the point of mastery, begin to develop familiarity with the analog clock dial and the associated minute values. Reference the *Introduction to the 5× Whole-to-Part Multiplication Facts* in the following section for a detailed explanation of this process.

Accuracy Benchmark Pretest - Untimed

Complete this sheet with 100% accuracy before taking the related timed *Fluency Assessment*.

1) Complete each diagram. Have them scored.
2) Correct diagrams if needed.
3) Write a multiplication fact and a division fact for each.
4) Archive this pretest in your Fact Notebook as a record.

Name _____
Date _____
Day _____

Diagram Accuracy: _____/10

Sentence Accuracy: _____/20

2) 2 _____   2) 12 _____

2) 4 _____   2) 14 _____

2) 6 _____   2) 16 _____

2) 8 _____   2) 18 _____

2) 10 _____   2) 20 _____

© 2013 C. Woodin & Landmark School

Fluency Assessment - Timed

Administer this test after the student scores 100% accuracy on the related *Accuracy Benchmark Pretest*.

1) Complete each diagram. Note time and accuracy.
2) Correct diagrams as needed.
3) Write a multiplication fact and a division fact for each. Note time and accuracy.
4) Archive this in your Fact Notebook as a record.

Name _____
Date _____
Day _____

Diagram Accuracy: ____/10   Time: ____
Sentences Accuracy: ____/20   Time: ____

(2) [5] _____   (2) [7] _____

(2) [3] _____   (2) [10] _____

(2) [2] _____   (2) [9] _____

(2) [6] _____   (2) [8] _____

(2) [1] _____   (2) [4] _____

© 2013 C. Woodin & Landmark School

Vertical Fact Practice

Name _____
Date _____
Day _____

Timed quiz
_____ seconds

◯ /10

```
   | 1            | 6
 x | 2          x | 2
---|           ---|

   | 2            | 7
 x | 2          x | 2
---|           ---|

   | 3            | 8
 x | 2          x | 2
---|           ---|

   | 5            | 9
 x | 2          x | 2
---|           ---|

   | 4           1| 0
 x | 2          x | 2
---|           ---|
```

© 2013 C. Woodin & Landmark School   97

Fact Mosaics

This jigsaw-type puzzle reinforces number facts, the sequential instructions, directionality, problem-solving strategies, and perception of multiple reference frames. Students can play either individually or in small groups. Start by having each student complete a worksheet for the fact family you want to address. Correct students' worksheets to ensure that the facts are accurate. These number facts are the only clues for reassembling the puzzle once it is cut into pieces.

Give each student a blank Fact Mosaic puzzle. Using the corrected fact worksheets, have the students write a product (for example, 6) on one side of a grid line, and the multiplication problem (2 × 3) on the other. To make an easy version of the puzzle, have students leave the outside edge of the large square blank. To make the puzzle more challenging, students can write other facts and products around the outside edge. When students have labeled all grid lines with a problem and an adjoining product, have them cut out the large 3 × 3 square and then have them cut the square along the grid lines to produce a mosaic of nine pieces.

Ask students to reassemble this jigsaw-type puzzle by connecting each fact problem with its product. Once a student has assembled his or her mosaic, the student can trade mosaics with another student.

SAMPLE PAGE

Note: Omit the facts and products on the outside edges to make an easier version.

EXAMPLE OF A COMPLETED FACT MOSAIC

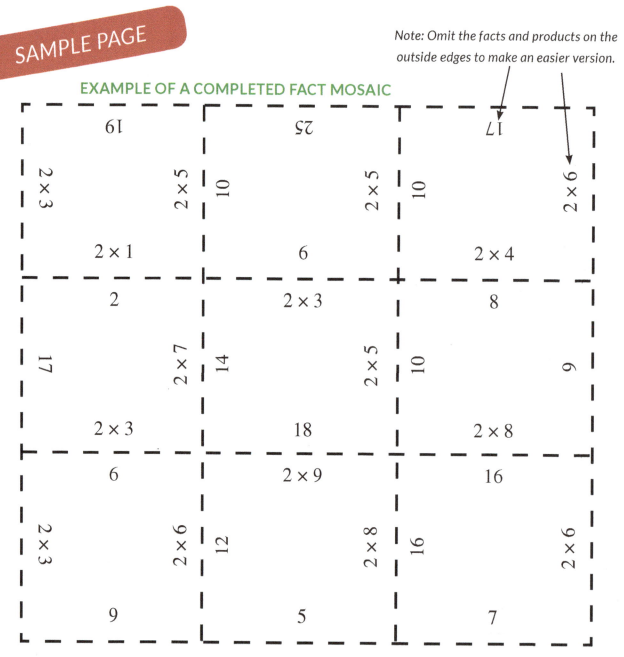

2× Fact Mosaic

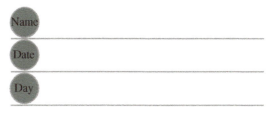

- Write a product—6, for example—on one side of a dashed grid line and the related multiplication problem ("2 x 3") on the other.
- After writing both parts of each fact on either sides of each line, cut this puzzle along the dashed lines into nine square pieces.
- Shuffle the pieces.
- Try to reassemble them using the multiplication problems and products as a guide.
- Trade puzzles with another student and challenge each other!

GAME

Baseball Fact Game

The baseball fact game provides an activity-based way for students to practice facts. The game is played on a game board that resembles Boston's Fenway Park. Students generate facts based on a factor (a number 1 through 10) determined by the drawing of a playing card. Limit the length of the innings by limiting the deck students draw from, the "pitch deck," to ten cards (each card corresponds to a number 1 through 10). Add cards to expand the pitch deck and add variety to the game.

This is a two player game, or may be adapted for two "teams".

Materials:
- Baseball fact game worksheet (for use as a gameboard)
- Facedown deck of playing cards with face cards removed or Woodmark Numeric Icons
- Dried beans to use as players "human beans," and counters

Goal:
The goal of the game is to score the most runs.

The example provided features the 2× facts; however, the scoring rubric may be adjusted to create a game based on any fact family. The ten possible products are apportioned so that the three lowest multiples (1×, 2×, and 3× products) produce outs. The 4× and 5× products are singles; the 6× and 7× products are doubles; the 8× and 9× products are triples. Home runs are generated by the 10× product.

1) Player 1 is the batter. He or she places a bean on home plate. Player 2 is the pitcher. He or she "pitches" a card by flipping the top card from the facedown deck.

2) The batter (Player 1) must use the factor on the card, or "pitch," in a corresponding 2× fact sentence. For example, if the pitcher (Player 2) pitches a 3, the batter would say, "Two times three is six." The pitcher will either affirm the response or politely disagree. (You serve as the umpire. Students may consult with you to settle any disagreements over the accuracy of the fact, or players may refer to a corrected fact sheet. Before the start of play, model polite disagreement.)

3) The product defines the outcome of the play. Drawing a low-value pitch (factors 1, 2, 3) results in an out, while higher factors generate higher products and result in base runs or home runs as defined by the scoring rubric. The players should consult the scoring rubric at the top of the game board to determine the result of a pitch.

Scoring Rubric For 2× Facts

2, 4, 6	Out	Move the "batter" bean from home plate to one of the three Out spaces.
8, 10,	Single	Move the "batter" bean to first base. If a bean is already on first base, advance it to second base. Beans on other bases are advanced similarly if forced.
12, 14	Double	Move the "batter" bean to second base, advancing other runners if forced.
16, 18	Triple	Move the "batter" bean to third base, advancing other runners if forced.
20	Home Run	"Yee haw!" Clear the bases, place all beans that score on the "Runs Scored" spaces.

4) Use the beans to represent base runners. In the example above, if a 3 is pitched, Player 1 responds with, "Two times three is six." Since a product of 6 corresponds to an out according to the scoring rubric, Player 1 takes the bean off home plate and puts it in one of the *Out* circles on the game board. That player now has one out.

5) Player 2 now pitches another card. Beans that are on base can be advanced to score runs as the batter responds with products that equate to base hits or

home runs. (Note that a bean advances from a base only when another bean must land on that base. For example, if a batter gets a double on his or her first turn, the batter would place a bean on second base. If the batter gets a single on his or her second turn, he or she would place a bean on first base, and the bean on second base would *not* advance to third.) As runs are scored, players place beans in the Runs section on the game board. The batter continues to receive pitches, verbalize facts, and advance runners (beans) to score until there are three outs.

6) At the end of the inning, players cross off the three outs on the game board. Player 1 should take the beans out of the *Runs* section, count them, and then write the number in the *Runs* section. The beans then get passed to Player 2.

7) Player 2 is now up at bat, Player 1 pitches the cards, and the inning continues until Player 2 gets three outs.

Beans can't pass each other on the base path or share bases. There is no stealing, and runner beans advance only if a bean that has been put into action by a hit forces them.

Description of a sample game:

A 6 is pitched. The product is 12. The batter says, "Two times six is twelve." This is a double, as 12 corresponds to a double on the scoring rubric. If the pitcher agrees that the verbalized fact is correct, the batter moves the bean along the base path counterclockwise from home plate, first to first base and then to second base. The batter places a new bean on home plate.

The next pitch is a 5. The batter says, "Two times five is ten." This is a single, so the batter moves the bean from home plate to first base. The bean on second base stays there until forced to advance. The batter places a new bean on home plate.

The next pitch is a 2. The batter says, "Two times two is four." Four corresponds to an out, so the batter places the bean on one of the *Outs* circles. The batter places a new bean on home plate.

The next pitch is a 7. The batter says, "Two times seven is fourteen." A product of 14 corresponds to a double. The batter moves the bean from home plate to second base and advances the bean on first base to third base. The bean that was on second base is now home. This bean should be placed in the *Runs* section of the board.

Play continues until there are beans covering all three *Outs* spaces. Have the batter write the number of beans that have scored in the *Runs* section. The player who was pitching becomes the batter, and he or she moves the beans around the game board.

Notes:
- The length of the game can be altered by shortening the number of innings. Also, the game can be played for a short amount of time each class, over a few days.
- It's important that each player agree that the answer is correct. This will keep both students engaged, as it's possible that one person could be at bat for a long time (if they're lucky!).
- This game can be adapted to use as practice with any specific fact family.

Baseball Fact Game

2×

OUT = __2, 4, 6__
SINGLE = __8, 10__
DOUBLE = __12, 14__
TRIPLE = __16, 18__
HOME RUN = __20__

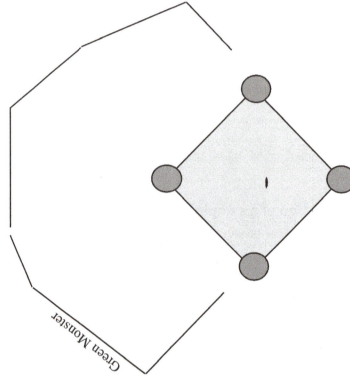

Name _____
Date _____
Day _____

Visiting Team _____		
Outs		Runs
ooo	1	
ooo	2	
ooo	3	
ooo	4	
ooo	5	
ooo	6	
ooo	7	
ooo	8	
ooo	9	
	Final Score	

Home Team _____		
Outs		Runs
ooo	1	
ooo	2	
ooo	3	
ooo	4	
ooo	5	
ooo	6	
ooo	7	
ooo	8	
ooo	9	
	Final Score	

Woodmark Numeric Icons for use as Baseball Deck of Cards
Cut around the rectangular borders to separate the icons.

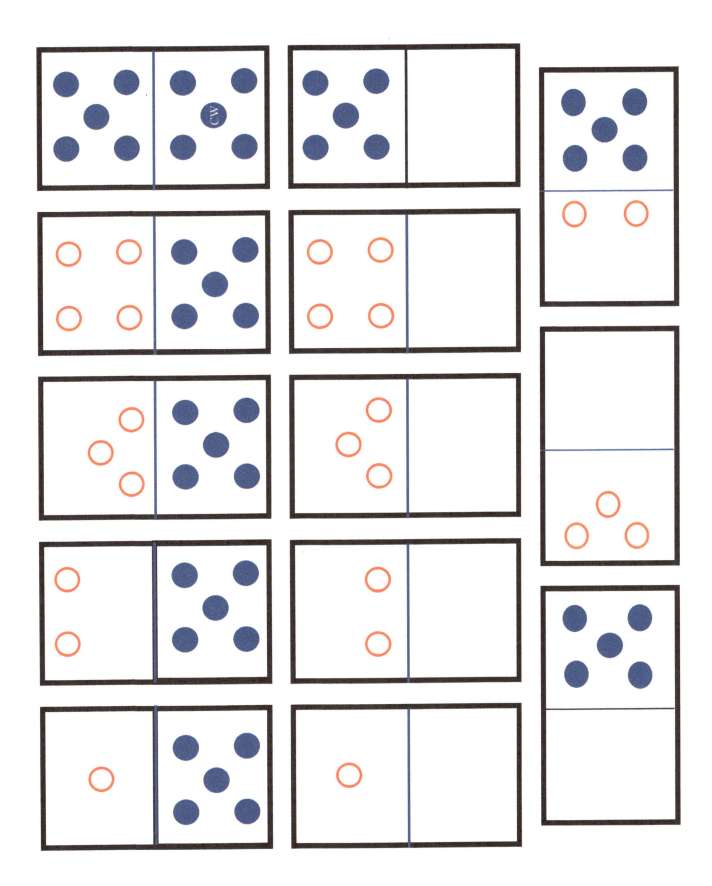

Teach the 5× Multiplication and Division Facts

Consider a student to be **functionally fluent** with 2× facts **if he or she can complete all of the Fluency Assessment Worksheet diagrams accurately in under 1 minute, then write the 20 related fact sentences with 100% accuracy in under three minutes.** At this point the student may move to the next fact family; however, continue to administer fluency tests to concurrently review the 2× facts while learning new fact families. Review these facts periodically with students to ensure students retain them.

Once students have mastered the 2× facts, they should write the 2× facts on their multiplication grids in ink. Also, color in the yellow 2× portion of the giant thermometer.

After students have mastered the 2× facts, it's time for students to begin learning the 5× fact family. Start a new section in each student's Fact Notebook binder for the 5× fact family. The divider tab should be red. Begin by using the 0–100 chart to help students discover the divisibility rule for the 5× fact family. Use the same 0–100 chart that has the 2× multiples highlighted in yellow. This should be in the front of the student's Fact Notebook.

You will now work with students to highlight the 5× multiples in red.

Have students color all of the 5× fact products red. **Make sure that students start with 5!** As before, students may start this process by skip counting, but they should soon see the pattern of the multiples and alter their coloring strategy.

- Pattern: The 5× products will emerge as two columns of red. The multiples of 10 that were previously colored yellow during the 2× shading process will appear somewhat orange with the addition of the red.
- Divisibility rule to generate collaboratively and then write individually on the 5× Divisibility Rule Sheet:

A number is divisible by 5 if it has 0 or 5 in the ones place.

Even multiples of 5 (produced by multiplying 5 by an even number) end in 0. **Odd multiples of five (produced by multiplying 5 by an odd number) end in 5.**

Have students complete a Divisibility Rule Sheet for their fact binders. This completed divisibility rule poster for the 5× fact family will be the first sheet in the new 5× section of their Fact Notebooks. Also, ask students to give examples of numbers that are multiples of 5 and explain how they know the numbers are multiples of 5. Ask students to generate numbers that are not multiples of 5. **Post the Rule Poster for 5 in a visible place in the classroom for later reference.**

Use the divisibility rule to check a product with the class. For example, ask, "Does five times eighteen equal ninety or ninety-four? How do you know?" Students should note that 5 × 18 cannot equal 94 because there is not a 0 or 5 in the ones place.

Next, have students lightly color the 5× row and column on their multiplication grids with the color red. They should fill in the row and column of 5× products in pencil. Once they have learned these facts, students will write them in ink.

To practice the divisibility rule, students can play the divisibility rule game similar to musical chairs that was taught with the 2× fact family.

Teach the 5× Multiplication and Division Facts

5× Pattern 0 - 100 Chart

0	1	2	3	4	5	6	7	8	9
10	11	12	13	14	15	16	17	18	19
20	21	22	23	24	25	26	27	28	29
30	31	32	33	34	35	36	37	38	39
40	41	42	43	44	45	46	47	48	49
50	51	52	53	54	55	56	57	58	59
60	61	62	63	64	65	66	67	68	69
70	71	72	73	74	75	76	77	78	79
80	81	82	83	84	85	86	87	88	89
90	91	92	93	94	95	96	97	98	99
100									

Multiplication Grid with 5× Shading Pattern

	1	2	3	4	5	6	7	8	9	10
1					5					
2					10					
3					15					
4					20					
5	5	10	15	20	25	30	35	40	45	50
6					30					
7					35					
8					40					
9					45					
10					50					

Gain 17 facts by learning the 5× facts.

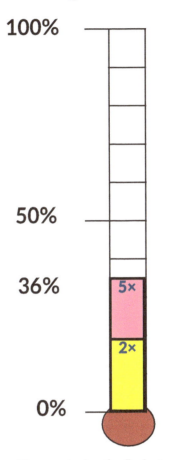

After mastering the 5× facts, 36% of the 100 facts have been learned.

At the end of this unit, have the student color this additional red portion of the big graphic organizer, originally found on page 22. This big progress chart should be stored in the front of the student's Fact Notebook.

Use a red tab to flag a new section in the Fact Notebook to store completed worksheets relating to the 5× facts.

© 2013 C. Woodin & Landmark School

Divisibility Rule Poster

DIVISIBLE BY 5

A number is **divisible by 5** if it has 5 or 0 in the ones place.

Examples: 2<u>5</u>   6<u>0</u>   7<u>5</u>   30<u>0</u>   111<u>5</u>

If a number is a **multiple** of 5, it will end in 5 or 0.
Some multiples of 5:   1<u>5</u>   4<u>0</u>   5<u>5</u>   10<u>0</u>   23<u>5</u>

5 is a **factor** of any number that ends in 5 or 0.

Multiple		Factors
20	=	5 × 4
65	=	5 × 13
300	=	5 × 60
425	=	5 × 85

Divisibility Rule Sheet

Fill in the divisibility rules as you learn them.

Name
Date
Day

A number is **divisible by 5** if . . .

_____

_____

EXAMPLES:

USE THIS DIVISIBILITY POSTER TO START SECTION #2 OF YOUR FACT NOTEBOOK

© 2013 C. Woodin & Landmark School

Use Divisibility Rules to Identify Multiples of 5

These are car license plates.
Multiples of 5 have 0 or 5 in the ones place.

- Color multiples of 5 with red.
- Draw an X over numbers not divisible by 5.

425	450	135	440
430	163	431	944
465	130	645	149
831	138	503	430
765	998	937	445
836	270	580	922

Use Divisibility Rules to Identify Multiples of 5

Multiples of 5 have 0 or 5 in the ones place.

- Color multiples of 5 with red.
- Put an "X" over numbers not divisible by 5.

Name
Date
Day

Teachers: customize this template by filling in blanks with appropriate values.

Introduction to the 5× Whole-to-Part Multiplication Facts

While continuing to review the 2× facts, begin to develop familiarity with the analog clock dial and the associated minute values. Students will use the common, familiar structure of the clock to learn about the 5× fact family within a relational context. Numbered clock positions have corresponding minute values that are multiples of 5. Students will become familiar with the relative positions of these in a manner that promotes comparison through a spatial medium.

Students will learn the twelve clock positions through a series of gross motor kinesthetic activities that initially place the student at the center of a large clock dial, facing the twelve o'clock position. From this student-centered location, each student learns the relative number locations from his or her primary reference frame. As the student internalizes this spatial organization, he or she is able to externalize, or project the positions to the center of a desk, a piece of paper, or an actual clock dial on the wall. Students then associate minute values with these positions. Clock positions are merged with minute values to create 5× facts in a relational format.

Make a clock dial with a diameter of approximately 6 ft. Outside during summer the dial may be drawn in sidewalk chalk or spray-painted on the pavement. During winter, the dial may be made by packing down a circle in the snow. Inside, the clock face may be fabricated using chalk on the carpet or by placing a parachute, circular tarp, or plastic wading pool on the floor. On a basketball court, the circle around the free throw line at the top of the free throw lane, or "key," also provides a great circular structure to accommodate a clock face.

If the clock is being constructed outside, it is helpful to place the clock on a slight incline with twelve o'clock at the highest position. It is also helpful to orient the clock so that the twelve o'clock position is oriented toward the sun. If the clock is positioned optimally, the student standing at the center facing the twelve o'clock position will be leaning uphill with the warmth of the sun on his or her face. Both of these conditions will help the student internalize the twelve o'clock position as being at the top of the dial and think of all the other positions relative to that upper (twelve o'clock) position.

The clock dial should have a large or obvious point of focus placed at the twelve o'clock position. This focal point will further serve to orient the student to that location. Throughout the activities, the student will be prompted to remain focused on this point or object. It is essential that the student maintain his or her orientation to the twelve o'clock position so that he or she will associate all the other numbers relative to this seminal point of reference. Students will develop a consistent association of the number 12 being in front of them, 6 being behind them, 3 to the right, and 9 to the left. Once students learn these four benchmark locations, they will determine that all of the other numbers are located one position away.

> **NECESSARY MATERIALS:**
> - Something to define the circular clock face:
>   - a play parachute with a six-foot diameter
>   - a tarp that has had its corners cut-off
>   - a circle drawn on carpet with chalk (it will vacuum out)
>   - a circle drawn on the pavement with sidewalk chalk or spray paint
>   - the circle around the free throw line on a basketball court.
> - Cones or markers to establish benchmark clock number locations, placed at the three o'clock, six o'clock, and nine o'clock positions (hereafter referred to as positions 3, 6, and 9).
> - Prompt cards: paper or dry erase boards. Write the benchmark clock positions of three o'clock, six o'clock, and nine o'clock on one side and the numbers 15, 30, and 45, respectively on the backs.
> - An object to place at the twelve o'clock position, hereafter referred to as the 12 position. You may hang a large object, such as a target, at eye level on the wall, or you may place a cone or chair at the 12 position. *This object will serve as a point of focus to hold students' gaze when they are standing at the center of the clock face. Remind students as necessary to face this object while pointing to the clock positions. Do not allow them to turn their bodies. If outside, orient the clock so that the sun is at the 12 position.*

Teach the Clock's Benchmark Positions of 3, 6, and 9 relative to the 12

Draw a line at the center of the clockface. Have the class line up behind the 6 position of the large clock. From this position, students not actively engaged in the activity can view the students who are.

The 3 Position

a) Have the first student stand at the line at the center of the clock face.

b) Remind the student to face forward—toward the 12 position—and not to turn his or her body.

c) Stand at the 3 position, to the student's right.

Say, "I'm on the three. Point to three."

The student, while maintaining his or her orientation to the 12 position, should extend his or her right arm to point to the 3 position.

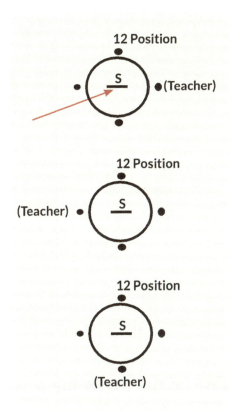

The 9 Position

- Remind the student to face forward, toward the 12 position.
- Stand at the 9 position, to the student's left.

Say, "I'm on the nine. Point to nine."

The student, while maintaining his or her orientation to the 12 position, should extend his or her left arm to point to the 9 position.

The 6 Position

- Remind the student to face forward, toward the 12 position.
- Stand at the 6 position, behind the student.

Say, "I'm on the six. Point to six."

The student, while maintaining his or her orientation to the 12 position, should extend an arm to point to the 6 position.

This student then moves to the back of the line as the next student moves to the center of the clock face.

Repeat this drill over three days.

Teach Student to Identify Benchmark Positions without a Visual Cue

In order to move toward independence, place additional motor planning demands on the student. Move immediately behind the student so that you can prompt the student with a verbal cue, such as, "Point to the three." If the student is unable to point to the position after five seconds, provide a directional cue by tapping on the appropriate shoulder to prompt the correct pointing response.

For example, if the student does not point after five seconds, tap the student on the right shoulder and again say, "Point to the three." The student should then point to the 3.

- Say, "Point to the nine." If the student is unsure, tap the student's left shoulder. Usually, the first cue provided for the 3 is enough to prompt the correct responses.
  The student should point left, to the 9 position.

- Say, "Point to the six." The student should point backward, to the 6 position. Now that the student has practiced pointing to the three position, have him or her move to a position.
- Move immediately behind the student and say, "Point to the three."

After the student points to the 3, say, "Side step to the three."

If necessary, guide the student to side step (right) to the 3 position, while facing the top of the clock. Hand the student a sign that has a 3 written on it, and ask the student to stay at the 3 position. Have the next two students fill the 9 and 6 positions in a similar fashion. Again, remind them to remain facing the 12 position while stepping to their positions.

The fourth student steps to the center of the clock and is asked to point to the three benchmark positions (3, 6 and 9). After the student is able to point to each of these positions without hesitation, have him or her step to one of these positions and take that student's card. The replaced student goes to the back of the line. Rotate through until all students have had a chance to stand in one of the three benchmark positions.

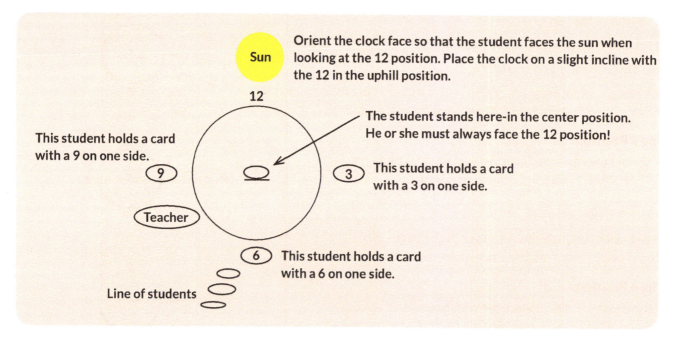

Teach the Number Positions relative to the 3, 6, and 9 Benchmark Positions

After the students can reliably identify the 3, 6, and 9 positions from a verbal prompt, have them extend this knowledge to learn the positions that are located on either side of the benchmark clock numbers. The following exercises should be done on one day, and then repeated on a second day. On the second day, note if the students are able to recall all of the positions without additional assistance. Occasionally, it may take longer than two days for students to process and integrate all positions.

Teach positions 4 and 2 relative to the 3 position.

Have a student stand at the center of the clock and face the 12 position. Stand slightly behind and to the right of the student.

- Say, "Point to the three." The student should point to his or her right.
- Move the student's hand clockwise to the 4 position. Say, "Now you are pointing to the four."
- Release the student's hand and say, "Point to the three." Wait for the student's response (pointing).
- Say, "Point to the four." Wait for the students' response.
- Say, "Point to the three." Wait for the student's response.
- Say, "Point to the two." Wait for the student's response. Usually students will do this without assistance.

* If the student fails to point to the 2 position, say, "Point to the three." Wait for the student's response. Move the student's hand counterclockwise to the 2 position. Say, "Now you are pointing to the two."

- Repeat the previous step, asking the student to point first to the 3 position and then to the 2 position.

Each student should have a chance to do this, as it important for them to develop the kinesthetic memory of the process. This motor memory will later be used to trigger the expression of a 5× fact.

Teach positions 7 and 5 relative to the 6 position.

At this point make the student self-impose structure by stepping away from the student. You will no longer move his or her hand as a cue. Instead, you will be standing on the numbers of the clock face.

- Move to the 6 position of the clock and say, "Point to the six." The student should point behind himself or herself. Make sure the student does not turn around!
- With a loud stomp, step one step clockwise to the 7 position and say, "Good, now point to seven." The student should move his or her arm one position clockwise. Wait for the pointing response.
- Say, "Point to the six," and wait for the pointing response.
- Say, "Point to the seven," and wait for pointing response.
- Say, "Point to the six." Wait for the pointing response.
- Move to the 5 position of the clock and say, "Point to the five." Wait five seconds for the pointing response. If the student needs a prompt, stomp at the five location to cue the pointing response.
- Give the following instructions. Wait for the pointing response before giving each subsequent instruction.

"Point to the six."

"Point to the seven."

"Point to the six."

"Point to the five."

Again, ensure that all students get a chance to practice this.

Teach positions 10 and 8 relative to the 9 position.

- Move to the 9 position of the clock and say, "Point to the nine." The student points to the left.
- With a loud stomp, step one step clockwise to the 10 position and say, "Good, now point to the ten." The student should move his or her arm one position clockwise.
- Say, "Point to the nine." The student again points to the left.
- Say, "Point to the eight." The student should move his or her arm one position counterclockwise and point to the 8 position. Again, if the student does not point after five seconds, cue the student with a stomp at the 8 position.
- Give the following instructions in fairly rapid succession. Wait for the pointing response before giving each subsequent instruction.

"Point to the nine."

"Point to the ten."

"Point to the nine."

"Point to the eight."

- Repeat teaching these relative positions to the other students in line.

SPEED ROUND

After walking students through all the positions with the previous drill, work on the efficiency of students' motor planning. Do the following drill until students are able to automatically locate all of the positions within their primary reference frame.

Link the three benchmark positions (3, 6, and 9) to their relative positions as units of three.

Give the following instructions in fairly rapid succession. Wait for the pointing response before giving each subsequent instruction. Pause between each set of grouped instructions.

"Point to the three."

"Point to the four."

"Point to the three."

"Point to the two."

PAUSE

"Point to the six."

"Point to the seven."

"Point to the six."

"Point to the five."

PAUSE

"Point to the nine."

"Point to the ten."

"Point to the nine."

"Point to the eight."

Teach the Student to Verbalize the Clock Positions from His or Her Primary Reference Frame

Until now, you have named a position, and the student has responded by pointing to that position. The next step is to have the student locate and point to a position and then label it verbally. This step will be challenging for students with expressive language difficulties, but it is necessary to the process of verbalizing entire 5× fact sentences.

- Stand at the 3 position, clap once, and say, "Point to the clap. What number is here?"
- The student should respond, "Three." It is imperative that you provide ample wait time for a response—up to five seconds before cueing, "Say three." Wait for the student to say, "Three."
- Then say, "I am going to move to other positions and clap. Point to the clap you hear, and then say the number." Take one noisy step clockwise, clap, and wait for the student to point and give the verbal response, "Four."
- After that, move back one noisy step to the benchmark 3 position. Clap and wait for the student to point and give the verbal response, "Three."
- Next, move one step counterclockwise to the 2 position. Clap and wait for the student to point and give the verbal response, "Two."
- Move to a new benchmark location (6 or 9), clap, and wait for the student to point and give a verbal response. Then, move one noisy step clockwise, clap, and wait for the student to point and give a verbal response. After that, move back one noisy step to the benchmark position, clap, and wait for the student to point and give a verbal response.
- Next, move one noisy step counterclockwise, clap, and wait for the student to point and give a verbal response.
- Finally, move to another benchmark position to repeat the above process.

Repeat this exercise with each student three times, on subsequent days.

Externalize Learned Gross Motor Kinesthetic Skills to Paper and Pencil Tasks

To integrate the recently developed kinesthetic directional skills involving clock positions with visual processing and fine motor production, have students practice locating the clock positions with the Clock Number Positions worksheet that follows. Teach each student to project his or her internal understanding of the clock positions from the primary frame of reference to the center of the clock face printed on the paper.

Give each student a Clock Number Positions worksheet. Tape your copy to the chalkboard at the front of the class so that all the students may see it.

Point to the center of the clock face, marked with an asterisk (*), with one finger, and ask students to copy you.

- Say, "Start with your finger on the center of the clock face."
Slowly drag your fingertip from the center of the clock face to the 3 position.

- Say, "Watch my finger move from the center to a position." "Copy the same motion. Be ready to name the position."
Observe students, who should be pointing to the 3 position.

- Say, "What number are you pointing to?" Students should respond, "Three."
Next, move your finger back to the center of the clock face, and ask students to copy you.

- Say, "Start with your finger on the center of the clock face."
Slowly drag your fingertip from the center of the clock face to the 3 position, and then move your finger clockwise one position to the 4.

- Say, "Watch my finger move from the center to a position and then down one position. Copy the same motion. Be ready to name the position."

Observe students, who should be pointing to the 4 position. Make sure they are not moving diagonally to four, but first to the three position, then down. Select a student who has his or her finger at the correct spot.

- Say, "You have the right spot. What number are you pointing to?" The student should respond, "Four."

Move your finger from the center to each benchmark position (3, 6, and 9), and have students name the benchmark position. Next, select a position to name that is adjacent to the benchmark position. Start with your fingertip at the center of the clock face, slide your finger to a benchmark, move one position clockwise or counterclockwise, and then have students name that position.

In this manner, all positions, 1 through 10, will be located and labeled by the students.

Teach the Positions of 15, 30, and 45 Minutes

Write the minute values 15, 30, and 45 on the backs of the corresponding 3, 6, and 9 cards. Bring the students back to the large clock and run students through the drill to fill these three benchmark clock positions. As three students take their clock positions, tell them to read the minute amounts that have been written on the backs of their cards. Next, have the fourth student take the center position. Have him or her point to the 3 position. Ask him to say the number of minutes that correspond to that position. Have the person holding the 3 card turn the 15 toward the center. Ask the same student (in the center) to state the minutes that correspond to 6 and 9. Have the 3, 6, and 9 people cue with their minute cards as necessary. Repeat this drill daily until each student can point to and label the three minute or clock positions without cueing.

Extend the Knowledge of the Benchmark Minute Values

Stand on the 3 benchmark position. Ask the student at the center to point at you and label your benchmark location and associated minute value. The student should respond, "You are on the 3, which is 15 minutes." Then, with a loud stomp, step clockwise one step. Ask the student to point to and identify the new clock position that you are standing on and give the number of minutes corresponding to that position. Next, go back to the benchmark and again ask the student to point and label the position and minute amount for the benchmark. Lastly, step counterclockwise and have the student point and label. Continue with this student for the 6 and 9 benchmarks (and surrounding positions) as well. Then repeat the entire drill with each student. Repeat this activity on several occasions until the students can perform these tasks on a consistent basis. Usually this can be accomplished with three presentations over the course of three days.

Link Benchmark Positions to Minute Values to Create Multiplication Facts

- Put it all together. Make 5× facts from a minute prompt. Ask a student to point to a minute location.
- For example, stand at the 9 position, clap your hands, and say, "Point to forty-five minutes."
- Once the student points to the 9 position, say, "What number are you pointing to?" The student should respond, "Nine."
- Then, prompt the student to say the entire 5× fact that relates the two quantities.
- Say, "Forty-five equals five times what?" The student responds, "Forty-five equals five times nine."
- If the student pauses, prompt, "Forty-five is five times..." Take the student's pointing hand and gently tug it toward you at the 9 position. This kinesthetic prompt will usually result in the student saying "nine."
- Have the student repeat the fact: "Forty-five equals five times nine."
  Affirm by saying, "Yes! Nine times five equals forty-five."
- Repeat the drill to reference the 6 position and the 30 minute value and the 9 position and the 45 minute value.

Clock Number Positions

Start with your finger on the center (*).

Watch your teacher's finger move from the center to a position.

Copy the same motion. Be ready to name the position.

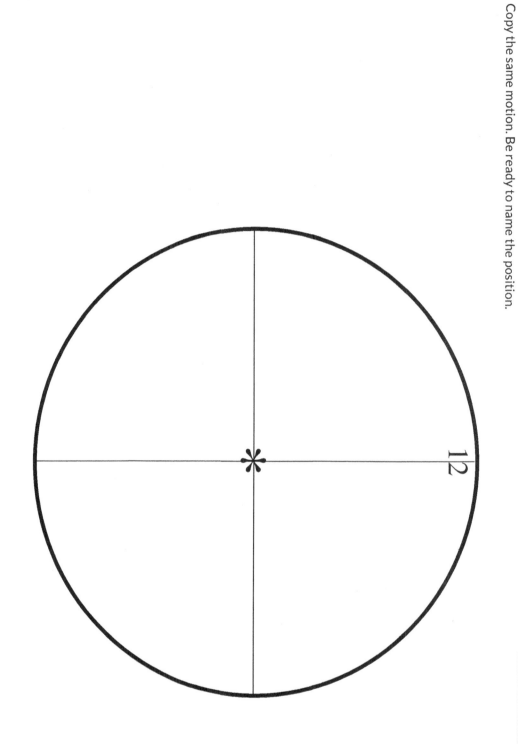

116 © 2013 C. Woodin & Landmark School

Link All Positions to Minute Values to Create Multiplication Facts with Fewer Prompts

As with the benchmark positions, make 5× facts from a minute prompt.

- Stand on the 9 position and ask the student to point to that minute location. Say, "Point to forty-five minutes."

- Once the student has acquired the association between the 9 position and forty-five minutes, then say, "Say the five times fact that equals forty-five."

If needed, prompt with, "Forty-five equals five times…" Take the student's hand and gently tug it toward you at the 9 position.

- Then move to the 10 position and say, "I'm on fifty minutes. Point to me."

- Ask, "Which clock number corresponds to fifty." The student should respond, "Ten."

- Say, "Fifty equals five times…" The student says, "Fifty equals five times ten." Affirm: "Ten times five equals fifty."

- Say, "Point to forty-five minutes." Once the student has acquired the association between the 9 position and forty-five minutes, say, "Say the five times fact that equals forty-five." The student should respond, "Forty-five equals five times nine." Say, "Good. Say the fact again, now start with five times." The student should respond, "Five times nine equals forty-five."

- Move to the 8 position and say, "I'm on forty minutes. Point to me."

- Once the student has acquired the association between the 8 position and forty minutes, say, "Say the five times fact that equals forty." The student should respond, "Forty equals eight times five."

- Repeat this drill for the other two benchmark positions (3 and 6). Go to the 3 position, the 4 position, back to the 3 position, and then the 2 position. After that, go to the 6 position, the 7 position, back to the 6 position, and then the 5 position. Repeat this drill on three different occasions.

Externalize the Kinesthetic-Based Skills to Paper-and-Pencil Tasks

To integrate students' recently developed kinesthetic skills with visual processing and fine motor production, have students practice making 5× facts with the *5× Facts: Large Clock* worksheet. This worksheet helps students externalize their understanding of the clock from a primary frame of reference to a point on a piece of paper. If a student needs to be cued to verbalize a fact, have the student point to the clock or minute position as he or she has done in the past. This kinesthetic act will usually prompt an accurate response.

The number 12 is written on the clock face to provide a reference point. The face is divided into quadrants to provide some organizational structure, while eliminating the opportunity to skip count. Students must activate and process their background knowledge in order to fill in the missing components. The desired effect is achieved when students transfer their internal kinesthetic memory of the 3, 6, and 9 positions to the externalized center of the printed clock face. The initial activities are designed to accomplish this feat.

Establish the benchmark positions of 3, 6 and 9, as well as their corresponding minute values

The 6 position is the easiest position for students to externalize because it is the polar opposite of the 12 written at the top of the clock face. The large clock face enables you to monitor the performance of many students simultaneously and correct them individually as needed. Draw a matrix diagram on the chalkboard, and then write 30 inside the rectangular portion and write 5 in the left circle. (See fig. A.)

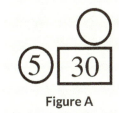

Figure A

- Ask the students to point to 30 minutes on their worksheets.

If a student is not pointing to the 6 position, tell the student to picture himself or herself at the center of the clock face. Snap your fingers behind the student's head or gently position the student's arm so that it is pointing behind the student. These actions should prompt the student to remember the correct position. Ask the student to point to the 6 position on the clock face.

- On the bottom of the circle that encloses the number 5 in the matrix diagram, color a dot to correspond with the 6 position. (See fig. B.)

Figure B

Impose a constant time delay procedure when linking the minute values to the clock positions. Tell students that you will be asking them to answer together, immediately after you clap your hands—not before. This imposed wait time provides necessary processing time for the students who need it. It also benefits all students as the information must be held in short-term memory and repeatedly rehearsed with the inner voice.

- When all students are pointing to the 6 position, say, "Wait for my clap. What number are you pointing to?" Pause five seconds, and then clap your hands. Students should say, "Six."

Write a 6 in the top circle of the matrix diagram. (See fig. C.)

- Ask, "Who can make a multiplication sentence based on thirty?"
Choose a student, tap the 30 and then prompt him or her by saying "Thirty equals…"

Repeatedly tap on the 6 portion of the diagram and say, "Start here."

After the student says, "Six," say, "times," and tap the 5 in your diagram.

After the student says, "Five," ask him or her to say the entire fact.

Figure C

- Say, "Now start here," as you prompt by tapping the 6, then the 5, and then the 30 to drive the student's production of the fact sentence, "Six times five equals thirty."

Ask another student to make a similar sentence.

- Say, "Start here," as you prompt by tapping the 5, then the 6, and then the 30 to drive each successive element of the student's production of the fact sentence, "Five times six equals thirty."

Ask students to finish the multiplication sentence on the middle space of the center column of their *Large Clock Number Positions* worksheet: 30 = 6 × 5. Proceed in a similar manner to have students produce 45 = 9 × 5 on the middle space of the left column, and then 15 = 3 × 5 on the middle space of the right column. During the first presentations, have students complete each column with two related part-to-whole sentences: 15 = 3 × 5; 3 × 5 = 15; 5 × 3 = 15 (see below).

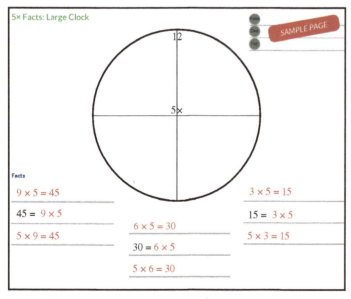

On subsequent days, use a blank copy of the same worksheet, but ask students to complete each column using the middle benchmark fact as a reference. Have students first point to a benchmark fact, such as 15 = 3 × 5, and then have them locate, verbalize, and then write the facts that surround it: 10 = 2 × 5 above, and 20 = 4 × 5 below (see following sample page).

After students have mastered the introductory clock activities, the clock can be used as a reference. When a student gets stuck, remind the student to visualize the clock. Kinesthetic "tug prompts" are also helpful. For instance, if the student is struggling to say, "Five times three equals…" lightly tug the student's right hand. You will probably be rewarded with "Fifteen…. Five times three equals fifteen." The student's kinesthetic or motor memory will drive the verbal production of the fact. Often, students who are slow to name things that they see are more accurate and efficient at labeling a familiar action that they perform.

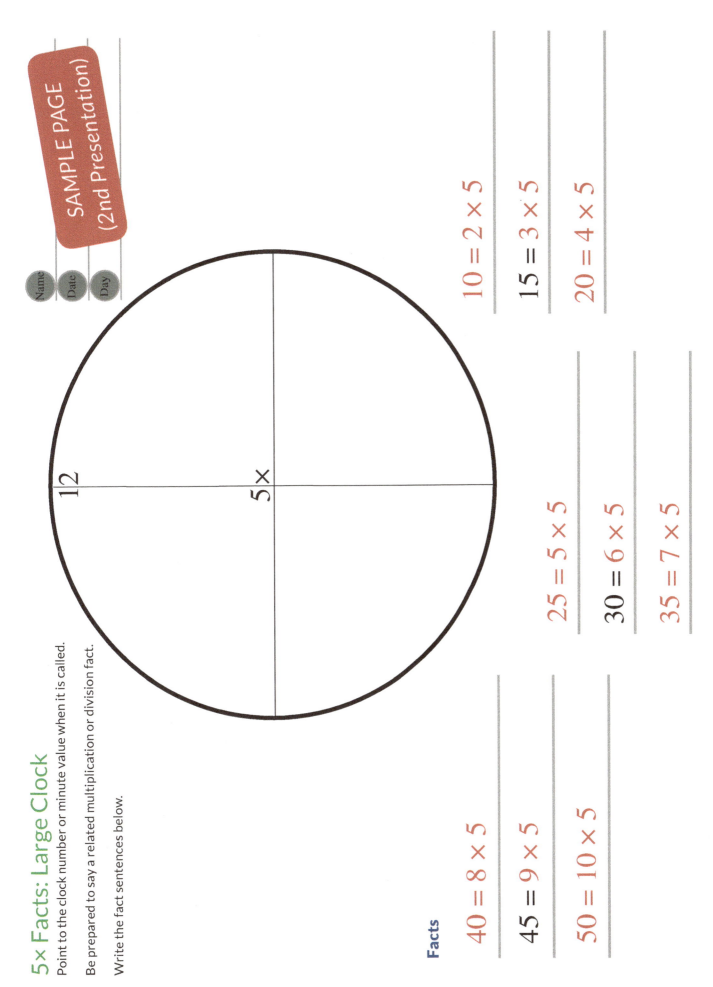

5× Facts: Large Clock

Point to the clock number or minute value when it is called.

Be prepared to say a related multiplication or division fact.

Write the fact sentences below.

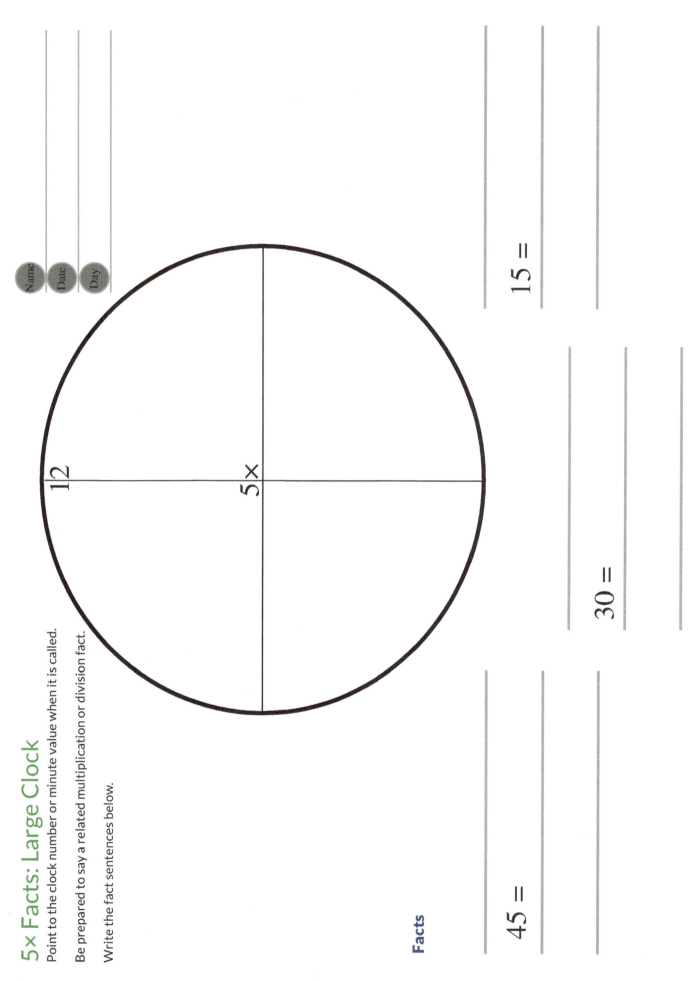

Facts

45 = _____

30 = _____

15 = _____

Other Applications of the Clock as a Graphic Organizer

Revisit the clock dial to help students organize and compare relative information. The large clock dial may be used to teach the (chronological) concepts of *before* and *after*. Have a student point to hour positions on the clock to reference a specific time of day or event and then move his or her arm clockwise to point to an event that happens after or counterclockwise to point to an event that occurred before.

Start by associating three consecutive hour locations to habitual activities specific to the student.

Use a benchmark position as the middle number.

> **EXAMPLE**
>
> For example, a given student, Johnny, is in school until 3 o'clock and then takes the bus home.
>
> Ask Johnny to point to the time he gets on the bus to go home. Johnny should point to the 3 position.
>
> Say, "Point to the 2. What do you do **before** 3?" Johnny should point to 2 and answer, "I'm in school, learning."
>
> Say, "Point to the 3. What are you doing at 3 o'clock when the last bell rings?" Johnny should point to 3 and answer, "I'm getting on the bus."
>
> Say, "Point to the 4. "What are you doing at 4 o'clock **after** the bus ride?" Johnny should point to 4 and answer, "I'm at home, relaxing."
>
> Repeat this activity, identifying activities occurring to either side of dinner time (six o'clock), bedtime (nine o'clock), and lunch (noon).

The 5× Fact Family Flash Cards

Complete the following worksheet prior to using the 5× flash cards to continue to integrate students' recently developed kinesthetic skills with visual processing and fine motor production. They will then use flash cards that reference the clock as a valuable tool for practice. Use the dry erase *Fact Production* template to help generate fact sentences using the flash cards.

5× Area problems

As with the 2× facts, students will practice solving word problems related to area by masking a multiplication grid. Remember, as you read a problem aloud, students will mask the multiplication grid with two index cards to frame the rectangle described by the word problem. They use the grid to find the answer, then transfer the information to the diagram and label the answer with the appropriate units.

The 5× Reference Bank

Next, students complete the *Reference Bank for the 5× Fact Family* showing items (nouns and attributes) that come in groups of five. Students should keep this reference bank in their fact binders in the same manner as their 2× reference banks. The reference banks will provide nouns that can be used to model facts semantically or to create word problems.

One 5× noun that is easy to practice with is a nickel. Grouping the fives in nickels is a way to practice multiplication facts while also developing money skills.

5× Facts: Fine Motor Practice

Draw the minute hand from the center to the given minute value. Write a related 5× fact.

30

5 × _____

15

35

_____

20

_____

45

50

_____

25

40

_____

55

10

_____

122 © 2013 C. Woodin & Landmark School

Use the Clock Face Position as a Factor Cue on 5× Flash Cards

On the following page of flash cards, the dot on the circled 5 represents the clock position to be verbalized.

In the above example, the student should recognize that the dot is in the 6 position. Ideally this visual cue should trigger the student's motor memory of pointing to that spot during previous clock activities. As a result, the student should be prompted to say, "Six times five equals thirty."

© 2013 C. Woodin & Landmark School   123

5× Facts: Cut out these flash cards along the dotted lines. Use the dot as a cue to trigger the student's motor memory of pointing to that spot during previous clock activities. Then verbalize the related facts.

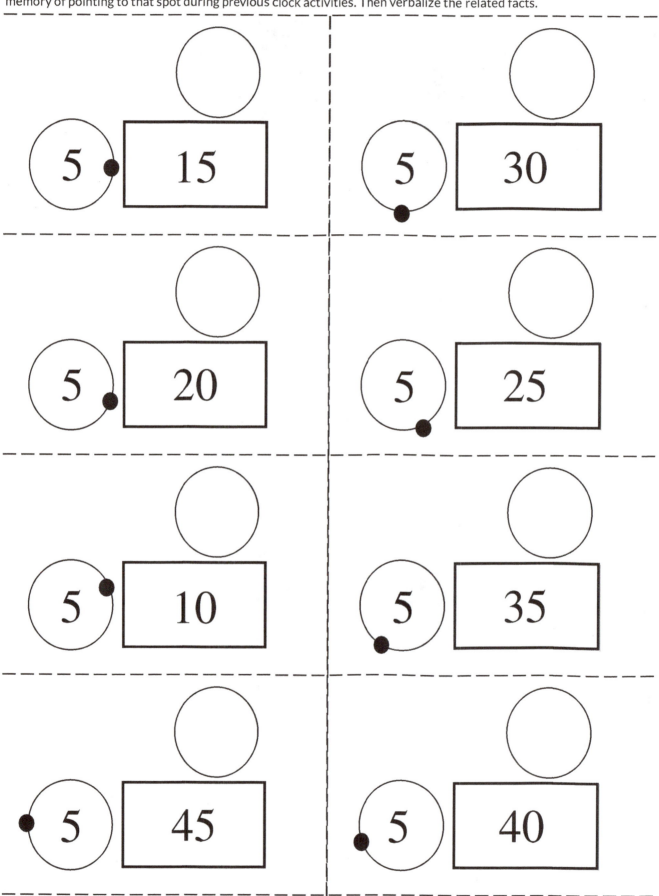

Word Problems Related to Area: 5× Facts

- Mask the multiplication grid with two index cards to frame the rectangle described by the word problem.
- Use the grid to find the answer.
- Transfer the information to the diagram and label the answer with the appropriate units.

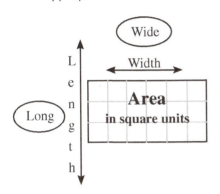

	1	2	3	4	5	6	7	8	9	10
1					5					
2					10					
3					15					
4					20					
5	5	10	15	20	25	30	35	40	45	50
6					30					
7					35					
8					40					
9					45					
10					50					

Problem #1

The rectangular table is 6 feet long.

The table has an area of 30 square feet.

How wide is the table?

Diagram

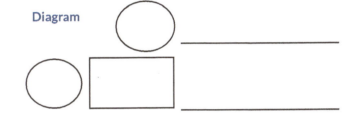

Problem #2

The rectangular rug is 5 feet long.

The area of the rug is 45 square feet.

How wide is the rug?

Diagram

Problem #3

The garden has an area of 35 square feet.

The garden is 5 feet long.

How wide is the garden?

Diagram

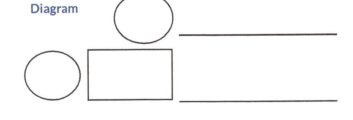

Problem #4

The wall is 5 feet wide.

It is 8 feet long.

What is the area of the wall?

Diagram

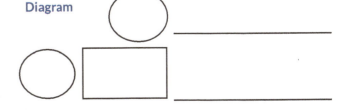

© 2013 C. Woodin & Landmark School

Teachers: customize this template by filling in blanks with appropriate values.

Word Problems Related to Area: 5× Facts

- Mask the multiplication grid with two index cards to frame the rectangle described by the word problem.
- Use the grid to find the answer.
- Transfer the information to the diagram and label the answer with the appropriate units.

Name _____
Date _____
Day _____

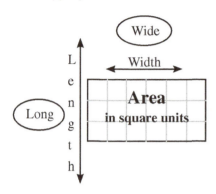

	1	2	3	4	5	6	7	8	9	10
1					5					
2					10					
3					15					
4					20					
5	5	10	15	20	25	30	35	40	45	50
6					30					
7					35					
8					40					
9					45					
10					50					

Problem #1

The rectangular table is _____ feet long.

The table has an area of _____ square feet.

How wide is the table?

Diagram

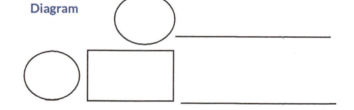

Problem #2

The rectangular rug is 5 feet long.

The area of the rug is _____ square feet.

How wide is the rug?

Diagram

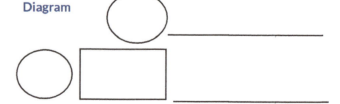

Problem #3

The garden has an area of _____ square feet.

The garden is 5 feet long.

How wide is the garden?

Diagram

Problem #4

The wall is 5 feet wide.

It is _____ feet long.

What is the area of the wall?

Diagram

© 2013 C. Woodin & Landmark School

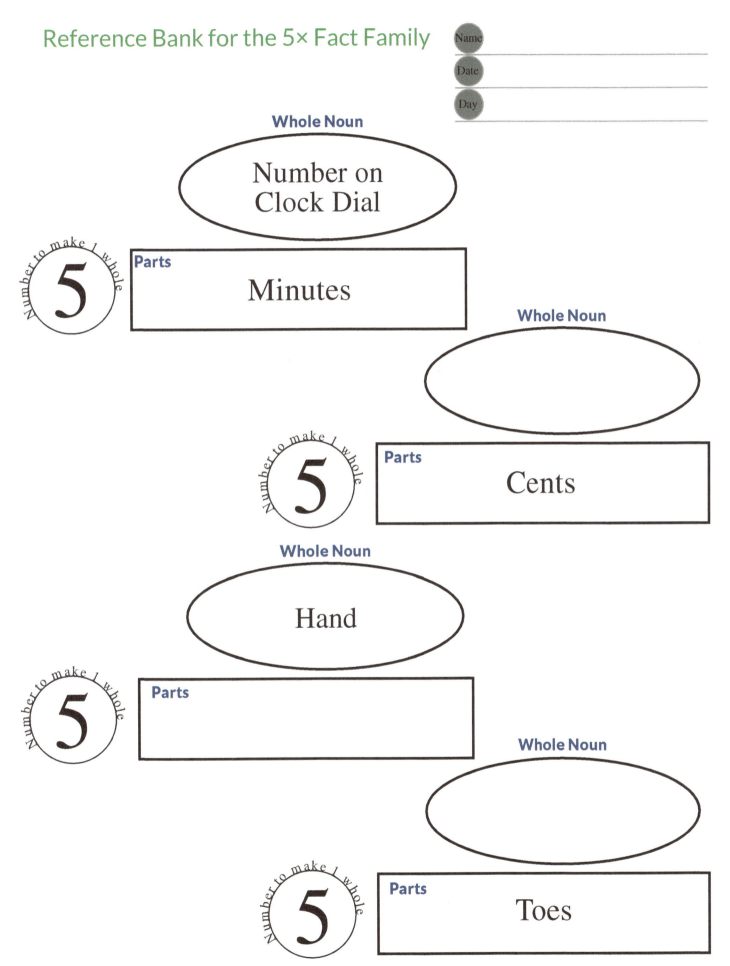

Semantic-Based 5× Multiplication Facts and Matrix Diagrams

- Circle the number of whole things.
- Circle the number of parts needed to make one whole.
- Box the number that represents all of the parts.
- Complete the diagram and write two related facts.

Name _____
Date _____
Day _____

Fill in the diagram:

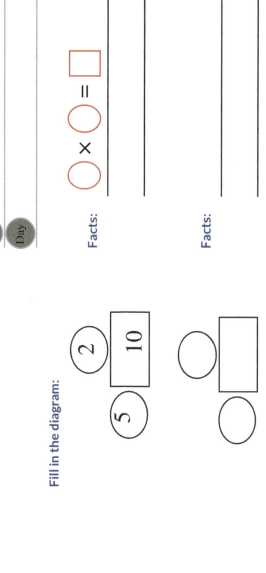

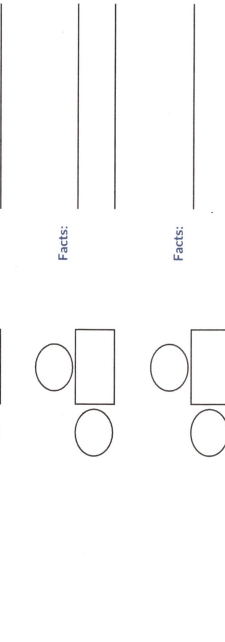

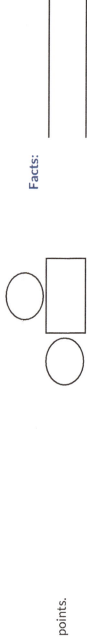

Facts: ○ × ○ = □
_____

Nickels are worth ⑤ cents each.

If there are ② nickels, there are [10] cents.

Facts: _____
_____

Starfish have 5 legs each.

If there are 3 starfish, there are 15 legs.

Facts: _____
_____

Hands have 5 fingers each.

If there are 4 hands, there are 20 fingers.

Facts: _____
_____

Pentagons have 5 sides each.

If there are 5 pentagons, there are 25 sides.

Facts: _____
_____

Stars have 5 points each.

If there are 6 stars, there are 30 points.

Semantic-Based 5× Multiplication Facts and Matrix Diagrams

- Circle the number of whole things.
- Circle the number of parts needed to make one whole.
- Box the number that represents all of the parts.
- Complete the diagram and write two related facts.

Name Date Day

Fill in the diagram:

○ × ○ = □

Nickels are worth ⑤ cents each.
If there are ③ nickels, there are [15] cents.

Facts: _____

Starfish have 5 legs each.
If there are 7 starfish, there are 35 legs.

Facts: _____

Hands have 5 fingers each.
If there are 8 hands, there are 40 fingers.

Facts: _____

Pentagons have 5 sides each.
If there are 9 pentagons, there are 45 sides.

Facts: _____

Stars have 5 points each.
If there are 10 stars, there are 50 points.

Facts: _____

© 2013 C. Woodin & Landmark School 129

Semantic-Based 5× Word Problems

- Circle the number of whole things.
- Circle the number of parts needed to make one whole.
- Box the number that represents all of the parts.
- Complete the diagram to find the answer to the question.

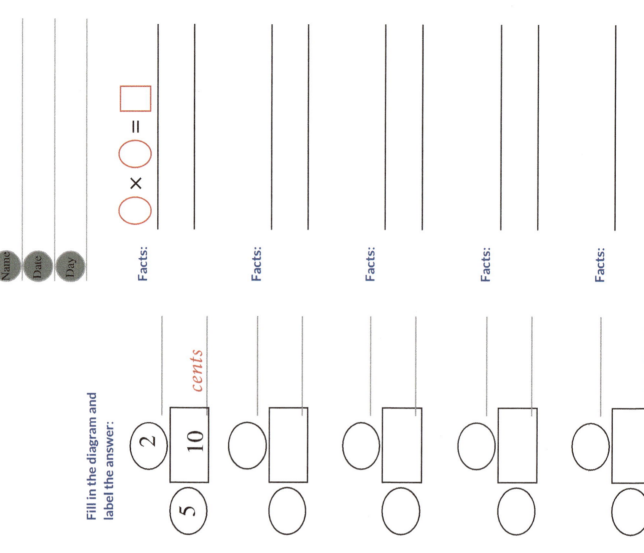

Fill in the diagram and label the answer:

Nickels are worth ⑤ cents each.

If there are ② nickels, [how many cents] are there?

Facts: ___ × ___ = ___

Starfish have 5 legs each.

If there are 7 starfish, how many legs are there?

Facts: _____

Hands have 5 fingers each.

If there are 8 hands, how many fingers are there?

Facts: _____

Pentagons have 5 sides each.

If there are 9 pentagons, how many sides are there?

Facts: _____

Stars have 5 points each.

If there are 10 stars, how many points are there?

Facts: _____

130   © 2013 C. Woodin & Landmark School

Name
Date
Day

Semantic-Based 5× Word Problems

- Circle the number of whole things.
- Circle the number of parts needed to make one whole.
- Box the number that represents all of the parts.
- Complete the diagram to find the answer to the question.

Fill in the diagram and label the answer:

Facts: ◯ × ◯ = ☐

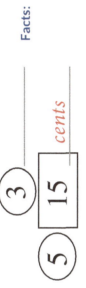   *cents*

Nickels are worth ⓢ cents each.

If there are ③ nickels, [how many cents] are there?

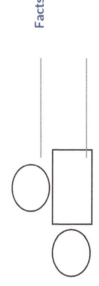

Facts: _____

Starfish have 5 legs each.

If there are 3 starfish, how many legs are there?

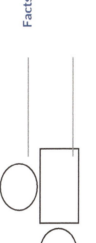

Facts: _____

Hands have 5 fingers each.

If there are 4 hands, how many fingers are there?

Facts: _____

Pentagons have 5 sides each.

If there are 5 pentagons, how many sides are there?

Facts: _____

Stars have 5 points each.

If there are 6 stars, how many points are there?

Facts: _____

© 2013 C. Woodin & Landmark School

Directions for the Template Using Nickels (or Five Icons)

Grouping fives in nickels is a way to practice multiplication facts while also developing money skills. Alternatively, students who have had exposure to icons may find icons easier, as the value is more concrete. The concept to be developed in the following activities is that even multiples of 5 create tens. Odd multiples have a 5 in the ones place.

EXAMPLE - WHOLE TO PART:

- Announce a quantity for the students to make with nickels. For example, say, "Make fifteen cents."
- Say, "Fifteen is an odd number."
- Prompt students to write "15" with their finger in the large grey and white boxes.
- Ask, "How many tens did you write?" (1). "How many ones did you write?" (5) Prompt students to place a pair of nickels for each ten. If there are 5 ones, a nickel also goes in the ones nickel space.
- Select a student with a correct number of nickels to verbalize the quantity as a 5× fact. The student should say, "Fifteen equals five times three."
- Say, "The factor 3 is odd and therefore the product 15 is also odd."
- Repeat the exercise with varying odd and even products.

EXAMPLE - PART TO WHOLE:

- Give a student one nickel. Ask the student what it is worth (five cents).

- Ask, "How many ones?" Have the student place the nickel on the vacant ones spot and then use his or her finger to write its value (5) in the white box for the ones place.

- Give the student a second nickel. There is no spot to place the nickel in the ones place.

The student should move the first nickel and combine it with the new nickel to fill one entire tens place.

- Ask, "How many tens?" There is one ten. Have the student use his or her finger to write the numeral 1 in the box for the tens place. As you point to the vacant ones spot, ask, " How many additional ones are there?"

There are zero additional ones. Have the student use his or her finger to write the numeral 0 in the box for the ones place.

Have the student "rewrite" the two digits with his or her finger: 1 ten and 0 ones. Then, have the student verbalize the value of one ten and zero ones ("ten").

- Give the student a third nickel. Have him or her place the nickel on the vacant ones spot. Ask, " How many tens?" There is one ten. Have the student use his or her finger to write the numeral 1 in the box for the tens place. As you point to the recently filled ones spot, ask, "How many additional ones are there?"

There are five additional ones. Have the student "write" the numeral 5 in the box for the ones place.

Have the student rewrite the two digits: 1 ten and 5 ones. Now ask the student to verbalize the value of one ten and five ones (fifteen).

- Ask the student to state the number of nickels needed to make 15 cents, then create a "five times" sentence to match.
- e.g., "5 × 3 =15"

Nickels and 5 Icons for use on the 5× Place Value Template

Use real nickels if possible, otherwise photocopy these on card stock and cut them out.

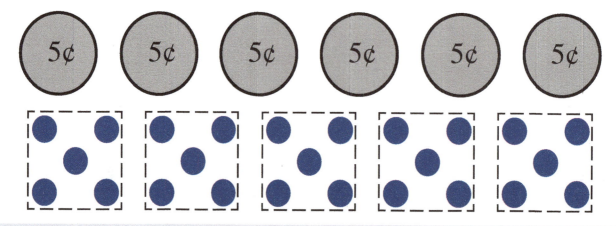

5× Place Value Template Using Nickels or Icons

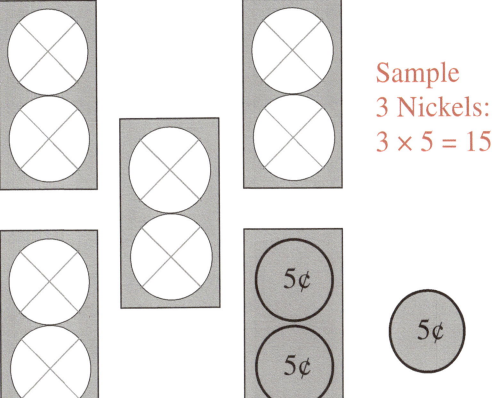

Sample
3 Nickels:
3 × 5 = 15

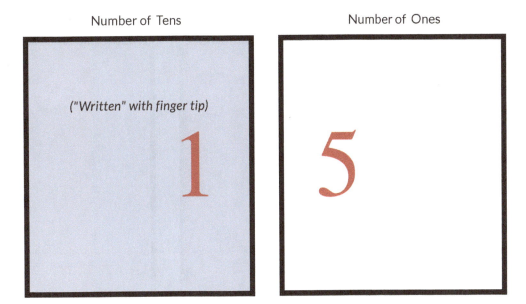

Write the digits with your index finger.

5× Place Value Template Using Nickels or Icons

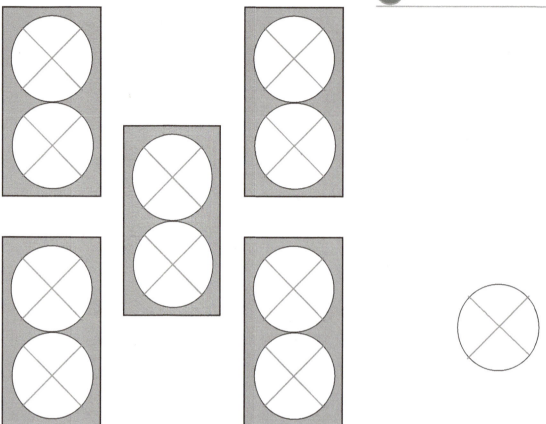

Number of Tens	Number of Ones

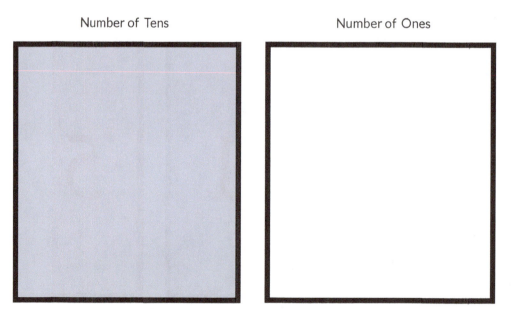

Write the digits with your index finger..

Iconic Grouping of Nickels and Multiplication

Identify the number of nickels in the diagram.

Then, link pairs of nickels (tens) with a line.

These pairs of nickels will generate the number of tens in the product. An odd (lone) nickel represents five additional units.

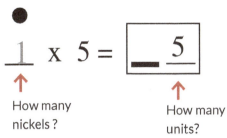

$\underline{1}$ x 5 = $\boxed{\underline{}\ \underline{5}}$

How many nickels?   How many units?

$\underline{2}$ x 5 = $\boxed{\underline{1}\ \underline{0}}$

How many nickels?

How many groups of ten?   How many additional units?

___ x 5 = $\boxed{\underline{}\ \underline{}}$

___ x 5 = $\boxed{\underline{}\ \underline{}}$

___ x 5 = $\boxed{\underline{}\ \underline{}}$

___ x 5 = $\boxed{\underline{}\ \underline{}}$

___ x 5 = $\boxed{\underline{}\ \underline{}}$

___ x 5 = $\boxed{\underline{}\ \underline{}}$

___ x 5 = $\boxed{\underline{}\ \underline{}}$

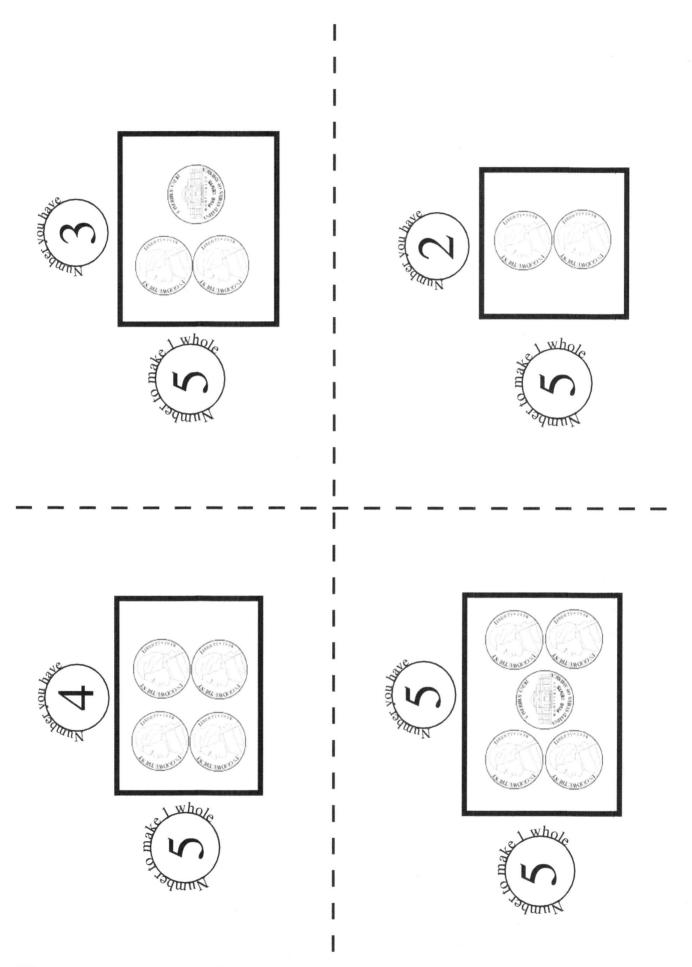

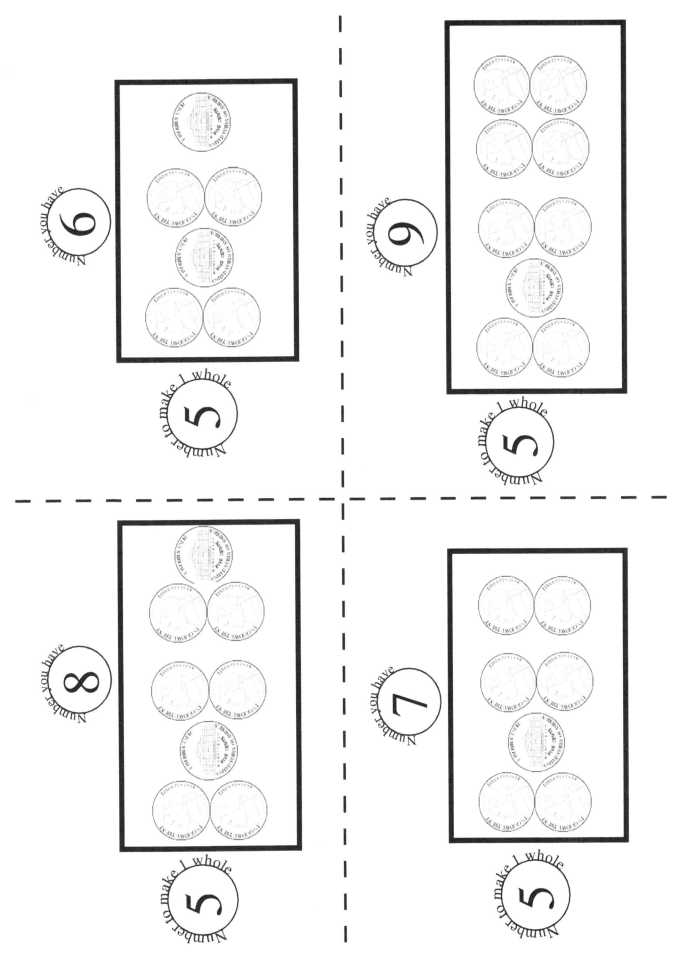

5× Fact Mosaic

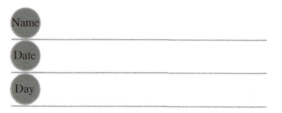

- Write a product (for example, 10) on one side of a dashed grid line and the other part of the face sentence (2 × 5) on the other side of the dashed line.
- Repeat this process for each of the grid lines.
- Then cut the puzzle along the dashed lines to make nine square pieces and shuffle the pieces.
- Try to put them back together using the fact sentences and products as a guide.
- Trade puzzles with another student and challenge each other!

Baseball Fact Game

5×

OUT = 5, 10, 15
SINGLE = 20, 25
DOUBLE = 30, 35
TRIPLE = 40, 45
HOME RUN = 50

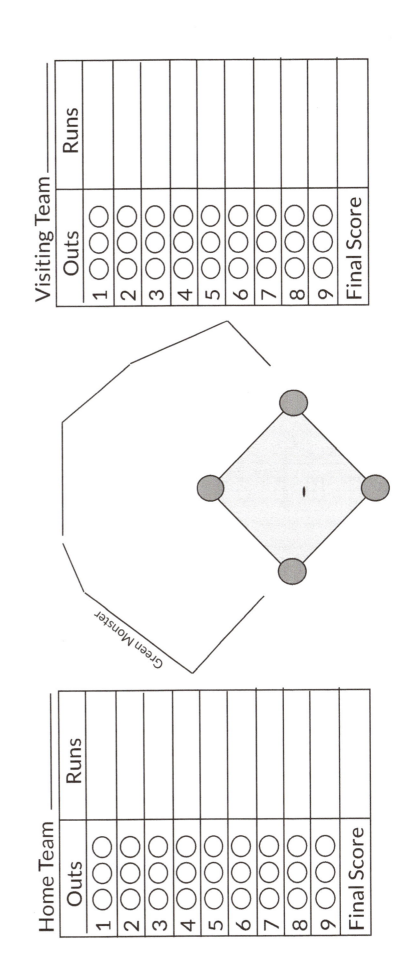

Accuracy Benchmark Pretest - Untimed

Complete this sheet with 100% accuracy before taking the related timed *Fluency Assessment*.

Name
Date
Day

1) Complete each diagram. Have them scored.

2) Correct diagrams if needed.

3) Write a multiplication fact and a division fact for each.

Diagram Accuracy: ____/10

4) Archive this in your Fact Notebook as a record.

Sentence Accuracy: ____/20

5 | 5

5 | 30

5 | 10

5 | 35

5 | 15

5 | 40

5 | 20

5 | 45

5 | 25

5 | 50

140   © 2013 C. Woodin & Landmark School

Fluency Assessment - Timed

Administer this test after the student scores 100% accuracy

1) Complete each diagram. Note time and accuracy.

2) Correct diagrams as needed.

3) Write a multiplication fact and a division fact for each. Note time and accuracy on the related *Accuracy Benchmark Pretest*.

4) Archive this in your Fact Notebook as a record.

Name _____
Date _____
Day _____

Diagram Accuracy: _____/10 Time: _____

Sentences Accuracy: _____/20 Time: _____

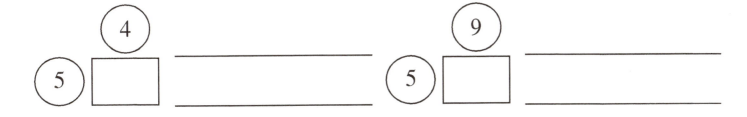

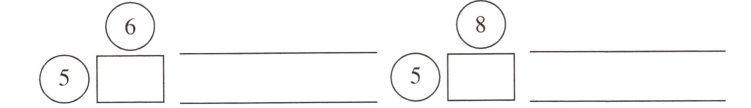

© 2013 C. Woodin & Landmark School   141

Vertical Fact Practice

Timed quiz

_____ seconds

◯/10

	1
×	5

	2
×	5

	3
×	5

	4
×	5

	5
×	5

	6
×	5

	7
×	5

	8
×	5

	9
×	5

	1	0
×		5

Teach the 10× Multiplication and Division Facts

Consider a student to be functionally fluent with the 5× facts if he or she can complete all of the Fluency Assessment Worksheet diagrams accurately in under 1 minute, then write the 20 related fact sentences with 100% accuracy in under three minutes. At this point the student may move to the next fact family; however, continue to administer fluency assessments to concurrently rehearse the production of the 2× and 5× facts while learning new fact families. Review these facts periodically with students to ensure students retain them.

Once functionally fluent, it's time to use pen to fill in the 5× facts on the multiplication grid. Also, color in the red 5× fact portion of the giant thermometer. Don't forget to continue reviewing them, along with the 2× facts, as you move ahead. Now the focus shifts to the 10× facts. Again, use the 0–100 chart to help students discover the divisibility rule for the 10× fact family. Start a new section in the student's Fact Notebook with an orange tab divider.

Students should look at the 0–100 chart and find the 10× facts. Students should notice that because of the 2× and 5× facts that are already colored, the tens are orange. Have students describe the pattern they see that applies to all multiples of ten.

- **Pattern:** The 10× products will emerge as one column of orange.
- **Divisibility rule to generate collaboratively** and then write individually on the 10× Divisibility Rule Sheet:

A number is divisible by 10 if it has 0 in the ones place.

- Have students fill in a Divisibility Rule Sheet for their indexed Fact Notebook binders. Again, ask students to give examples of numbers that are multiples of 10 and to explain how they know that the number is a multiple of 10. Also, ask students to generate numbers that are not multiples of 10.
- Post the Divisibility Rule Poster for 10 in a visible place in the classroom for later reference.
- Use the divisibility rule to check a product with the class. Ask, "Does ten times twenty-one equal two hundred ten or two hundred eleven?" Students should recognize that 10×21 cannot equal 211 because there is not a zero in the ones place.
- Next, have students lightly color the 10× row and column on their multiplication grids orange. They should fill in the row and column of 10× products in pencil. Once they have learned the products, students will write over them in ink.
- Students should practice the divisibility rule for 10 and complete the Reference Bank for the 10× Fact Family to store in their Fact Notebooks.
- Students will practice the 10× facts using patterns of base ten sticks and dimes. The worksheets that follow can be used to practice 10× facts and their division counterparts in a variety of ways.

Teach the 10× Multiplication and Division Facts

10× Pattern 0 - 100 Chart

0	1	2	3	4	5	6	7	8	9
10	11	12	13	14	15	16	17	18	19
20	21	22	23	24	25	26	27	28	29
30	31	32	33	34	35	36	37	38	39
40	41	42	43	44	45	46	47	48	49
50	51	52	53	54	55	56	57	58	59
60	61	62	63	64	65	66	67	68	69
70	71	72	73	74	75	76	77	78	79
80	81	82	83	84	85	86	87	88	89
90	91	92	93	94	95	96	97	98	99
100									

Gain 15 more facts by learning 10× facts.

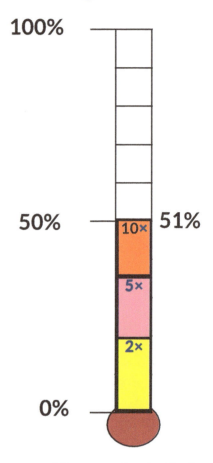

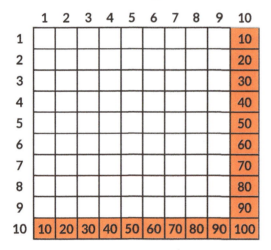

Multiplication Grid with 10× Shading Pattern

After mastering the 10× facts, 51% of the 100 facts have been learned.

At the end of this unit, have the student color this additional orange portion of the big graphic organizer. This progress chart should be stored in the first section of the student's Fact Notebook.

144 © 2013 C. Woodin & Landmark School

Divisibility Rule Poster

A number is **divisible by 10** if it has 0 in the ones place.

Examples: 2<u>0</u>   6<u>0</u>   17<u>0</u>   30<u>0</u>   451<u>0</u>

If a number is a **multiple** of 10, it will end in 0.

Some multiples of 10:   3<u>0</u>   4<u>0</u>   7<u>0</u>   10<u>0</u>   22<u>0</u>

10 is a **factor** of any number that ends in 0.

Multiple		Factors
20	=	10 × 2
60	=	10 × 6
120	=	10 × 12
340	=	10 × 34

Divisibility Rule Sheet
Fill in the divisibility rules as you learn them.

A number is **divisible by 10** if . . .

_____

_____

EXAMPLES:

USE THIS DIVISIBILITY POSTER TO START A NEW SECTION OF YOUR FACT NOTEBOOK

Use Divisibility Rules to Identify Multiples of 10

These are car license plates. Multiples of 10 have 0 in the ones place. Multiples of 10 are also multiples of 2 and 5.

- Color multiples of 2 yellow and multiples of 5 red.
- Multiples of 10 will be orange- a mix of red & yellow.
- Draw an X over numbers not divisible by 10.

130	455	130	449
430	160	431	940
460	150	648	140
830	130	503	430
760	990	937	440
830	275	580	922

Divisibility Rules to Identify Multiples of 10

These are car license plates. Multiples of 10 have 0 in the ones place.
Multiples of 10 are also multiples of 2 and 5.

- Color multiples of 2 yellow and multiples of 5 red.
- Multiples of 10 will be orange- a mix of red & yellow.
- Put an "X" over numbers not divisible by 10.

Name
Date
Day

Teachers: customize this template by filling in blanks with appropriate values.

Reference Bank for the 10× Fact Family

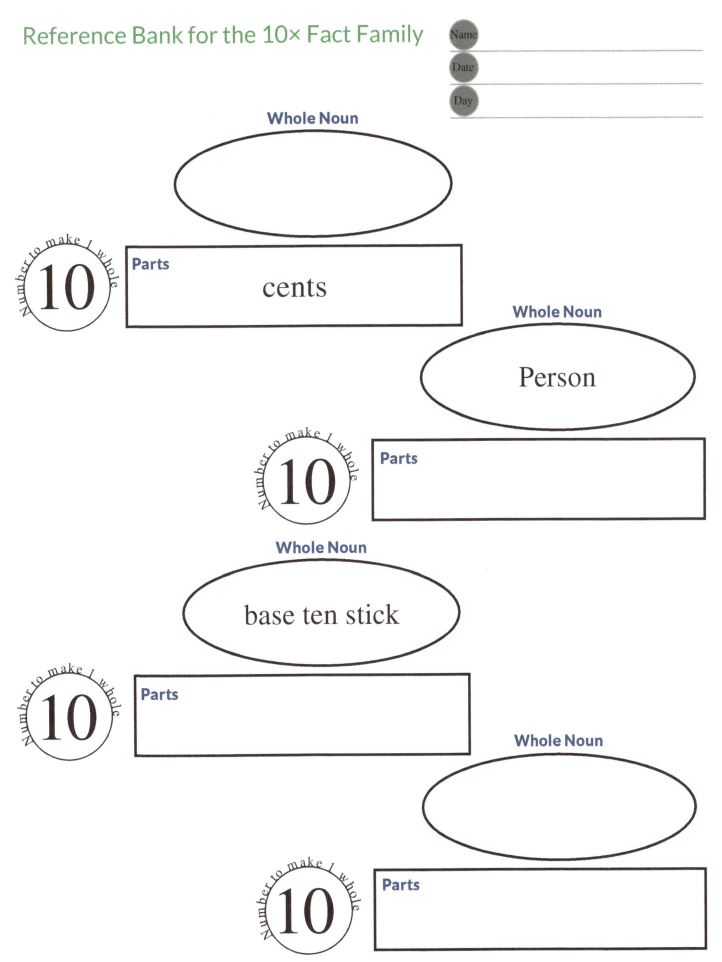

Multiplying By Ten

In the following worksheets, you will use a variety of semi-concrete visual models to prompt the expression of multiplication and division facts relating to 10.

Semi-concrete matrix model **Abstract (standardized) matrix diagram**

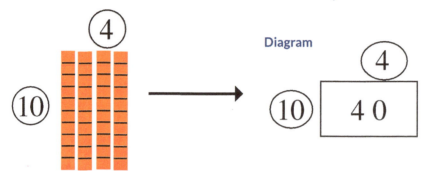

Procedure appended to matrix diagram **Scaffolded verbal expression**

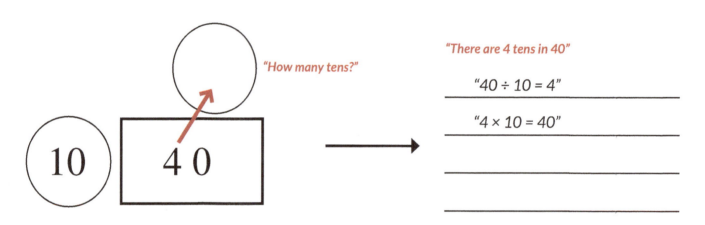

Semi-concrete Iconic model **Semantic-based template**

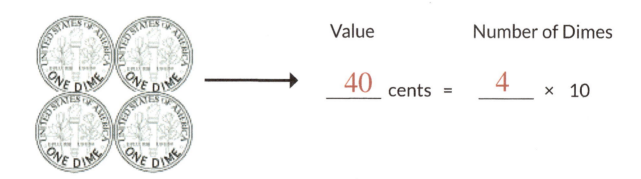

150 © 2013 C. Woodin & Landmark School

Learning 10× Facts Using a Matrix
Diagram of Base Ten Sticks

Use base ten sticks to help produce facts.

SAMPLE PAGE

Name | Date | Day

Give students different amounts of base ten blocks. Have them place the blocks on the paper. Then have the students complete the diagrams to match.

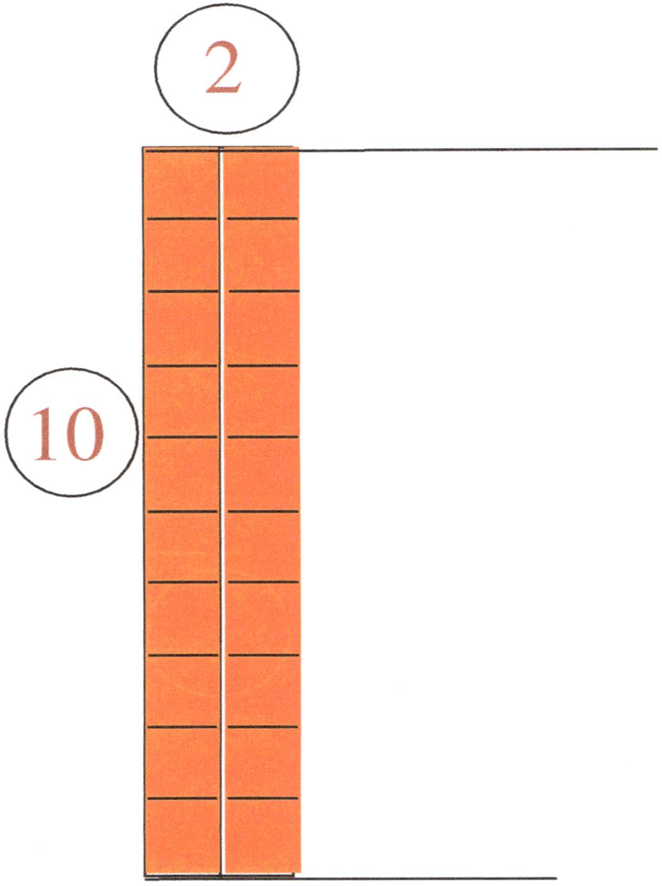

Diagram

(10)   (2)
       [20]

10 × 2 = [20]
2 × 10 = 20
[20] ÷ 10 = (2)
20 ÷ 2 = 10

(2)
(10)

© 2013 C. Woodin & Landmark School

Learning 10× Facts Using a Matrix
Diagram of Base Ten Sticks

Use base ten sticks to help produce facts.

Name _____ Date _____ Day _____

Diagram

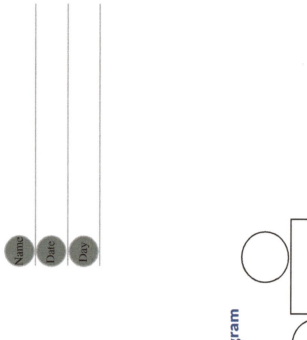

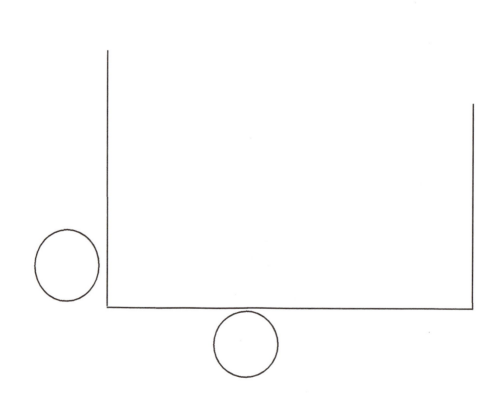

Facts with Base Ten Sticks

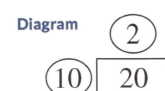
Diagram
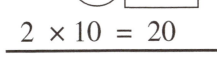

2 × 10 = 20

10 ×   =

20 ÷ 10 = 2

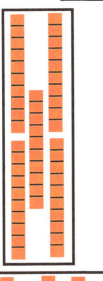
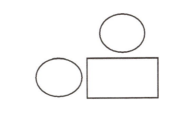

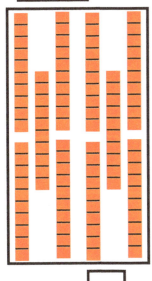
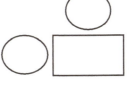

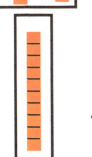
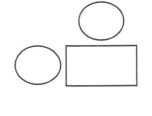

Facts with Base Ten Sticks

Diagram

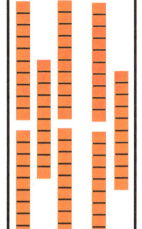

$4 \times 10 = 40$

$10 \times = $

$40 \div 10 = 4$

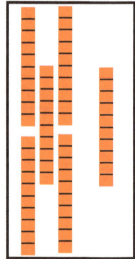

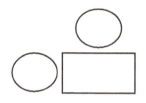

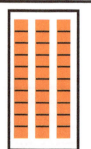

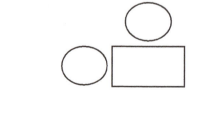

Facts with Base Ten Sticks

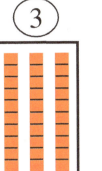

Diagram
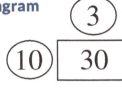

$3 \times 10 = 30$ $30 \div 10 = 3$

$10 \times \quad =$

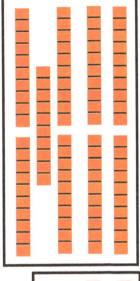

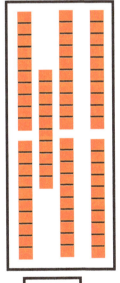

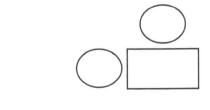

© 2013 C. Woodin & Landmark School   155

Word Problems: Base Ten Sticks

- Circle the number of whole things (sticks).
- Circle the number it takes to make 1 whole stick.
- Box "all the stuff," or total value of the sticks.
- Transfer the numbers to the diagram.

Use the diagram to generate the fact that solves the problem.

Each stick is worth (10) units.
There are (4) sticks.
What is the value of all the sticks?

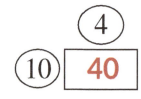

$4 \times 10 = 40$

There are (4) sticks.
All the sticks are worth [40] units.
What is the value of a stick?

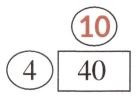

$40 \div 4 = 10$

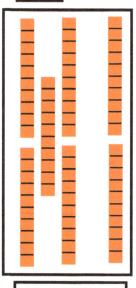

There are 7 sticks.
Each stick is worth 10 units.
What is the value of all the sticks?

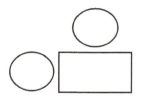

All the sticks are worth 70 units.
There are 7 sticks.
What is the value of a stick?

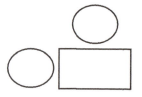

Each stick is worth 10 units.
All the sticks are worth 60 units.
How many sticks are there?

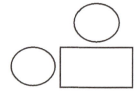

There are 6 sticks.
Each stick is worth 10 units.
What is the value of all the sticks?

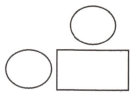

Word Problems: Base Ten Sticks

- Circle the number of whole things (sticks).
- Circle the number it takes to make 1 whole stick.
- Box "all the stuff," or total value of the sticks.
- Transfer the numbers to the diagram.

Use the diagram to generate the fact that solves the problem.

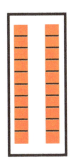

Each stick is worth ⑩ units.
There are ② sticks.
What is the value of all the sticks?

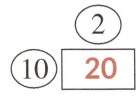

$2 \times 10 = 20$

There are ② sticks.
All the sticks are worth ☐20☐ units.
What is the value of a stick?

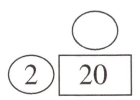

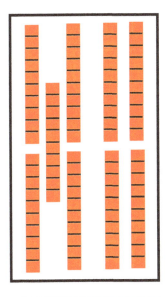

There are 9 sticks.
Each stick is worth 10 units.
What is the value of all the sticks?

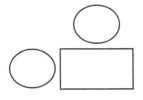

All the sticks are worth 90 units.
There are 9 sticks.
What is the value of a stick?

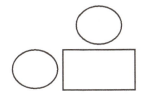

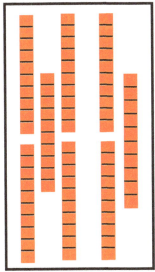

Each stick is worth 10 units.
All the sticks are worth 80 units.
How many sticks are there?

There are 8 sticks.
Each stick is worth 10 units.
What is the value of all the sticks?

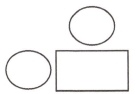

Dime Values

- Fill in the blanks, then transfer the values to the diagram.

Value   **Number of Dimes**

_____ cents = _____ × 10

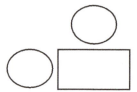

Value   **Number of Dimes**

_____ cents = _____ × 10

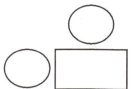

Value   **Number of Dimes**

_____ cents = _____ × 10

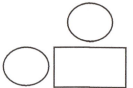

Value   **Number of Dimes**

_____ cents = _____ × 10

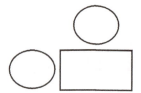

Dime Values

- Fill in the blanks, then transfer the values to the diagram.

    Value   Number of Dimes

_____ cents = _____ × 10

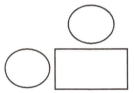

    Value   Number of Dimes

_____ cents = _____ × 10

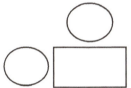

    Value   Number of Dimes

_____ cents = _____ × 10

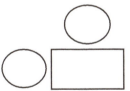

    Value   Number of Dimes

_____ cents = _____ × 10

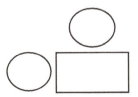

© 2013 C. Woodin & Landmark School

Dime-Based Facts

- Fill in the blank diagrams.
- Write four related facts for each diagram.

Diagram

$3 \times 10 = 30$ $30 \div 10 = 3$

$10 \times = $ $30 \div = $

   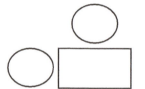

   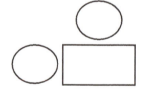

   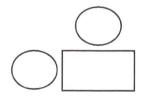

160   © 2013 C. Woodin & Landmark School

Dime-Based Facts

- Fill in the blank diagrams.
- Write four related facts for each diagram.

Diagram

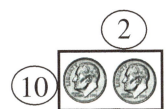
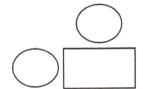

$2 \times 10 = 20$

$20 \div 10 = 2$

$10 \times \quad =$

_____

_____

_____

_____

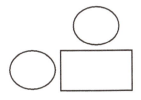

_____

_____

_____

_____

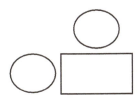

_____

_____

_____

_____

Dime-Based Facts

- Fill in the blank diagrams.
- Write related multiplication and division facts for each diagram.

Name
Date
Day

Diagram

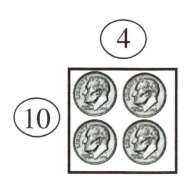

$4 \times 10 = 40$

$10 \times = $

$40 \div 10 = 4$

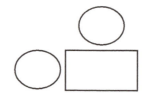

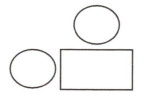

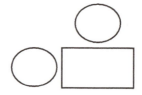

162 © 2013 C. Woodin & Landmark School

Dime-Based Fact Problems

- Circle the number of whole things.
- Circle the number it takes to make 1 whole.
- Box "all the stuff," or total value.
- Transfer the numbers to the diagram. Use the diagram to generate the fact that solves the problem.

Name _____
Date _____
Day _____

There are ②　dimes.
Each dime is worth ⑩ cents.
What is the value of all the coins?

　　　⑩
②　| 20 |
$2 \times 10 = 20$

There are ② dimes.
The coins are worth | 20 | cents.
What is the value of a dime?

　　　⑩
②　| 20 |
$20 \div 2 = 10$

The coins are worth 20 cents.
Each dime is worth 10 cents.
How many dimes are there?

　　　◯
⑩　| 20 |

There are 5 dimes.
Each dime is worth 10 cents.
What is the value of all the coins?

◯
◯ | □ |

Each dime is worth 10 cents.
The coins are worth 50 cents.
How many dimes are there?

◯
◯ | □ |

The coins are worth 50 cents.
There are 5 dimes.
What is the value of a dime?

◯
◯ | □ |

Each dime is worth 10 cents.
The coins are worth 30 cents.
How many dimes are there?

◯
◯ | □ |

The coins are worth 30 cents.
There are 3 dimes.
What is the value of a dime?

◯
◯ | □ |

There are 3 dimes.
Each dime is worth 10 cents.
What is the value of all the coins?

◯
◯ | □ |

© 2013 C. Woodin & Landmark School　　163

Dime-Based Fact Problems

- Circle the number of whole things.
- Circle the number it takes to make 1 whole.
- Box "all the stuff," or total value.
- Transfer the numbers to the diagram. Use the diagram to generate the fact that solves the problem.

Name _____
Date _____
Day _____

There are ③ dimes.
Each dime is worth ⑩ cents.
What is the value of all the coins?

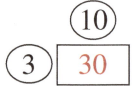

$3 \times 10 = 30$

There are ③ dimes.
The coins are worth ☐30☐ cents.
What is the value of a dime?

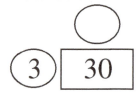

The coins are worth 30 cents.
Each dime is worth 10 cents.
How many dimes are there?

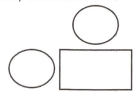

There are 7 dimes.
Each dime is worth 10 cents.
What is the value of all the coins?

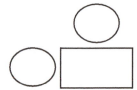

Each dime is worth 10 cents.
The coins are worth 70 cents.
How many dimes are there?

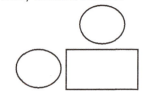

The coins are worth 70 cents.
There are 7 dimes.
What is the value of a dime?

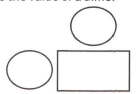

Each dime is worth 10 cents.
The coins are worth 90 cents.
How many dimes are there?

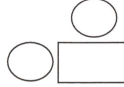

The coins are worth 90 cents.
There are 9 dimes.
What is the value of a dime?

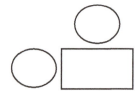

There are 9 dimes.
Each dime is worth 10 cents.
What is the value of all the coins?

164   © 2013 C. Woodin & Landmark School

Dime-Based Fact Word Problems

- Circle the number of whole things.
- Circle the number it takes to make 1 whole.
- Box "all the stuff," or total value.
- Transfer the numbers to the diagram. Use the diagram to generate the fact that solves the problem.

Name _____
Date _____
Day _____

There are (4) dimes.
Each dime is worth (10) cents.
What is the value of all the coins?

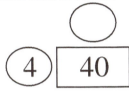

There are (4) dimes.
The coins are worth [40] cents.
What is the value of a dime?

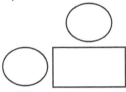

The coins are worth 40 cents.
Each dime is worth 10 cents.
How many dimes are there?

$4 \times 10 = 40$

There are 6 dimes.
Each dime is worth 10 cents.
What is the value of all the coins?

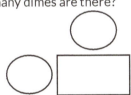

Each dime is worth 10 cents.
The coins are worth 60 cents.
How many dimes are there?

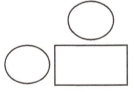

The coins are worth 60 cents.
There are 6 dimes.
What is the value of a dime?

Each dime is worth 10 cents.
The coins are worth 80 cents.
How many dimes are there?

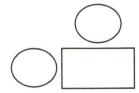

The coins are worth 80 cents.
There are 8 dimes.
What is the value of a dime?

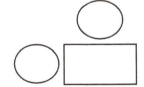

There are 8 dimes.
Each dime is worth 10 cents.
What is the value of all the coins?

© 2013 C. Woodin & Landmark School   165

Word Problems Related to Area: 10× Facts

- Mask the multiplication grid with two index cards to frame the rectangle described by the word problem.
- Use the grid to find the answer.
- Transfer the information to the diagram and label the answer with the appropriate units.

Name _____
Date _____
Day _____

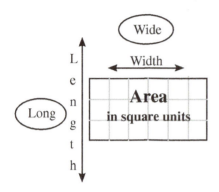

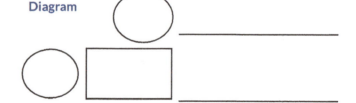

Problem #1

The rectangular table is 3 feet long.

The table has an area of 30 square feet.

How wide is the table?

Diagram

Problem #2

The rectangular rug is 10 feet long.

The area of the rug is 40 square feet.

How wide is the rug?

Diagram

Problem #3

The garden has an area of 80 square feet.

The garden is 8 feet long.

How wide is the garden?

Diagram

Problem #4

The wall is 5 feet wide.

It is 10 feet tall.

What is the area of the wall?

Diagram

166   © 2013 C. Woodin & Landmark School

Word Problems Related to Area: 10× Facts Template

- Mask the multiplication grid with two index cards to frame the rectangle described by the word problem.
- Use the grid to find the answer.
- Transfer the information to the diagram and label the answer with the appropriate units.

Teachers: customize this template by filling in blanks with appropriate values.

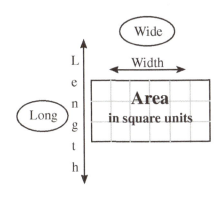

Problem #1

The rectangular table is ___ feet long.

The table has an area of ___ square feet.

How wide is the table?

Diagram

Problem #2

The rectangular rug is 10 feet wide.

The area of the rug is ___ square feet.

How wide is the rug?

Diagram

Problem #3

The garden has an area of ___ square feet.

The garden is ___ feet long.

How wide is the garden?

Diagram

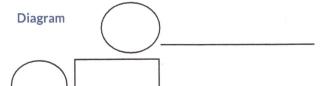

Problem #4

The wall is ___ feet wide.

It is 10 feet tall.

What is the area of the wall?

Diagram

© 2013 C. Woodin & Landmark School   167

10× Facts: Cut out these flash cards along the dotted lines. Use the tens digit in the product to cue the missing factor, then verbalize the related facts.

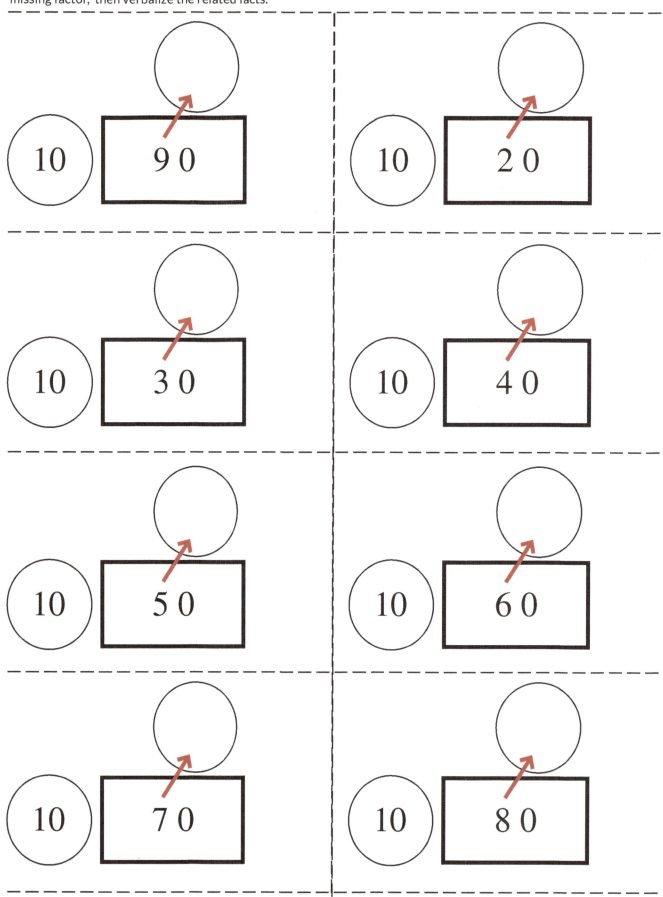

10× Fact Mosaic

- Write a product (for example, 20) on one side of a dashed grid line and the other part of the face sentence (2 × 10) on the other side of the dashed line.
- Repeat this process for each of the grid lines.
- Then cut the puzzle along the dashed lines to make nine square pieces and shuffle the pieces.
- Try to put them back together using the fact sentences and products as a guide.
- Trade puzzles with another student and challenge each other!

Name

Date

Day

© 2013 C. Woodin & Landmark School

Baseball Fact Game

10×

OUT = 10, 20, 30
SINGLE = 40, 50
DOUBLE = 60, 70
TRIPLE = 80, 90
HOME RUN = 100

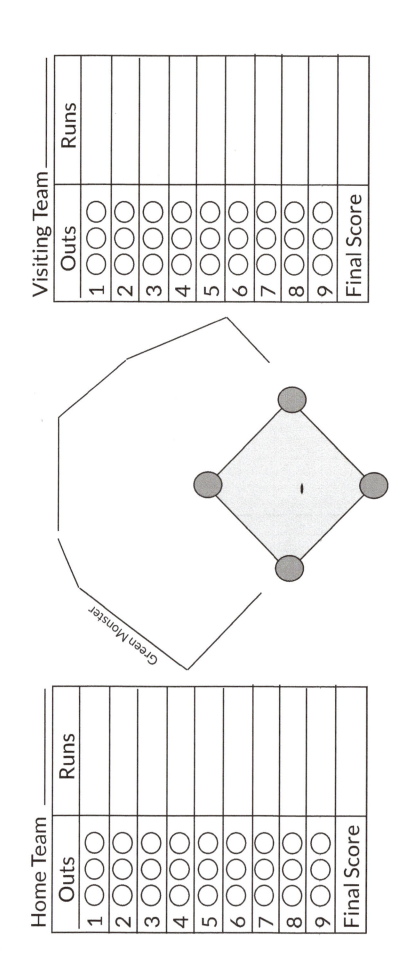

Accuracy Benchmark Pretest - Untimed

Complete this sheet with 100% accuracy before taking the related timed *Fluency Assessment*.

1) Complete each diagram. Have them scored.
2) Correct diagrams if needed.
3) Write a multiplication fact and a division fact for each.
4) Archive this in your Fact Notebook as a record.

Name _____
Date _____
Day _____

Diagram Accuracy: ____/10

Sentence Accuracy: ____/20

10) 10 _____

10) 60 _____

10) 20 _____

10) 70 _____

10) 30 _____

10) 80 _____

10) 40 _____

10) 90 _____

10) 50 _____

10) 100 _____

© 2013 C. Woodin & Landmark School

Fluency Assessment - Timed

Administer this test after the student scores 100% accuracy on the related *Accuracy Benchmark Pretest*.

1) Complete each diagram. Note time and accuracy.

2) Correct diagrams as needed.

3) Write a multiplication fact and a division fact for each. Note time and accuracy.

4) Archive this in your Fact Notebook as a record.

Name: _____
Date: _____
Day: _____

Diagram Accuracy: _____/10 Time: _____

Sentences Accuracy: _____/20 Time: _____

10 × 3	10 × 7
10 × 2	10 × 10
10 × 4	10 × 9
10 × 6	10 × 8
10 × 1	10 × 5

172   © 2013 C. Woodin & Landmark School

Vertical 10× Fact Practice

Name _____
Date _____
Day _____

Timed quiz

_____ seconds

◯/10

```
   1 0            1 0
 ×   1          ×   6
 ─────          ─────


   1 0            1 0
 ×   2          ×   7
 ─────          ─────


   1 0            1 0
 ×   3          ×   8
 ─────          ─────


   1 0            1 0
 ×   4          ×   9
 ─────          ─────


   1 0            1 0
 ×   5          × 1 0
 ─────          ─────
```

© 2013 C. Woodin & Landmark School

The 1× and 0× Families

Teach the 1× and 0× facts by their rules. The rule for multiplying by 1 is relatively simple. Any number times 1 is equal to the same number (1 × n = n). This rule is usually quite understandable to children at this point in their learning.

Multiplying by 0 is another story. Although any number times 0 is 0 (0 × n = 0), it is difficult to explain this process because there are no quantities to model with manipulatives. Neither the geoboard nor the 10 × 10 multiplication grid have spaces for the zero facts because these facts would corrupt the area model. It is helpful to demonstrate the multiplication of 0 using empty bowls to represent a quantity of zero. For example, you can demonstrate 3 × 0 = 0 by putting three empty bowls on a table.

After students automatize the 10×, 1×, and 0× facts, you can use facts students have already mastered to introduce them to problems involving single-digit numbers multiplied by multidigit numbers.

Multiplication Grid with 1× Shading Pattern

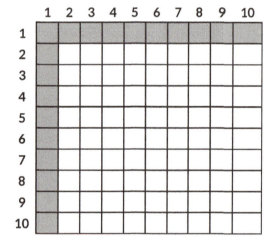

64% of the 100 facts have been learned.

After mastering the 1× facts, 64% of the 100 facts have been learned.

Have the student color this additional grey portion of the big graphic organizer found in the first section of their Fact Notebook.

Make a new grey-tabbed section in the student's Fact Notebook for the 1× and 0× facts.

Gain 13 more facts by learning 1× facts.

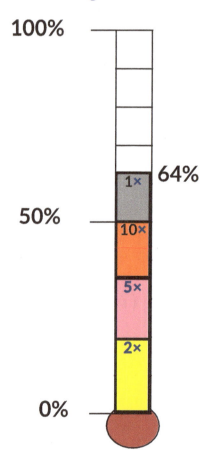

Semantic-Based 1× Facts and Matrix Diagrams

- Circle the number of whole things.
- Circle the number of parts needed to make one whole.
- Box the number that represents all of the parts.
- Complete the diagram and write four related facts.

Fill in the diagram: **Two × and two ÷ facts:**

How many wheels are on 1 tricycle?

Tricycles all have ③ wheels.

If there is ① tricycle, there are ☐3 wheels.

①×③=☐3   ☐3 ÷ ③ = ①

③×①=☐3   ☐3 ÷ ① = ③

How many legs are on 1 table?

Tables have 4 legs.

If there is 1 table, there are 4 legs.

How many shoes make 1 pair?

Shoes come in pairs of 2.

If there is 1 pair, there are 2 shoes.

How many sides are on 1 pentagon?

Pentagons have 5 sides each.

If there is 1 pentagon, there are 5 sides.

How many cents are in 1 dime?

Dimes are worth 10 cents each.

If there is 1 dime, it is worth 10 cents.

© 2013 C. Woodin & Landmark School   175

Semantic-Based 1× Facts and Matrix Diagrams

- Circle the number of whole things.
- Circle the number of parts needed to make one whole.
- Box the number that represents all of the parts.
- Complete the diagram and write four related facts.

Fill in the diagram: **Two × and two ÷ facts:**

How many fingers are on 1 hand?

Hands have (5) fingers.

If there is (1) hand, there are [5] fingers.

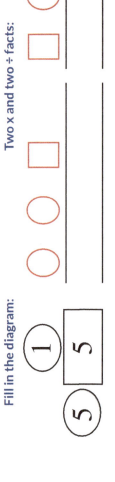

How many legs are on 1 ant?

Ants have 6 legs.

If there is 1 ant, there are 6 legs.

How many days make 1 week?

Weeks all have 7 days.

If there is 1 week, there are 7 days.

How many legs are on 1 spider?

Spiders all have 8 legs.

If there is 1 spider, there are 8 legs.

How many players are on 1 baseball team?

Baseball teams play 9 players at a time.

If there is 1 team, there are 9 players.

© 2013 C. Woodin & Landmark School

Accuracy Benchmark Pretest - Untimed

Complete this sheet with 100% accuracy before taking the related timed *Fluency Assessment*.

Name _____
Date _____
Day _____

1) Complete each diagram. Have them scored.

2) Correct diagrams if needed.

3) Write a multiplication fact and a division fact for each.

4) Archive this in the students fact notebook as a record..

Diagram Accuracy: ____/10

Sentence Accuracy: ____/20

1 × 4 _____

1 × 1 _____

1 × 9 _____

1 × 10 _____

1 × 2 _____

1 × 6 _____

1 × 3 _____

1 × 7 _____

1 × 5 _____

1 × 8 _____

© 2013 C. Woodin & Landmark School   177

Fluency Assessment - Timed

Administer this test after the student scores 100% accuracy on the related *Accuracy Benchmark Pretest*.

1) Complete each diagram. Note time and accuracy.

2) Correct diagrams as needed.

3) Write a multiplication fact and a division fact for each. Note time and accuracy.

4) Archive this in the students fact notebook as a record..

Name _____

Date _____

Day _____

Diagram Accuracy: _____/10 Time: _____

Sentences Accuracy: _____/20 Time: _____

178 © 2013 C. Woodin & Landmark School

Semantic-Based 0x Facts and Matrix Diagrams

Fill in the diagram: **Write two 0x facts:**

How many wheels are on 0 tricycles?

_____

_____

How many cans are in 0 6-packs?

_____

_____

How many shoes are in 0 pairs?

_____

_____

How many days are in 0 weeks?

_____

_____

How many paws are on 0 cats?

_____

_____

How many legs are on 0 spiders?

_____

_____

How many cents are in 0 nickels?

_____

_____

How many cents are in 0 dimes?

_____

_____

© 2013 C. Woodin & Landmark School   179

Introduction to Multidigit Multiplication

Now that students have a repertoire of facts, it is a good time to introduce multidigit multiplication. Use this higher level skill to reinforce the 2× and 5× facts that have been learned. Teach new fact families concurrently while using learned facts within these larger problems. Start by multiplying by magnitudes of 10 to relate large products to the familiar context of place value. Before starting procedural multidigit multiplication, students should be able to:

- Express the 2×, 5×, 10×, and 1× fact families in terms of multiplication and related division facts
- Express a multiplication fact from a matrix diagram

- Make a matrix diagram from a multiplication or division fact
- Make a matrix diagram from a rectangular array of base ten sticks and a rectangular array of units.

EXAMPLE

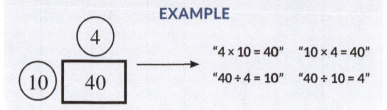

EXAMPLE

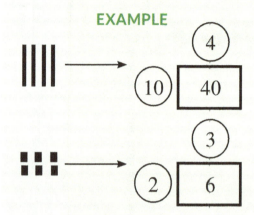

- Write a three digit number as it is dictated: "Two hundred thirty-six" ...
Student writes: 236

- Write a three digit number to represent a base ten model:

Student writes: 234

- Construct a base ten model to represent a three digit number: 124,
Student constructs:

- Extend the multiplication of a familiar fact by magnitudes of 10 (see following pages): →

EXAMPLE

Example: 2 × 4 = 8 → 2 × 40 = 80   Have students underline the fact portion of the problem and write the product. Then tell students to draw a dot in the center of the zero(s) within the problem. Next, have them draw the same number of dots beside the known part of the product. Finally, tell students to circle the dots in the product to make the appropriate number of zeros.

- Extend the multiplication of a familiar fact to the multiplication by a magnitude of 100. This skill is used to create estimates of multidigit products.:

↓

EXAMPLE

Example: 2 × 5 = 10 → 2 × 500 = 1000

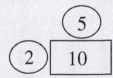

× Facts: $2 \times 5 = 10$

$5 \times 2 = 10$

$2 \times 50 = 100$

$2 \times 500 = 1000$

$20 \times 50 = 1000$

$20 \times 500 = 10000$

This is a selection from the Multiplying by Magnitudes of 10 worksheet series.

Multiplying 2 by Magnitudes of 10

- Underline the fact portion of the problem and write the product.
- Draw a dot in the center of the zero(s) within the problem.
- Draw the same number of dots beside the known part of the product.
- Circle the dots in the product to make the appropriate number of zeros.

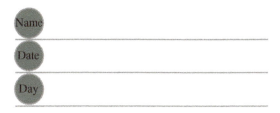

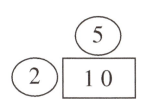

× Facts: $2 \times 5 = 10$

$5 \times 2 = 10$

$2 \times \underline{5}\,0 = \underline{1\,0}\,0$

$2 \times 500 =$

$20 \times 50 =$

$20 \times 500 =$

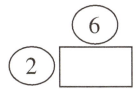

× Facts: _____

_____

$2 \times 90 =$

$2 \times 900 =$

$200 \times 90 =$

$20 \times 900 =$

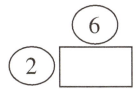

× Facts: _____

_____

$2 \times 60 =$

$2 \times 600 =$

$200 \times 60 =$

$20 \times 600 =$

© 2013 C. Woodin & Landmark School

Multiplying 2 by Magnitudes of 10

- Underline the fact portion of the problem and write the product.
- Draw a dot in the center of the zero(s) within the problem.
- Draw the same number of dots beside the known part of the product.
- Circle the dots in the product to make the appropriate number of zeros.

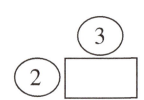

× **Facts:** _____

_____

$2 \times \underline{3\,0} = \underline{6}\,0$

$2 \times 3\,0\,0 =$

$2\,0 \times 3\,0 =$

$2\,0 \times 3\,0\,0 =$

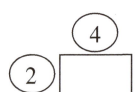

× **Facts:** _____

_____

$2 \times 4\,0 =$

$2 \times 4\,0\,0 =$

$2\,0\,0 \times 4\,0 =$

$2\,0 \times 4\,0\,0 =$

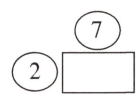

× **Facts:** _____

_____

$2 \times 7\,0 =$

$2 \times 7\,0\,0 =$

$2\,0\,0 \times 7\,0 =$

$2\,0 \times 7\,0\,0 =$

Multiplying 2 by Magnitudes of 10: Template

- Underline the fact portion of the problem and write the product.
- Draw a dot in the center of the zero(s) within the problem.
- Draw the same number of dots beside the known part of the product.
- Circle the dots in the product to make the appropriate number of zeros.

Teachers: customize this template by filling in blanks with appropriate values.

2 × __0 = _____

2 × __0 0 = _____

2 0 × __0 = _____

2 0 × __0 0 = _____

× **Facts:** _____

2 × __0 = _____

2 × __0 0 = _____

2 0 0 × __0 = _____

2 0 × __0 0 = _____

× **Facts:** _____

2 × __0 = _____

2 × __0 0 = _____

2 0 0 × __0 = _____

2 0 × __0 0 = _____

× **Facts:** _____

© 2013 C. Woodin & Landmark School   183

Use Iconic Diagrams to Model the Traditional Multidigit Multiplication Algorithm

Start multiplying quantities by 2 using base ten blocks.

- Make an iconic arrangement pattern of base ten blocks with fewer than five pieces in each place value - for example, 12, 44, 132, ...444. This will initially eliminate the regrouping process.

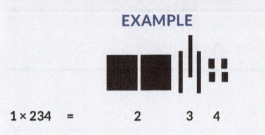

- Multiply the quantity by 2 by placing a duplicate arrangement of blocks below.

In this manner, you will show the student(s) the same quantity "two times."

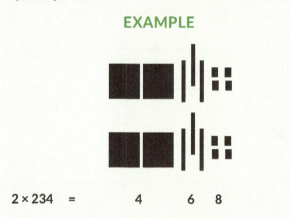

- Produce the requisite 2× facts in isolation 2 × (1, 2, 3, 4), using matrix diagrams or fact sentences on the board. They should be in sight of the student(s) for reference.

Example: For 2 x 234, have students produce the following

2 × 2 = 4, 2 × 3 = 6, 2 × 4 = 8

- Demonstrate the traditional multiplication algorithm to produce the identical product to the product found using base ten blocks.

On the board, set up the problem that has been diagrammed.

Solve and compare the product with the base ten model.

Increase the rigor of this process by introducing problems that involve a regrouping step using similar base ten block examples to model the regrouping process:

```
  2 3 4
x     2
-------
  4 6 8
```

```
  2 3 6
x     2
-------
```

Initially, place the factors that will result in a regrouped product in the ones place to limit the spatial demands caused by the size of the manipulatives that represent the tens and hundreds.

RECTANGULAR MATRIX DIAGRAMS (CONCRETE AREA MODELS)

After performing several of these problems, it is time to shift this iconic arrangement pattern to a rectangular compound matrix. At this point, the rectangular area model established by the compound matrix will be made of concrete materials (base ten blocks).

Use this concrete rectangular compound matrix to model two-digit by one-digit multiplication (1 × 11 through 9 × 99), but limit the model to a problem such as 2 × 23 due to spatial limitations of this model type. See the following pages for an example.

Area = Length × Width

Find the areas of each rectangle, then add them.

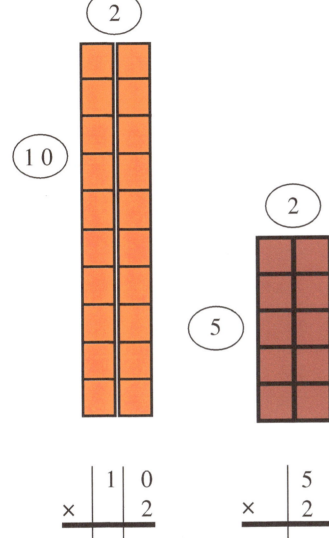
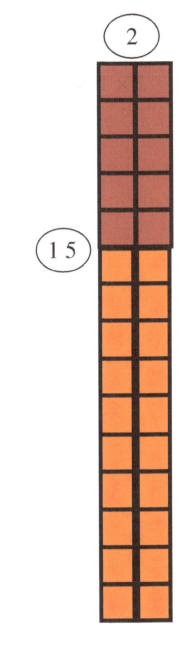

Combine the two areas:

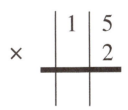

© 2013 C. Woodin & Landmark School   185

Multiplication Represented by the Compound Area Model

Write the related × facts for each diagram.

   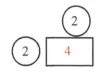

$2 \times 1 = 2$

$2 \times 10 = 20$

$2 \times 2 = 4$

$2 \times 20 = 40$

Use expanded notation to rewrite the top number.

$\underline{2\ 1}$ = $(2\ 0)$ + (1)

```
   2 1
×    2
-----
   4 2
```

Complete the diagram to match the problem. ⟶

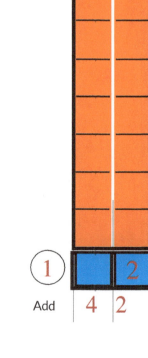

1) Warm up with requisite facts at the top of the page.

2) Rewrite the top number of the multiplication problem using expanded notation.

3) Use the expanded notation to write dimensions in the circles of the diagram.

4) Cover the area of the diagram using base-ten blocks as shown. Create the diagram so that the width is represented by the lower (bottom) factor of the problem - in this case "2". The height should represent the top number - in this case "21". This format aligns the two partial products so they can be added.

```
   40
+   2
-----
   4 2
```

5) Have the students locate the blocks that represent 2 × 1 (blue). Ask, "What is 2 × 1?" (2). Remove the two blocks and write the number 2 in their place.

6) Say, "Find 2 × 1 in the multiplication problem." Have students complete that step of the problem by writing 2 in the ones place.

7) Have the students locate the blocks that represent 2 × 20 (orange). Ask, "What is 2 × 20?" (40). Remove the four sticks and write the number 40 in their place.

8) Say, "Find 2 × 20 in the multiplication problem." Have the students complete that step of the problem by writing 4 in the tens place.

9) Have students add the partial products in the diagram and compare it to the product of their multiplication problem.

© 2013 C. Woodin & Landmark School

Multiplication Represented by the Compound Area Model

Write the related × facts for each diagram.

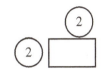

2 × 1 =

2 × 10 =

2 × 20 =

Use expanded notation to rewrite 21.

2 1 = ◯ + ◯

	2	1
×		2

Complete the diagram to match the problem. ⟶

Base-ten sticks and units fit on this diagram.

Add

© 2013 C. Woodin & Landmark School

Extend the Compound Area Model to Tabular Array Diagrams

Eventually, concrete rectangular compound matrixes become too large to be practical. Since base-ten sticks are ten centimeters long, any factor greater than or equal to one hundred would be larger than most school desks. The concrete materials necessary to construct a model of 102 × 2 would be over one meter long! The following steps clarify how to transition from the use of concrete models to diagrams.

1) In place of a concrete model, create a standardized diagram to represent the multiplication problem.

Use a semiconcrete (representational) diagram to model the factors as dimensions and the area as the product. This standardized matrix diagram will not be drawn to scale. It is more of a table, or tabular array, of the partial products. Label and complete a standardized tabular array to represent the factors, and label the dimensions in a standardized manner so that students can easily add the partial products.

- Write the first factor (the top factor in a vertically written multiplication problem) in expanded notation. The height of the array represents this number.
- The second factor (the bottom factor in a vertical multiplication problem) corresponds to the width of the array, labeled at the top of the array.

2) Produce an up-front estimate of the product on the basis of the factors' leading digits.

- Round the factors to their leading digits. For example, the problem 384 × 2 would be estimated as 400 × 2. This rough estimate is accurate enough to identify place value errors in the ensuing multidigit procedure.
- Multiply the leading digits. For example, estimate 400 × 2 as 4 × 2, which equals eight. The leading digit in the product of 400 × 2 will be 8.
- Adjust the product by appending zeros to it. For example, because there are two zeros in the factor 400, the product will expand by two place values—that is, two 0s must be appended to the product.

3) Before completing the standard multiplication procedure, fill in the tabular array.

Multiply the expanded factors, and then add the partial products.

4) Perform the standard multiplication procedure to compute the product.

- The computation's product should be the same as the sum of the partial products in the tabular array diagram.
- Check the computation's product by comparing it to the up-front estimate. For example, 768 is similar to 800.

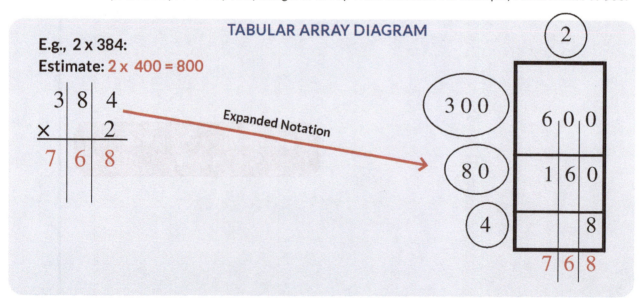

After practicing using a tabular array for many problems, students can then stick with the traditional method only. Begin with multiplying multidigit numbers by 2, then practice multiplying by 5.

2 × 21 Multiplication Sheet

Facts

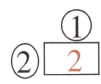

2 × 1 = 2	2 × 2 = 4
2 × 10 = 20	2 × 20 = 40

Diagram the number (21) using base-ten stick models, then write the number in expanded notation.

||.

2 1 = 2 0 + 1

Estimate: 2 × 20 = 40   **Tabular Array Diagram**

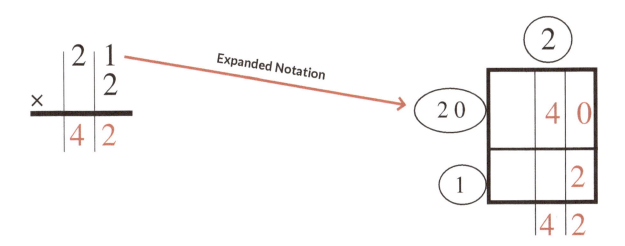

2 × 21 Multiplication Sheet
Facts

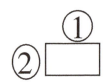
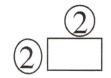

2 × 1 =   2 × 2 =

2 × 10 =   2 × 20 =

Diagram the number (21) using base ten block models, then write the number in expanded notation.

| |.

2 1 = __ __ + __

Estimate: 2 × 20 = _____   **Tabular Array Diagram**

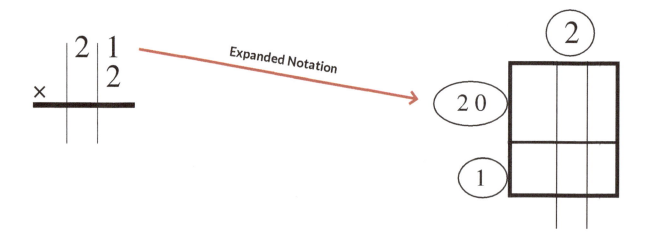

2 × 34 Warm-Up Sheet

Complete this before working on the 2 × 34 Multiplication Sheet.

Name
Date
Day

SAMPLE PAGE

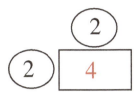

× Fact

2 × 2 = 4

× 10

2 × 20 = 40

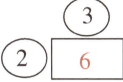

× Fact

2 × 3 = 6

× 10

2 × 30 = 60

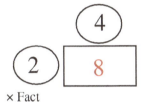

× Fact

2 × 4 = 8

× 10

2 × 40 = 80

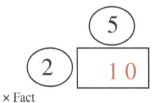

× Fact

2 × 5 = 10

× 10

2 × 50 = 100

Diagram the number using base-ten stick models, then write the number in expanded notation.

3 4 = 3 0 + 4

5 2 = 5 0 + 2

© 2013 C. Woodin & Landmark School   191

2 × 34 Multiplication Sheet

Facts

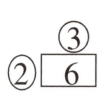 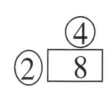

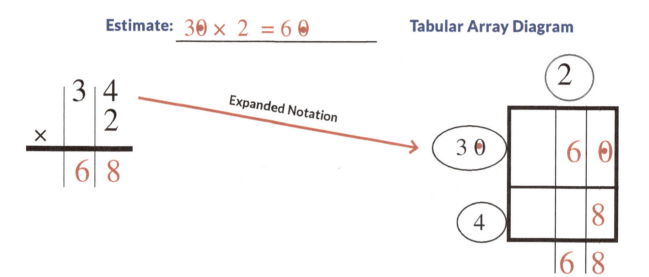

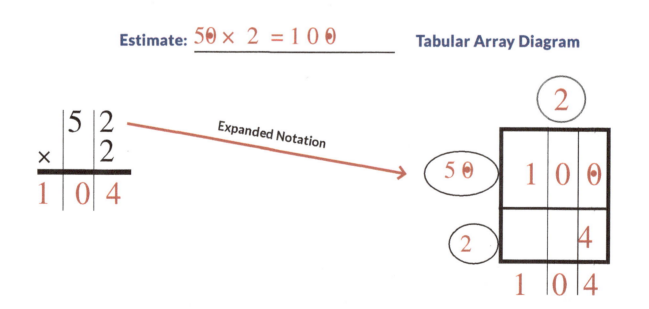

2 × 34 Warm-Up Sheet

Complete this before working on the 2 × 34 Multiplication Sheet.

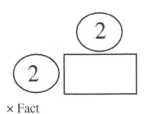

× Fact

2 × _____ = _____
× 10

2 × _____ = _____

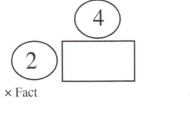

× Fact

2 × _____ = _____
× 10

2 × _____ = _____

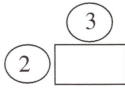

× Fact

2 × _____ = _____
× 10

2 × _____ = _____

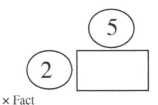

× Fact

2 × _____ = _____
× 10

2 × _____ = _____

Diagram the number using base-ten stick models, then write the number in expanded notation.

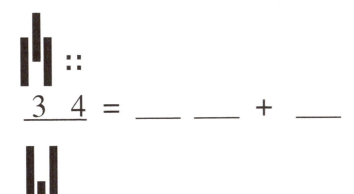

3 4 = ___ ___ + ___

5 2 = ___ ___ + ___

© 2013 C. Woodin & Landmark School

2 × 34 Multiplication Sheet

Facts

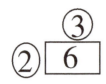 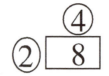

Estimate: 30 × 2 = _____   **Tabular Array Diagram**

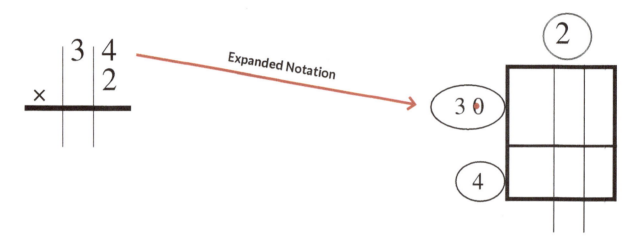

Estimate: _____   **Tabular Array Diagram**

2 × 24 Warm-Up Sheet

Complete this before working on the 2 × 24 Multiplication Sheet.

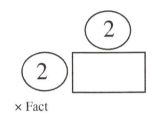

× Fact

2 × ___ = _____
       × 10

2 × 20 = _____

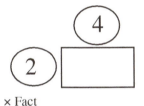

× Fact

2 × ___ = _____
       × 10

2 × ___ = _____

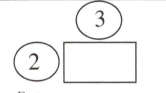

× Fact

2 × ___ = _____
       × 10

2 × ___ = _____

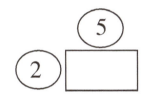

× Fact

2 × ___ = _____
       × 10

2 × ___ = _____

Diagram each number using base-ten stick models, then write the number in expanded notation.

| | ::

2 4 = 2 0 + ___

5 3 = ___ ___ + ___

© 2013 C. Woodin & Landmark School

2 × 24 Multiplication Sheet

Facts

 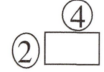

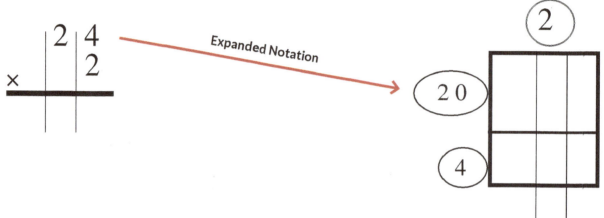

Estimate: 2 × 20 = _____

Tabular Array Diagram

Facts

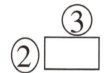 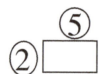

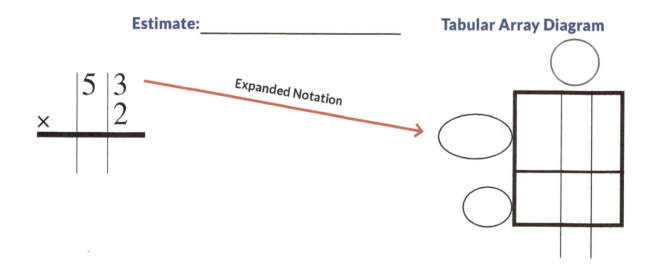

Estimate: _____

Tabular Array Diagram

2 × 54 Warm-Up Sheet

Complete this before working on the 2 × 54 Multiplication Sheet.

Name _____
Date _____
Day _____

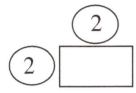
× Fact

2 × ___ = _____
   × 10

2 × 20 = _____

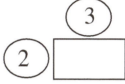
× Fact

2 × ___ = _____
   × 10

2 × ___ = _____

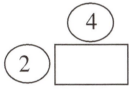
× Fact

2 × ___ = _____
   × 10

2 × ___ = _____

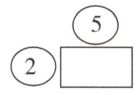
× Fact

2 × ___ = _____
   × 10

2 × ___ = _____

Diagram each number using base-ten stick models, then write the number in expanded notation.

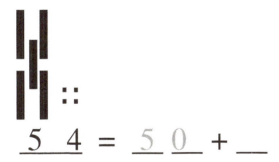

5 4 = 5 0 + ___

4 2 = ___ ___ + ___

2 × 54 Multiplication Sheet

Facts

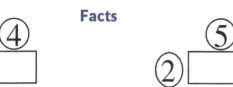

Estimate: $2 \times 50 = $ _____ **Tabular Array Diagram**

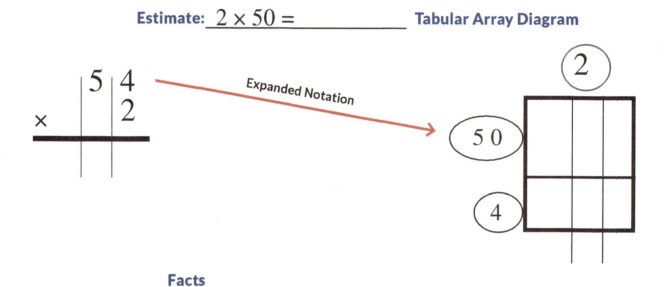

Facts

Estimate: _____ **Tabular Array Diagram**

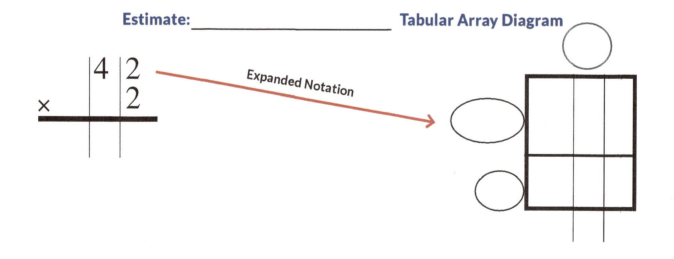

2 × 2-Digit Number Warm-up Sheet Template

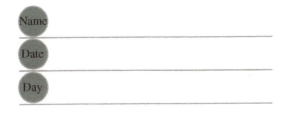

Teachers: customize this template by filling in blanks with appropriate values.

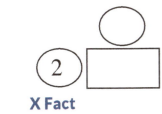

X Fact

2 × ___ = _____
   x 10

2 × ___ = _____

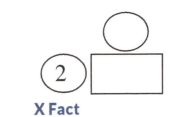

X Fact

2 × ___ = _____
   x 10

2 × ___ = _____

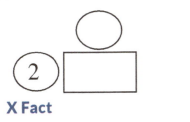

X Fact

2 × ___ = _____
   x 10

2 × ___ = _____

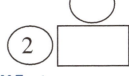

X Fact

2 × ___ = _____
   x 10

2 × ___ = _____

Diagram each number using base-ten stick models, then write the number in expanded notation.

___ = __ 0 + __

___ = __ __ + __

© 2013 C. Woodin & Landmark School   199

2 x 2-Digit Number Sheet Template

Teachers: customize this template by filling in blanks with appropriate values.

Name
Date
Day

Facts

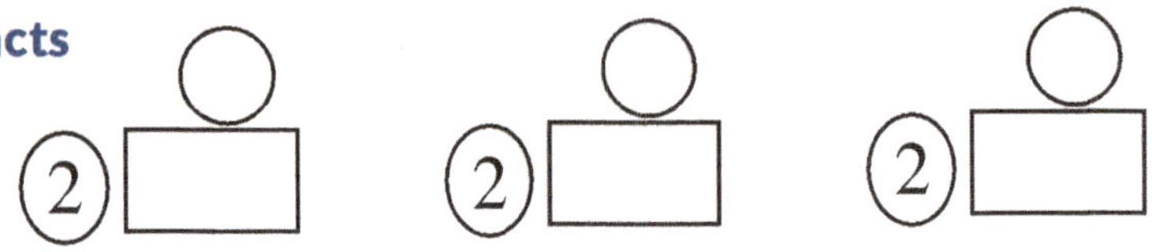

② ② ②

Estimate: _____

Tabular Array Diagram

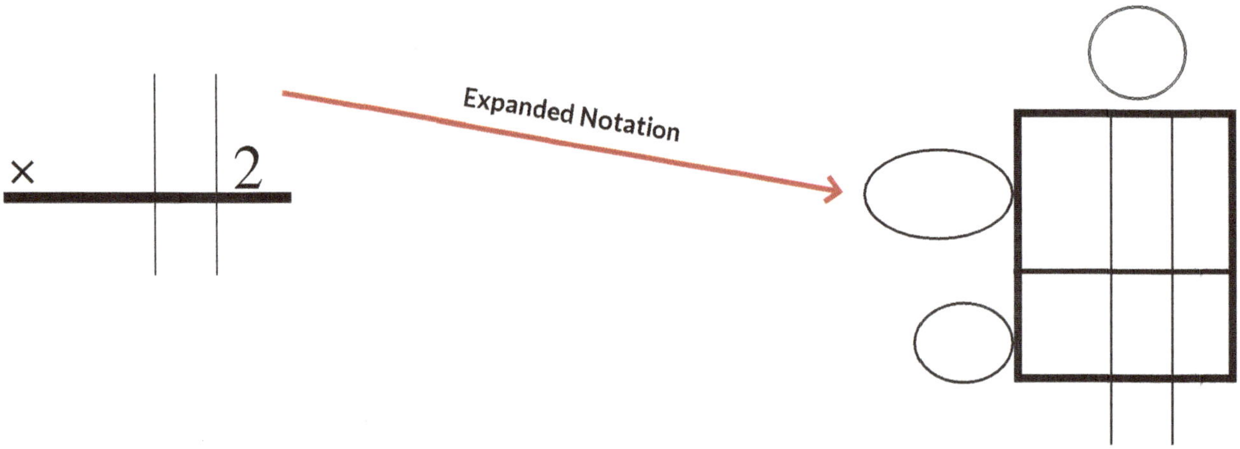

× ___ | ___ 2 ——— Expanded Notation ——→

Estimate: _____

Tabular Array Diagram

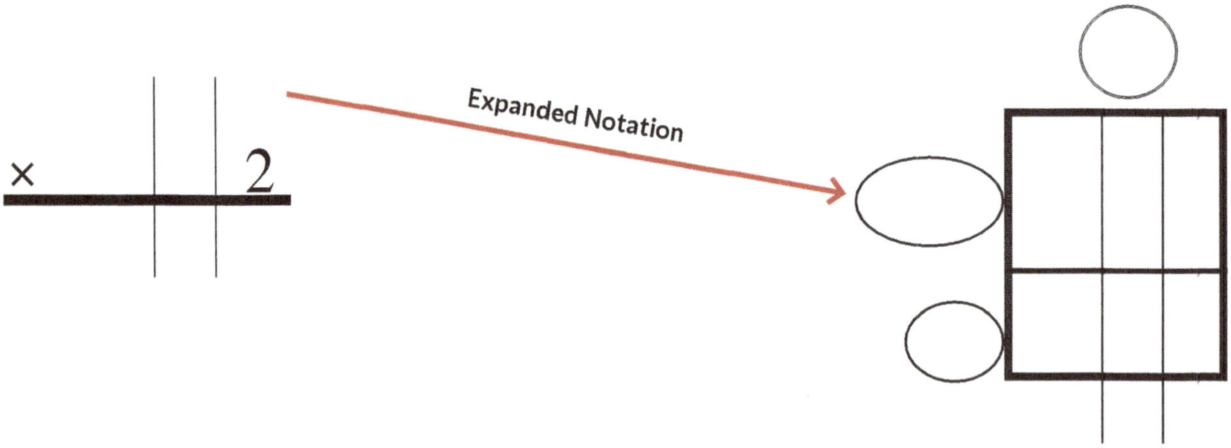

× ___ | ___ 2 ——— Expanded Notation ——→

200 © 2013 C. Woodin & Landmark School

5 × 2-Digit Number Warm-up Template

Teachers: customize this template by filling in blanks with appropriate values.

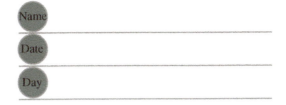

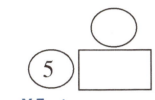

X Fact

5 × ___ = ___
   x 10

5 × 20 = ___

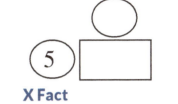

X Fact

5 × ___ = ___
   x 10

5 × ___ = ___

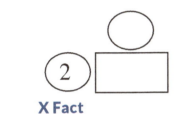

X Fact

5 × ___ = ___
   x 10

5 × ___ = ___

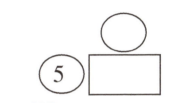

X Fact

5 × ___ = ___
   x 10

5 × ___ = ___

Diagram each number using base-ten stick models, then write the number in expanded notation.

___ = __0 + __

___ = __ __ + __

© 2013 C. Woodin & Landmark School

5 × 2-Digit Number Template

Teachers: customize this template by filling in blanks with appropriate values.

Name
Date
Day

Facts

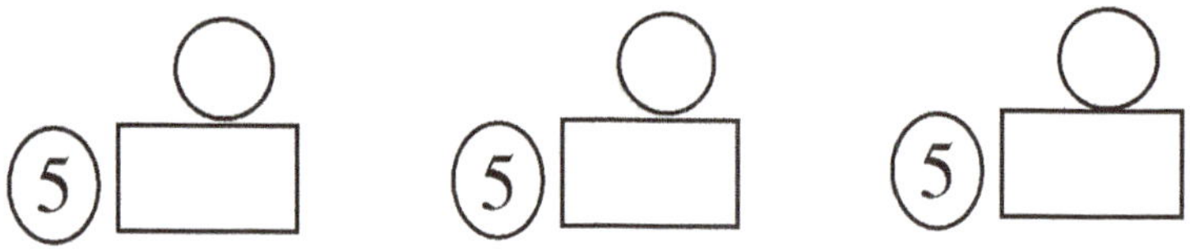

⑤ ⬜   ⑤ ⬜   ⑤ ⬜

Estimate: _____

Tabular Array Diagram

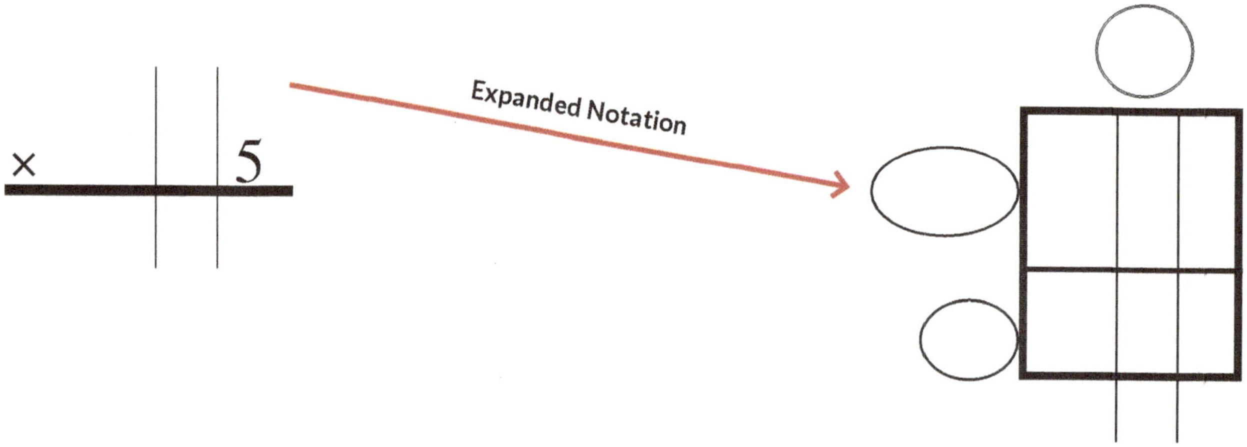

× __|__5 → *Expanded Notation*

Estimate: _____

Tabular Array Diagram

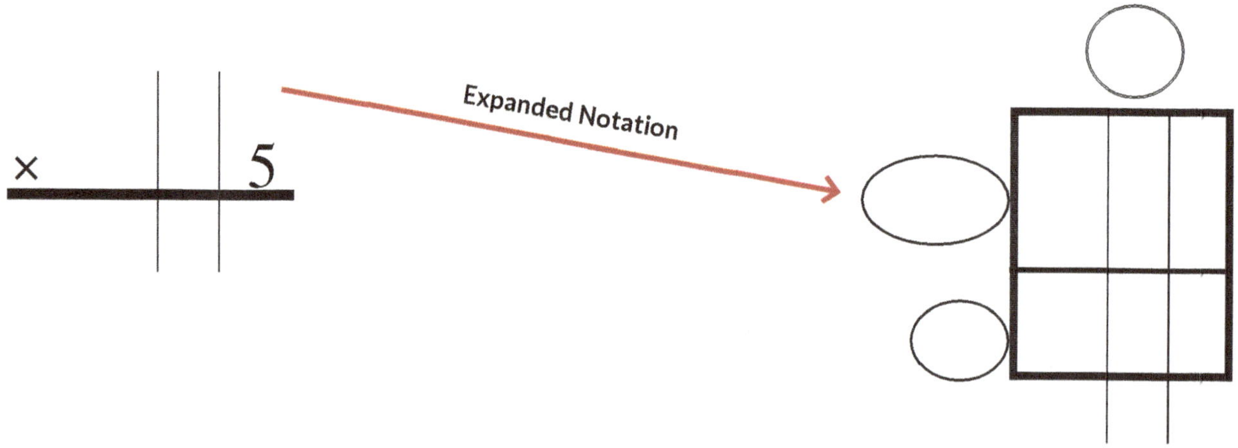

× __|5 → *Expanded Notation*

202 © 2013 C. Woodin & Landmark School

Single Digit x 2-Digit Number Warm-up Sheet Template

Teachers: customize this template by filling in blanks with appropriate values.

Name _____
Date _____
Day _____

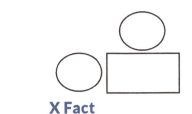

X Fact

× ___ =
_____
x 10

× __0 =
_____

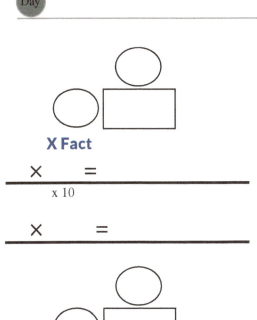

X Fact

× ___ =
_____
x 10

× ___ =
_____

X Fact

× ___ =
_____
x 10

× ___ =
_____

X Fact

× ___ =
_____
x 10

× ___ =
_____

Diagram each number using Base Ten Block models, then write the number in expanded notation.

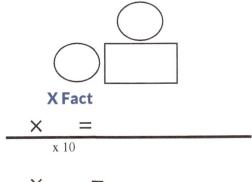

___ = __0 + __

___ = __ __ + __

© 2013 C. Woodin & Landmark School   203

Single Digit x 2-Digit Number Template

Teachers: customize this template by filling in blanks with appropriate values.

Name
Date
Day

Facts

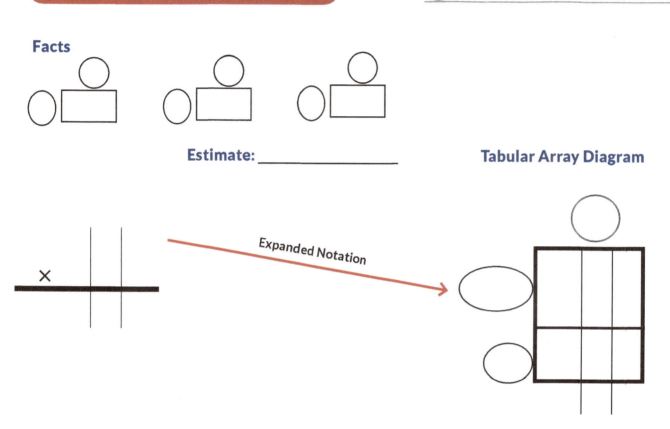

Estimate: _____   **Tabular Array Diagram**

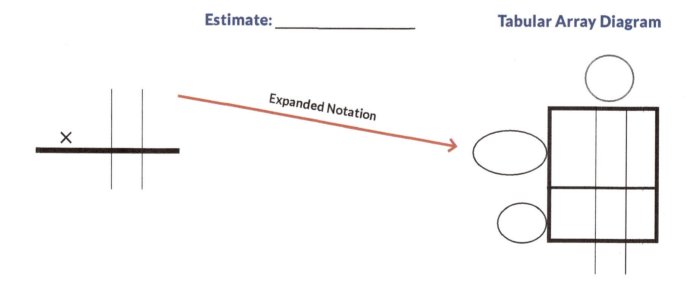

Estimate: _____   **Tabular Array Diagram**

204   © 2013 C. Woodin & Landmark School

Multiplying 1 by Magnitudes of 10: Form 1A

This fact sheet is to be done before 1x 3-Digit Multiplication Form 1A.

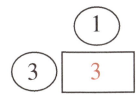

X Fact

1 × 3 =
_____
   x 10

1 × 3 0 =
_____
   x 100

1 × 3 0 0 =
_____

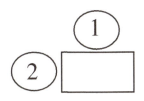

X Fact

1 × =
_____
   x 10

1 × =
_____
   x 100

1 × =
_____

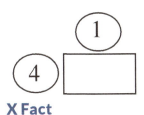

X Fact

1 × =
_____
   x 10

1 × =
_____
   x 100

1 × =
_____

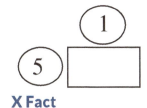

X Fact

1 × =
_____
   x 10

1 × =
_____
   x 100

1 × =
_____

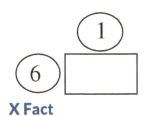

X Fact

1 × =
_____
   x 10

1 × =
_____
   x 100

1 × =
_____

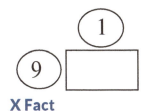

X Fact

1 × =
_____
   x 10

1 × =
_____
   x 100

1 × =
_____

1 × 3-Digit Multiplication: Form 1A

Facts

② [①]   ③ [①]   ④ [①]   ⑤ [①]   ⑦ [①]   ⑨ [①]

Standard Algorithm

Tabular Array Diagram

5 | 3 | 2 →

Expanded Notation

```
  5 0 0
    3 0
+     2
-------
  5 3 2
```

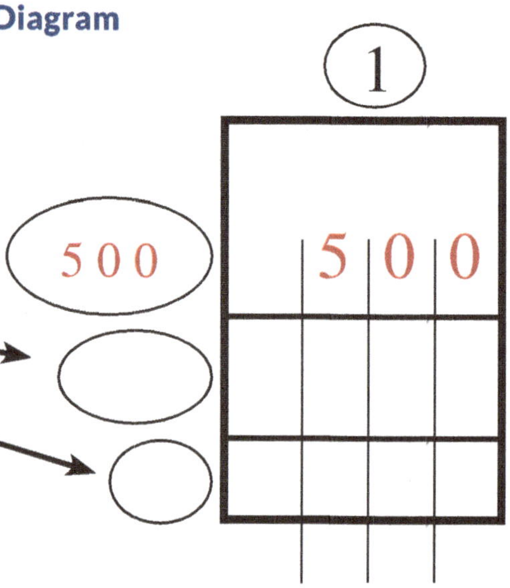

→ 5 0 0

①

5 0 0

Add these partial products.

× 1

6 | 4 | 3
× 1

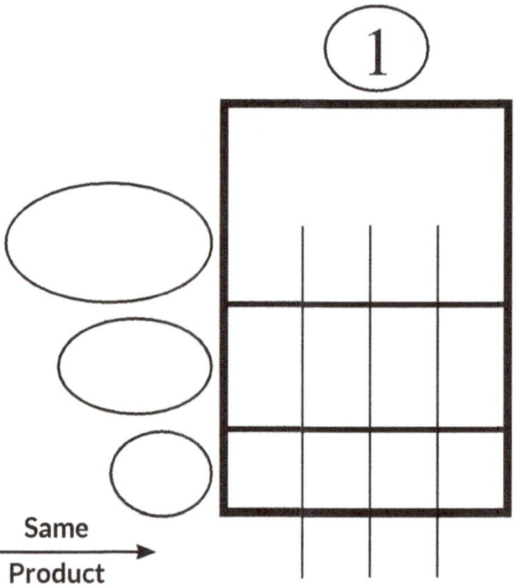

①

← Same Product →

9 | 2 | 7
× 1

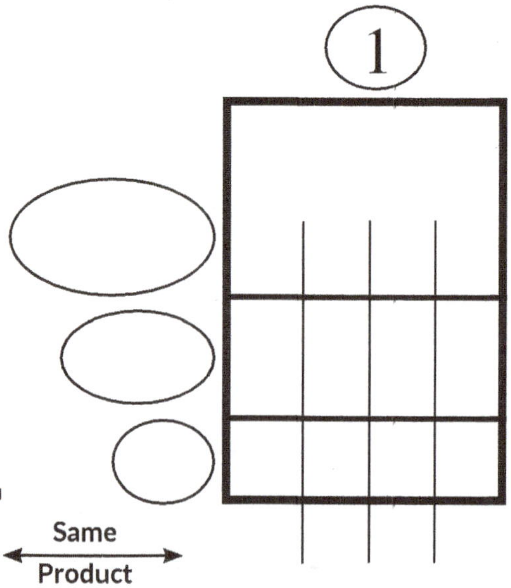

①

← Same Product →

206   © 2013 C. Woodin & Landmark School

Multiplying 2 by Magnitudes of 10: Form 2A

 Name
 Date
Day

This fact sheet is to be done before 2x 3-Digit Multiplication Form 2A.

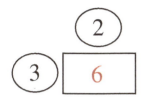

X Fact

2 × 3 = _____
x 10

2 × 3 0 = _____
x 100

2 × 3 0 0 = _____

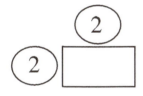

X Fact

2 × _____ = _____
x 10

2 × _____ = _____
x 100

2 × _____ = _____

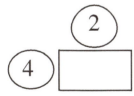

X Fact

2 × _____ = _____
x 10

2 × _____ = _____
x 100

2 × _____ = _____

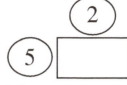

X Fact

2 × _____ = _____
x 10

2 × _____ = _____
x 100

2 × _____ = _____

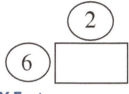

X Fact

2 × _____ = _____
x 10

2 × _____ = _____
x 100

2 × _____ = _____

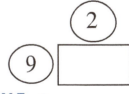

X Fact

2 × _____ = _____
x 10

2 × _____ = _____
x 100

2 × _____ = _____

© 2013 C. Woodin & Landmark School

2 x 3-Digit Multiplication
Form 2A
Facts

②2 ⃞(2)   ②3 ⃞(2)   ②4 ⃞(2)   ②5 ⃞(2)   ⃝7 |14| ②9 ⃞(2)

Standard Algorithm **Tabular Array Diagram**

```
  5 | 3 | 2
×     |   | 2
```
→ **Expanded Notation**

```
    5 0 0  →  ( 5 0 0 )    | 1 | 0 | 0 | 0 |
      3 0  →  (       )
  +     2  →  (       )
    5 3 2
```

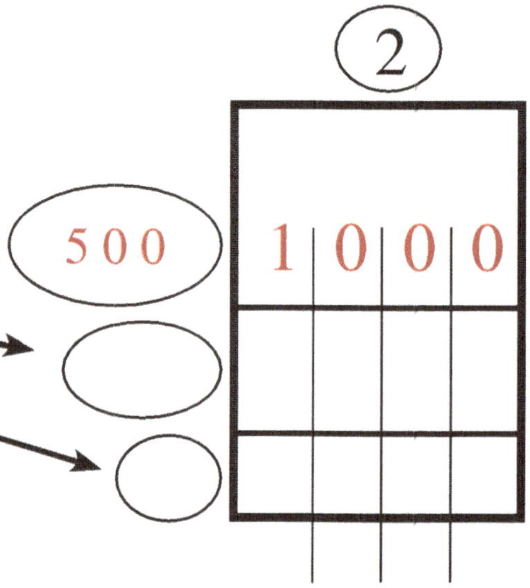

Add these partial products.

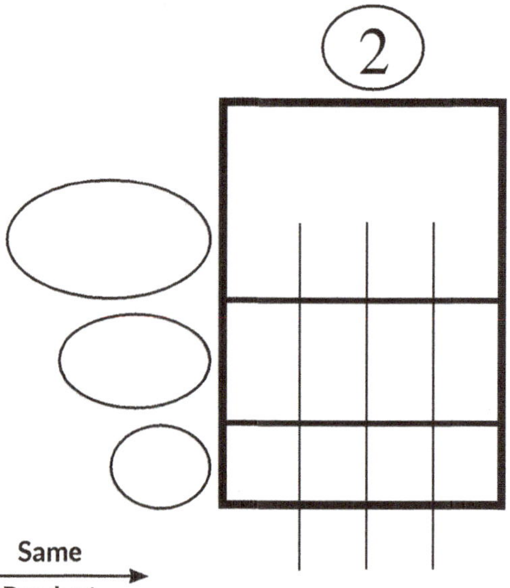

```
  4 | 4 | 3
×     |   | 2
```

Same Product

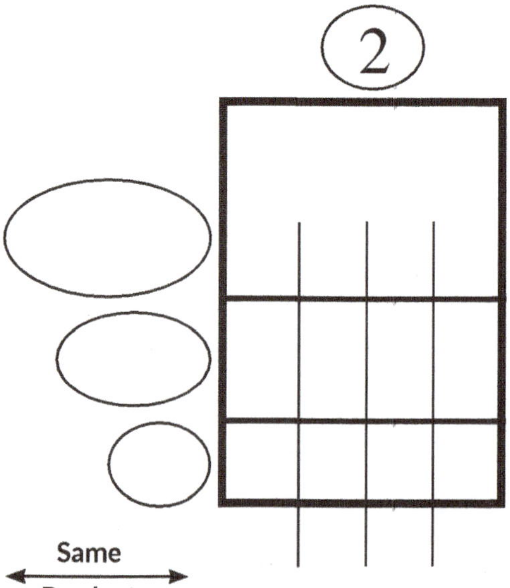

```
  9 | 2 | 7
×     |   | 2
```

Same Product

208 © 2013 C. Woodin & Landmark School

2 x 3-Digit Template

Facts

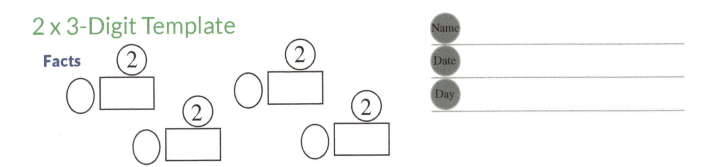

Teachers: customize this template by filling in blanks with appropriate values.

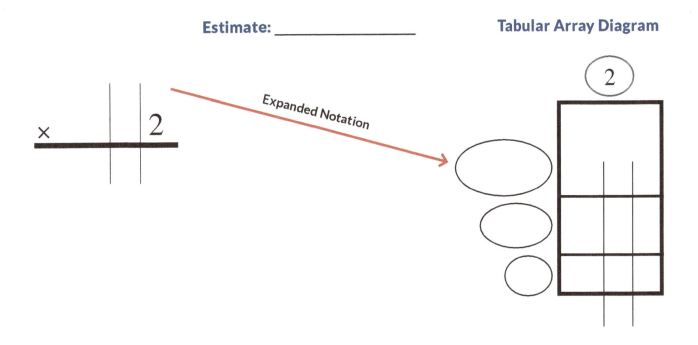

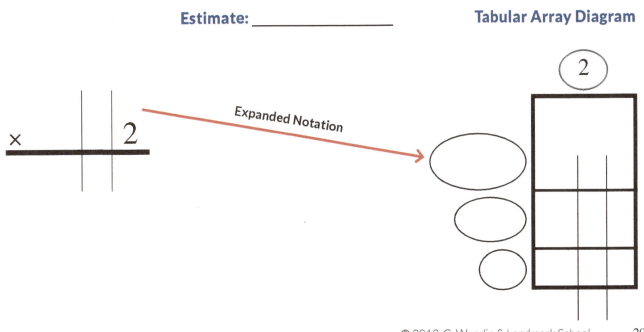

© 2013 C. Woodin & Landmark School

Multiplying 2 by Magnitudes of 10: Form 2B

This fact sheet is to be done before 2x 3-Digit Multiplication Form 2B.

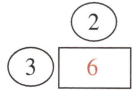

X Fact

2 × 3 =
----
x 10

2 × 30 =
----
x 100

2 × 300 =

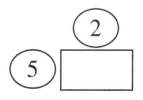

X Fact

2 ×   =
----
x 10

2 ×   =
----
x 100

2 ×   =

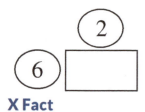

X Fact

2 ×   =
----
x 10

2 ×   =
----
x 100

        =

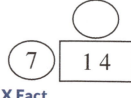

X Fact

2 ×   =
----
x 10

2 ×   =
----
x 100

2 ×   =

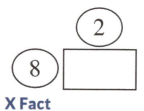

X Fact

2 ×   =
----
x 10

        =
----
x 100

        =

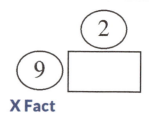

X Fact

2 ×   =
----
x 10

        =
----
x 100

        =
----

210   © 2013 C. Woodin & Landmark School

2 x 3-Digit Multiplication: Form 2B

Facts

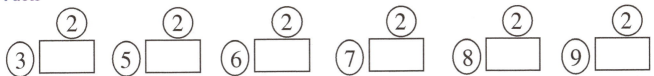

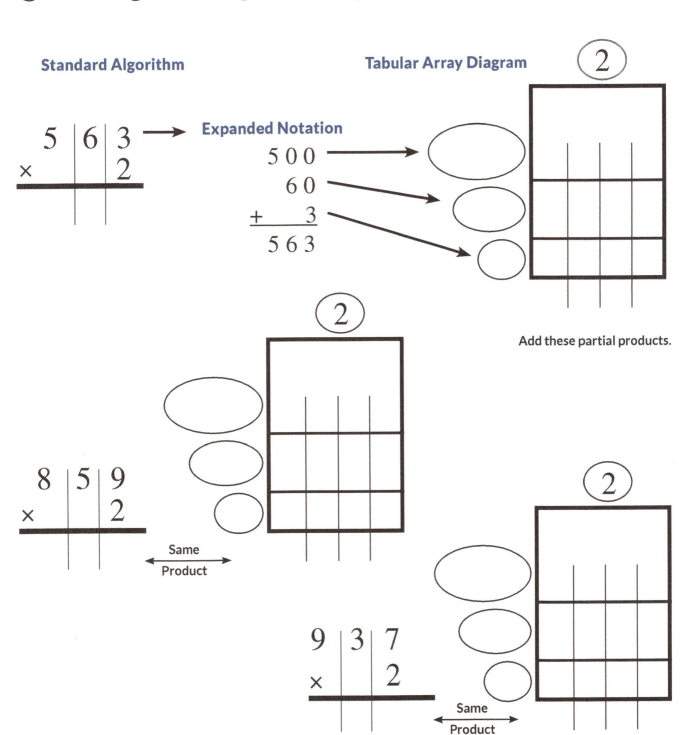

Single-Digit x 3-Digit Template

Teachers: customize this template by filling in blanks with appropriate values.

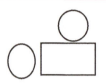 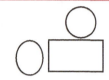 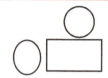 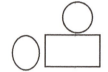

Estimate:  **Tabular Array Diagram**

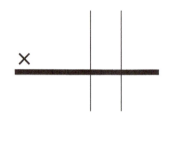 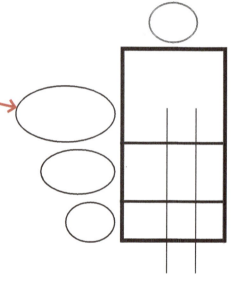

Estimate:  **Tabular Array Diagram**

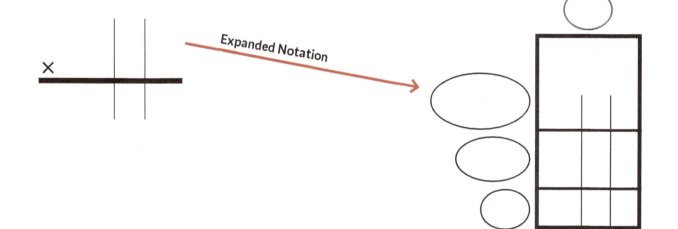

212   © 2013 C. Woodin & Landmark School

2× Multidigit Multiplication

× Facts

2 × 3 = _____

2 × 4 = _____

2 × 5 = _____

2 × 6 = _____

2 × 7 = _____

2 × 8 = _____

2 × 9 = _____

Name _____
Date _____
Day _____

All multiples of 2 are even numbers.

Estimate: _____

```
      1 3
  ×     2
  -------
```

√ Even number

Estimate: _____

```
    4 1 3
  ×     2
  -------
```

√ Even number

Estimate: _____

```
  7 4 1 3
  ×     2
  -------
```

√ Even number

© 2013 C. Woodin & Landmark School

Multiplying 5 by Magnitudes of 10

Use this skill to create estimates of multidigit products.

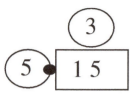

× **Facts:**

$3 \times 5 = 15$

$5 \times 3 = 15$

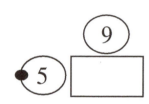

× **Facts:**

_____

_____

× **Facts:**

_____

_____

$5 \times 30 = 150$

$5 \times 300 =$

$50 \times 30 =$

$50 \times 300 =$

$5 \times 90 =$

$5 \times 900 =$

$500 \times 90 =$

$50 \times 900 =$

$5 \times 60 =$

$5 \times 600 =$

$500 \times 60 =$

$50 \times 600 =$

Multiplying 5 by Magnitudes of 10

Use this skill to create estimates of multidigit products.

Name
Date
Day

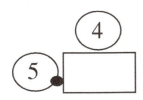

× Facts: _____

_____

$5 \times 40 = 200$

$5 \times 400 =$

$50 \times 40 =$

$50 \times 400 =$

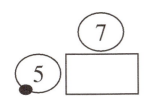

× Facts: _____

_____

$5 \times 70 =$

$5 \times 700 =$

$500 \times 70 =$

$50 \times 700 =$

× Facts: _____

_____

$5 \times 80 =$

$5 \times 800 =$

$500 \times 80 =$

$50 \times 800 =$

© 2013 C. Woodin & Landmark School

Multiplying 5 by Magnitudes of 10: Form 5A

Name
Date
Day

This fact sheet is to be done before 5 × 3-Digit Multiplication Form 5A.

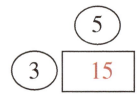

× Fact

5 × 3 =
―――――――
× 10

5 × 30 =
―――――――
× 100

5 × 300 =
―――――――

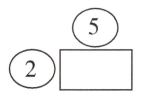

× Fact

5 × =
―――――――
× 10

5 × =
―――――――
× 100

5 × =
―――――――

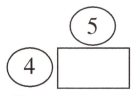

× Fact

5 × =
―――――――
× 10

=
―――――――
× 100

=
―――――――

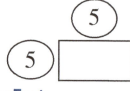

× Fact

5 × =
―――――――
× 10

5 × =
―――――――
× 100

5 × =
―――――――

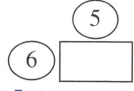

× Fact

5 × =
―――――――
× 10

=
―――――――
× 100

=
―――――――

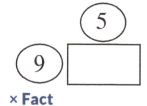

× Fact

5 × =
―――――――
× 10

=
―――――――
× 100

=
―――――――

216   © 2013 C. Woodin & Landmark School

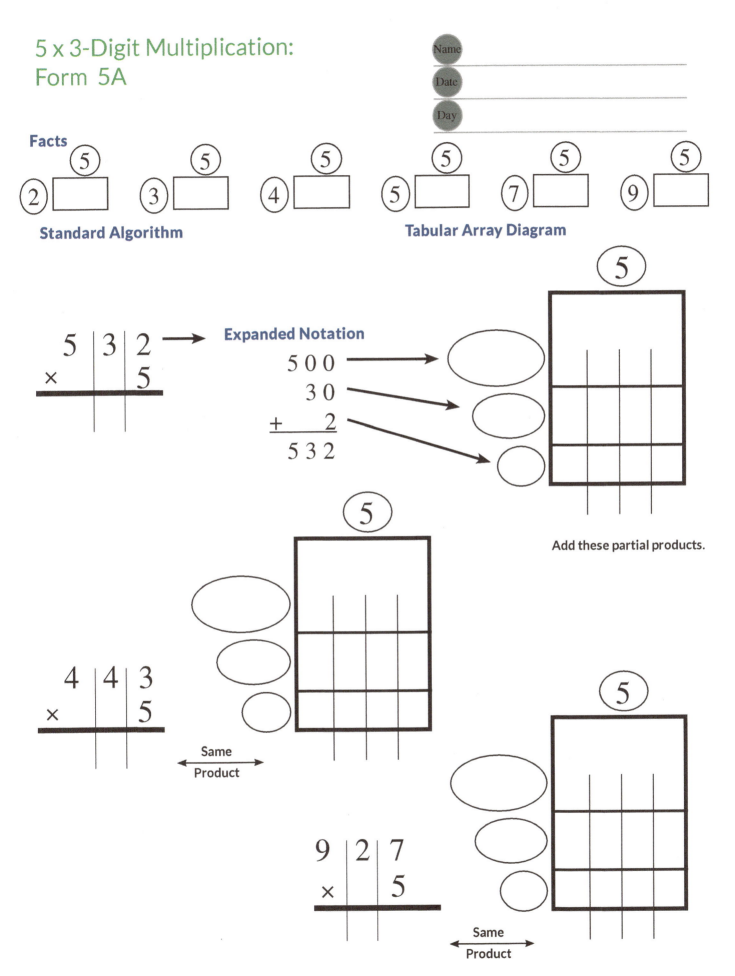

Multiplying 5 by Magnitudes of 10: Form 5B

This fact sheet is to be done before 5 x 3-Digit Multiplication Form 5B.

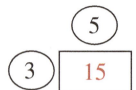

× **Fact**

5 × 3 =
―――――
x 10

5 × 3 0 =
―――――
x 100

5 × 3 0 0 =
―――――

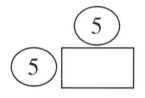

× **Fact**

5 × ___ =
―――――
x 10

5 × ___ =
―――――
x 100

5 × ___ =
―――――

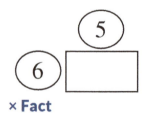

× **Fact**

5 × 6 =
―――――
x 10

5 × ___ =
―――――
x 100

___ =
―――――

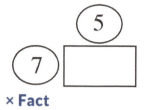

× **Fact**

5 × ___ =
―――――
x 10

5 × ___ =
―――――
x 100

5 × ___ =
―――――

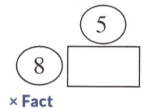

× **Fact**

5 × ___ =
―――――
x 10

___ =
―――――
x 100

___ =
―――――

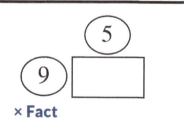

× **Fact**

2 × ___ =
―――――
x 10

___ =
―――――
x 100

___ =
―――――

5 x 3-Digit Multiplication: Form 5B

Facts

3 × 5 ☐   5 × 5 ☐   6 × 5 ☐   7 × 5 ☐   8 × 5 ☐   9 × 5 ☐

Standard Algorithm   **Tabular Array Diagram**

5 | 6 | 3
× | | 5

Expanded Notation

500 →
 60 →
+ 3 →
─────
563

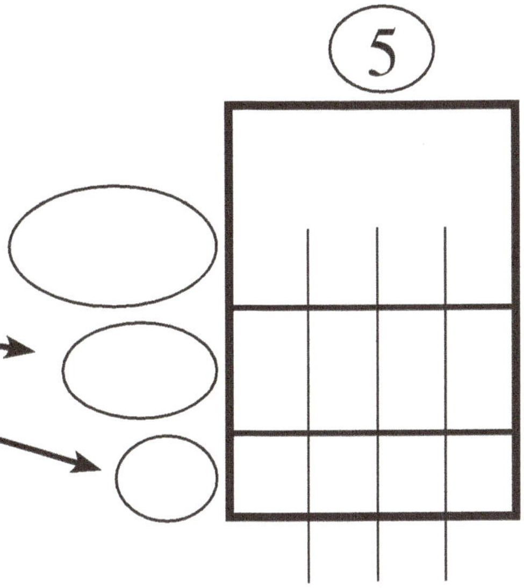

Add these partial products.

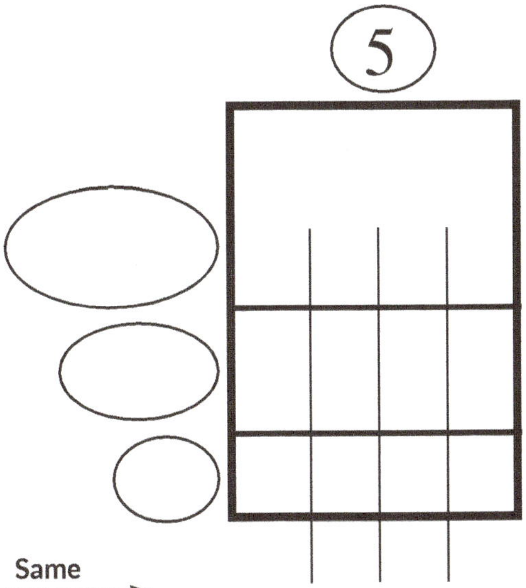

8 | 5 | 9
× | | 5

← Same Product →

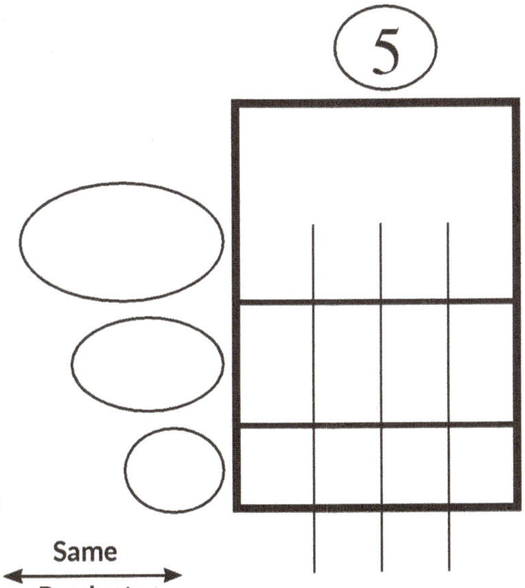

9 | 3 | 7
× | | 5

← Same Product →

© 2013 C. Woodin & Landmark School   219

Multiplying 5 by Magnitudes of 10

A skill used to create estimates of multidigit products

Name
Date
Day

Teachers: customize this template by filling in blanks with appropriate values.

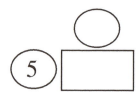

× Facts: _____

_____

5 × __0 = __

5 × __00 =

50 × __0 =

50 × __00 =

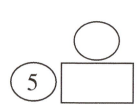

× Facts: _____

_____

5 × __0 =

5 × __00 =

500 × __0 =

50 × __00 =

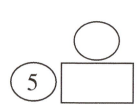

× Facts: _____

_____

5 × __0 =

5 × __00 =

500 × __0 =

50 × __00 =

220   © 2013 C. Woodin & Landmark School

5× Multidigit Multiplication

Name _____
Date _____
Day _____

× Facts

Even multiples of 5 end with "0."

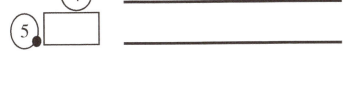

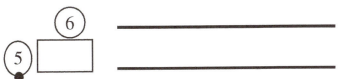

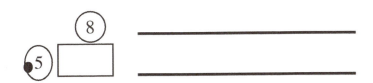

Odd multiples of 5 end with "5."

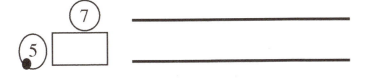

Even multiples of 5 end with "0."
Odd multiples of 5 end with "5."

Estimate: _____

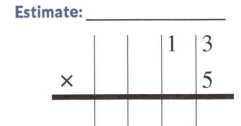

√ Ends in 5 or 0.

Estimate: _____

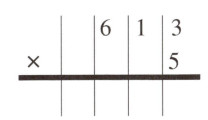

√ Ends in 5 or 0.

Estimate: _____

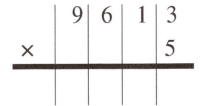

√ Ends in 5 or 0.

© 2013 C. Woodin & Landmark School

5× Multidigit Multiplication Template

Even multiples of 5 end with "0."
Odd multiples of 5 end with "5."

Name
Date
Day

Teachers: customize this template by filling in blanks with appropriate values.

Facts

Estimate: _____

√ Ends in 5 or 0.

Estimate: _____

√ Ends in 5 or 0.

Estimate: _____

√ Ends in 5 or 0.

222 © 2013 C. Woodin & Landmark School

The 9 × Fact Family

Consider a student to be **functionally fluent** with the 10× facts **if he or she can complete all of the Fluency Assessment Worksheet diagrams accurately in under 1 minute, then write the 20 related fact sentences with 100% accuracy in under three minutes.** At this point the student may move to the next fact family; however, continue to administer fluency tests to concurrently review the 2×, 5×, and 10× facts, and practice multiplying multidigit numbers by those factors while learning new fact families.

When students have mastered the 10× family, they should write the products in ink on their multiplication grids. Students will now focus on the 9× family. Continue to teach and practice multiplying two- and three-digit numbers by factors of 2 and 5 using the traditional algorithm coupled with the tabular array as a checking mechanism. The multidigit computation will demand that students access and express learned facts to increase their fluency with them.

The 9× family adds an additional 11 percent of facts, so students will have learned 75 percent of the multiplication grid when they add these facts. This fact family has a divisibility rule that involves adding the digits of the products.

All of the 9× products on the multiplication grid are comprised of digits that add up to 9. For example, in the fact sentence 9 × 2 = 18, the digits in the product, 1 and 8, add up to 9.

To learn these facts, students will follow the same process as when they learned other fact families:

- Use the 0–100 chart to discover the divisibility rule. Color all of the 9× products dark blue.
- **Pattern:** The 9× products will emerge as a diagonal line.
- **Divisibility rule to generate collaboratively** and then write individually on the 9× Divisibility Rule Sheet:

A number is divisible by 9 if it has digits that add to 9 or a multiple of 9.

- Students should fill in their Divisibility Rule Sheets. Hang the Rule Poster in the classroom.
- Have students use a pencil to fill in the fact family on the multiplication grid that is in the first section of their Fact Notebook.
- Start a new blue-tabbed 9× section in the student's Fact Notebook binder. The first page of the 9× section will be the Divisibility Poster for the 9× fact family.

Upcoming worksheets and activities will lead you to:

- Work with students to generate nouns that can be used to demonstrate the fact family.
- Have students solve and write basic multiplication and division word problems.
- Use the practice activities (flash cards, fact ball, fact mosaic puzzle, baseball game) to help students gain fluency with facts.

There are four versions of the 9× flash cards that are explained on the following pages. When students master the 9× facts, have students write them in ink on their multiplication grids. After that, students can start multiplying two- and then three-digit numbers by a factor of 9!

The 9 × Fact Family

**9× Pattern
0 - 100 Chart**

0	1	2	3	4	5	6	7	8	9
10	11	12	13	14	15	16	17	18	19
20	21	22	23	24	25	26	27	28	29
30	31	32	33	34	35	36	37	38	39
40	41	42	43	44	45	46	47	48	49
50	51	52	53	54	55	56	57	58	59
60	61	62	63	64	65	66	67	68	69
70	71	72	73	74	75	76	77	78	79
80	81	82	83	84	85	86	87	88	89
90	91	92	93	94	95	96	97	98	99
100									

Sum of Digits = 9 or a multiple of 9 (*Example:* 9 + 9 = 18). In turn the sum of those digits add to 9 (*Example:* 1 + 8 = 9)

Multiplication Grid with Highlighted 9× Facts

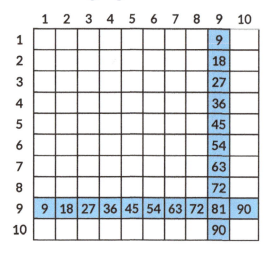

Gain 11 more facts after learning 9× facts....

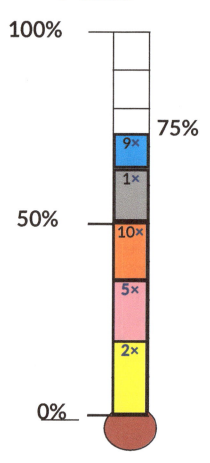

After mastering the 9× facts, 75% of the 100 facts have been learned.

When done with this section, have the student color this additional blue portion of the big graphic organizer found in the first section of the student's Fact Notebook.

Divisibility Rule Poster

DIVISIBLE BY 9

A number is **divisible by 9** if the digits add to 9 or a multiple of 9.

Examples:
- 18 → 1 + 8 = <u>9</u>
- 27 → 2 + 7 = <u>9</u>
- 459 → 4 + 5 + 9 = <u>18</u> → 1 + 8 = <u>9</u>
- 8991 → 8 + 9 + 9 + 1 = <u>27</u> → 2 + 7 = <u>9</u>

If a number is a **multiple** of 9, the digits will add to 9.

Some multiples of 9: 27   54   207
  2+7=9 5+4=9 2+0+7=9

9 is a factor of any number whose digits add to 9.

Multiple		Factors
18	=	9 × 2
36	=	9 × 4
72	=	9 × 8
108	=	9 × 12

© 2013 C. Woodin & Landmark School

Divisibility Rule Sheet

Fill in the divisibility rules as you learn them.

Name
Date
Day

A number is **divisible by 9** if . . .

_____

_____

EXAMPLES:

USE THIS DIVISIBILITY POSTER TO START A NEW SECTION OF YOUR FACT NOTEBOOK

Use Divisibility Rules to Identify Multiples of 9

Name
Date
Day

These are car license plates. Multiples of 9 have digits that add to 9.

- Color multiples of 9 blue.
- Draw an X over numbers not divisible by 9.

130	153	135	449
432	160	431	900
468	133	641	144
830	630	504	432
760	910	937	441
830	278	580	180

© 2013 C. Woodin & Landmark School

Use Divisibility Rules to Identify Multiples of 9

These are car license plates. Multiples of 9 have digits that add to 9.

- Color multiples of 9 blue.
- Draw an X over numbers not divisible by 9.

Teachers: customize this template by filling in blanks with appropriate values.

The 9×Finger Calculator

All of the 9× facts can be readily calculated with your fingers. Many people are familiar with this method. If you ask around in math teaching circles, you should find someone who can show you firsthand. This method is a means to an end, not a substitute for eventual automatization of the 9× facts. It is imperative that students rehearse the entire multiplication fact sentence after calculating the answer using this method. Remember, the idea is to provide a correct stimulus-response pattern that can be consistently reinforced. The 9× finger calculator is a reliable means of finding a correct product, as well as a way to reinforce the divisibility rule for 9. After all, the products are always being created with nine digits (phalanges).

To execute the 9× finger calculator, place your hands flat on a surface with your thumbs pointing toward each other. Number your digits one to ten from left to right. Your left ring finger is 2, your left thumb is 5, and your right index finger is 7. When you want, for example, to find the product of 9 × 7, bend finger 7, your right index finger. You should then have nine straight fingers, six to the left of finger 7 and three to the right. The digits to the left of the bent finger are the number of tens in the product, 6 in this example, and the digits to the right of the bent finger represent the ones, 3 in this example. The product of 9 × 7 is 63. When you demonstrate the execution of the 9× finger calculator, emphasize that it takes nine fingers to create the product, just as the divisibility rule for 9 states that the sum of the digits in a multiple of 9 is 9.

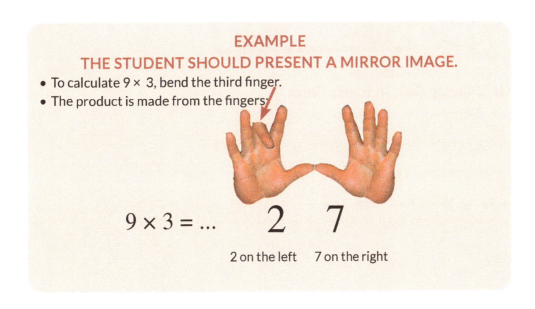

EXAMPLE
THE STUDENT SHOULD PRESENT A MIRROR IMAGE.
- To calculate 9 × 3, bend the third finger.
- The product is made from the fingers.

9 × 3 = ...   2   7

2 on the left   7 on the right

Semiconcrete Diagram Flashcards to Prompt the 9× Facts.

Set 1: Flash Cards Showing Finger Patterns

9× Finger Patterns: The sum of the digits (fingers) in the product is 9.

These finger patterns can be made by the student to produce the 9× facts, or you or the students may use these flash cards to prompt fact expression.

Have students identify the 9× factor by the position of the bent finger (fingers are numbered 1 through 10 from left to right).

Have students identify the product by looking at the nine fingers:

- The digit in the tens place of the product is represented by the sum of the fingers to the left of the bent finger.
- The digit in the ones place of the product is represented by the fingers to the right of the bent finger.

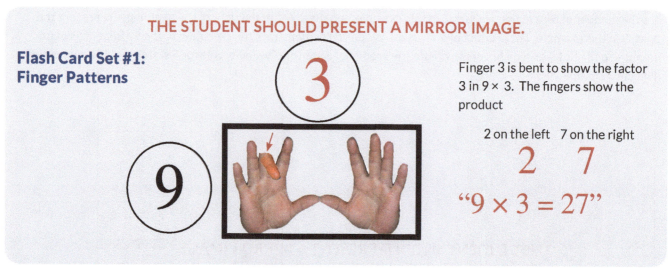

Set 2: Flash Cards Showing Dots in Iconic Form

9× Facts and Iconic Dots: The sum of the digits in the product is 9.

Have students identify the 9× factor by adding one to the number of red dots.

Have students identify the product by looking at the nine dots:

- The digit in the tens place of the product is represented by the sum of the red dots on the left.
- The digit in the ones place of the product is represented by the white dots on the right.

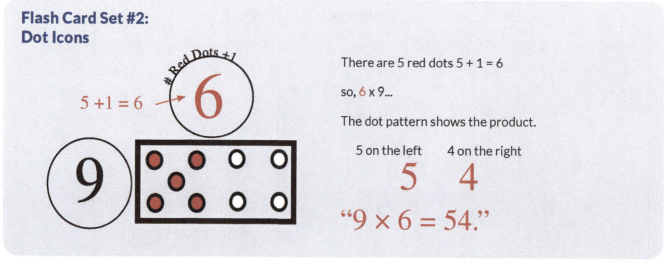

Set 1: 9× Finger Facts:
Identify the 9× <u>factor</u> by the position of the bent finger (fingers are numbered 1 through 10 from left to right). Identify the <u>product</u> by looking at the other fingers: the 10's digit of the product is represented by the fingers to the left of the bent finger. The 1's digit is represented by the fingers to the right.

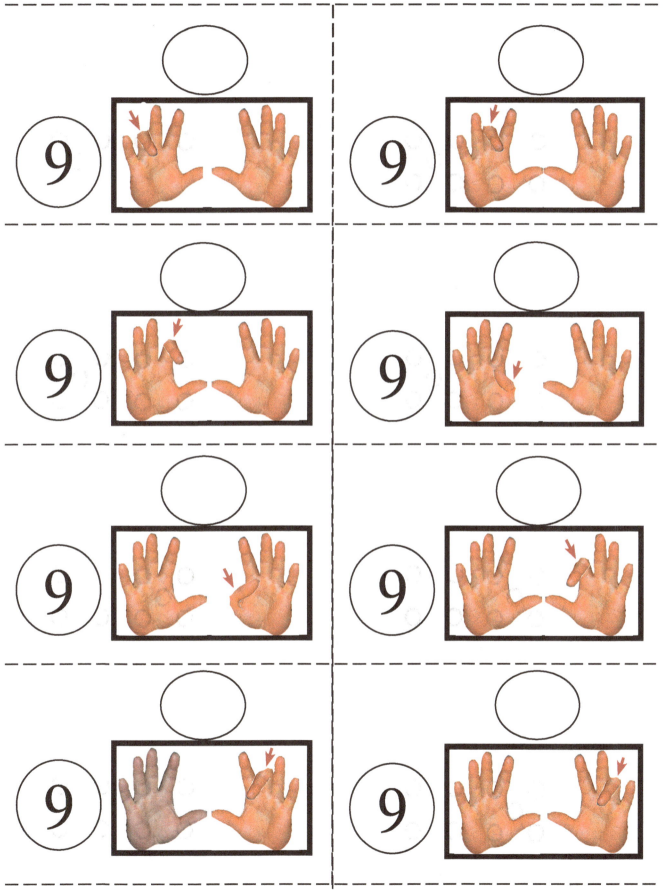

Set 2: 9× Icons:

The sum of the digits in the product is 9. Identify the 9× factor (by adding 1 to the number of red dots). Identify the product by looking at the 9 dots: the 10s digit is represented by the red dot, and ones digit is represented by the white dots.

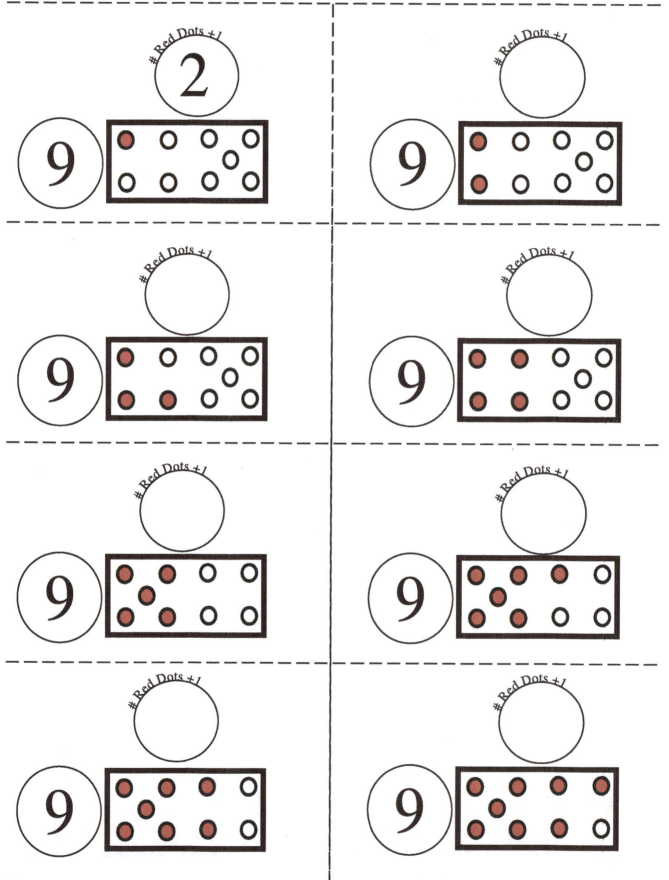

Abstract, Numeric-Based Flashcards to Prompt the 9× Facts

There are two additional sets of flashcards that can be used to practice the 9× fact family.

These cards use numbers rather than images to prompt the expression of the 9× facts.

Set 3: Flash Cards Showing The Product

The 9× facts are highly predictable when flash cards present the division form of the fact. The missing factor is equal to the digit in the tens place of the product plus one. When you present students with a division flash card based on the 9× fact family, cue the student to identify the digit in the tens place of the product (or dividend). Once students do this, they need only to add one to arrive at the missing factor. Have them recite the fact as a multiplication sentence that starts with this missing factor. Then ask them to recite the other three related facts.

Figure 4

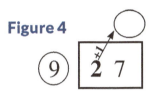

Add 1 to the ten's digit of the product:
2 + 1 = 3...... "3 x 9 = 27"

Prompt students to recite related facts, using the prompts as described below.

- Say, "Tell me a division fact. Start with the number twenty-seven."
  The student should respond, "Twenty-seven divided by nine equals three."
- Say, "Tell me a different division fact that has the number twenty-seven. Divide by three."
  The student should respond, "Twenty-seven divided by three equals nine."
- Say, "Tell me a multiplication fact. Start with the number twenty-seven."
  The student should respond, "Twenty-seven equals three times nine."
- Say, "Tell me a different multiplication fact that has the number twenty-seven. Start with nine."
  The student should respond, "Nine times three equals twenty-seven."
- Say, "Tell me a multiplication fact that has the number twenty-seven. Start with three."
  The student should respond, "Three times nine equals twenty-seven."

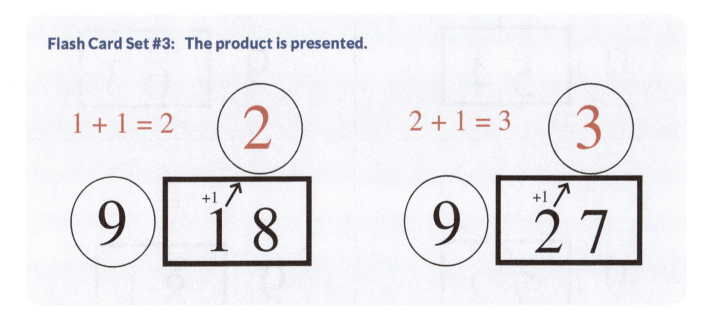

Set 3: 9× Facts Presenting the Product

The sum of the digits in the product is 9. Identify the 9× factor (by adding 1 to the number in the tens place).

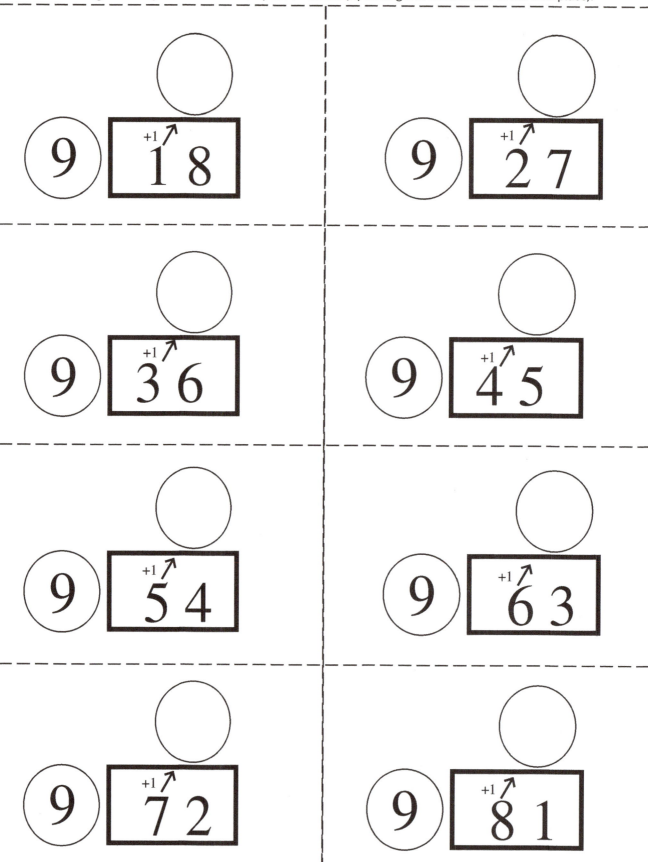

Set 4: Flash Cards Showing The Factors

When introducing the 9× flash cards that present the factors and a missing product, use a similar strategy as the one you used to introduce the 9× flash cards that present the product. The tens digit in the missing product is one less than the value of the top factor. Students should subtract one from the top factor and then say the resulting number as a decade. This action is usually enough to trigger the second digit of the product. If not, the second digit may be computed by finding the addend needed to reach a sum of nine.

Start using these flash cards after students have successfully practiced the Set 3 flash cards that feature the product. The Set 4 flash cards that provide the factors are most productive after the 9× products have become familiar through oral recitation.

Begin with Set 4 by using the flash card template as a worksheet. Have students write the products inside each rectangle. The trick is to have students first determine the tens digit by subtracting one from the number in the left circle. Students should then say this tens digit as a decade. For example, the student writes 2 but is prompted to say "twenty." If the fact is resident in the student's memory, saying "twenty" or writing 2 may trigger the associated ones digit—either the word "seven" stored in the student's auditory memory or number "7" stored in his or her visual memory. If the ones digit is not available for recall, tell the student that the digit in the ones place is the missing addend needed to make a sum of nine. Use the 9× finger calculator, as described earlier, to prompt the missing addend. If the student continues to have difficulty recalling the 9× products, have the student return to practicing the Set 2 flashcards that present the addends to nine in the iconic dot format.

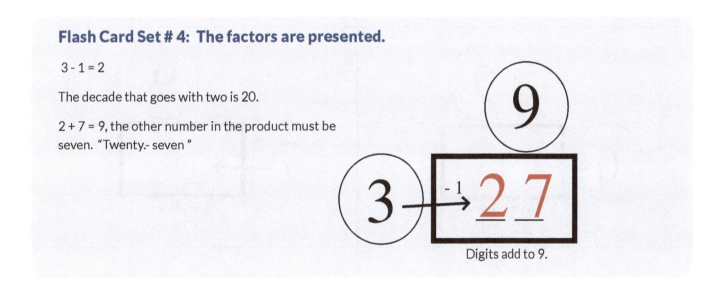

Set 4: 9× Facts Presenting the Factors
The tens digit is one less than the factor on the left. The sum of the digits in the product is 9.

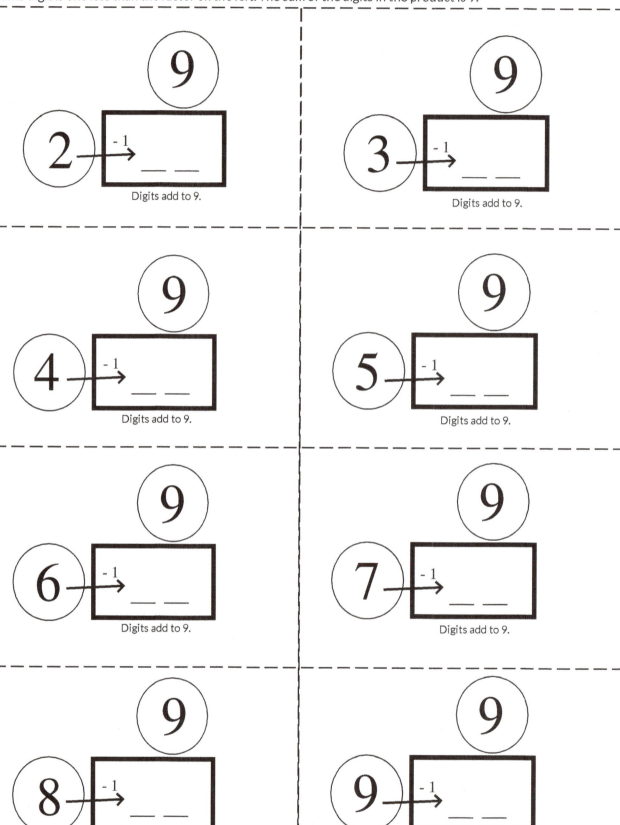

Solving Word Problems Involving 9× Facts: A Rule-Based Fact Family

Whole-Noun-Attribute Pairings

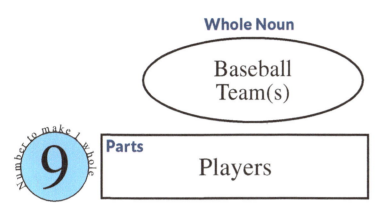

Multiplication Grid with Highlighted 9× Facts

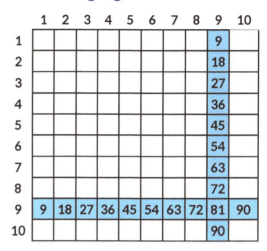

As you read each phrase of a word problem, have students mask the multiplication grid with two index cards to define a rectangular area on the grid. This rectangle will correspond to a matrix diagram and prompt the multiplication or division fact necessary to solve the word problem. A reference bank of strongly associated nouns will help students identify groups and parts, which facilitates the fact-making process necessary to solve the word problem.

In the case of the 9× facts, semantic relationships are few and far between. Baseball teams have nine players, and this relationship can be used as the first example of the reference bank. Squares on a tic-tac-toe board are another example, although possibilities include the nine lives of a cat and nine drummers drumming. At this point, it is most effective to define some noun-attribute pairings that are more arbitrary, such as cookies in a batch, pens in a box, students at a table, and passengers in a van. Work with students to complete the Reference Bank for the 9× Fact Family, and use the templates that follow to develop story problems.

EXAMPLE

A) Read the entire problem aloud: "All teams have nine players. There are three teams. How many players are there?"

B) Read aloud the first phrase: "All teams have 9 players." Students move their cards.

C) Read aloud the second phrase: "There are 3 teams." Students move their cards.

D) Prompt the students to fill in a matrix diagram to match the visible portion of the multiplication grid and label the answer (in this case, the product: 27 players).

When students begin working on the 9× facts, they can mask their multiplication grids to identify missing information and solve problems. Eventually students should be asked to diagram and solve problems without the use of multiplication grids.

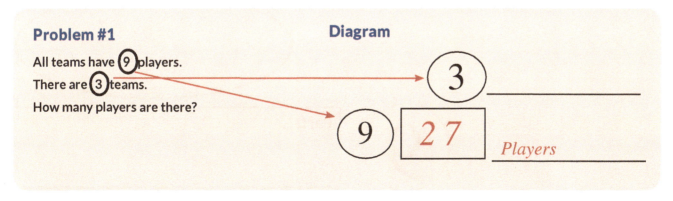

© 2013 C. Woodin & Landmark School

Reference Bank for the 9× Fact Family

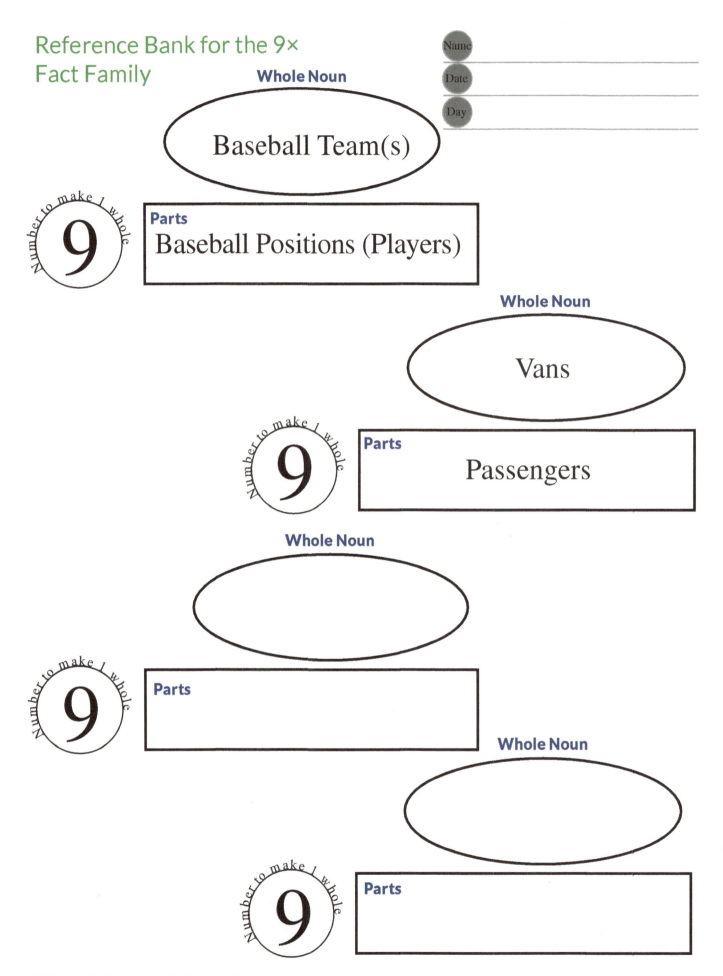

Solving Word Problems

- Circle the number of whole things.
- Circle the number of parts that make 1 whole thing.
- Box the total number of parts.
- Fill in the diagram and label the answer.

Name
Date
Day

Problem #1
A baseball team has 9 players.

There are 3 teams.

How many players are there?

Diagram
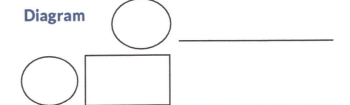

Problem #2
A van can carry 9 passengers.

There are 45 passengers.

How many vans are needed to carry them?

Diagram
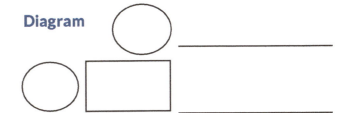

Problem #3
A baseball team has 9 players.

There are 6 teams.

How many players are there?

Diagram
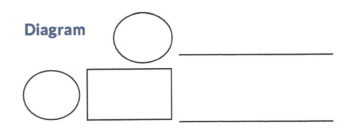

Problem #4
A van can carry 9 passengers.

There are 36 passengers.

How many vans are needed to carry them?

Diagram
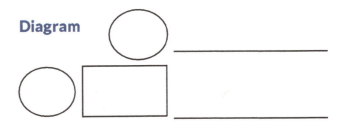

Problem #5
A baseball team has 9 players.

There are 72 players.

How many teams can be made?

Diagram

Solving Word Problems: Template

- Circle the number of whole things.
- Circle the number of parts to make 1 whole thing.
- Box the total number of parts.
- Fill in the diagram and label the answer.

Teachers: customize this template by filling in blanks with appropriate values.

Problem #1   **Diagram**

Problem #2   **Diagram**

Problem #3   **Diagram**

Problem #4   **Diagram**

Problem #5   **Diagram**

Semantic-Based 9× Matrix Diagram

- Circle the number of whole things.
- Circle the number of parts needed to make one whole.
- Box the number that represents all of the parts.
- Complete the diagram, label the answer and write four related facts.

Stars have 5 points each.
If there are 9 stars, how many points are there?

Fill in the diagram:

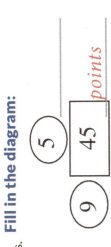

Facts:  x ◯ = ☐

_____
_____
_____
_____

9 students can sit at a lunch table. If there are 9 full lunch tables in the room, how many students are in the room?

Facts:
_____
_____
_____
_____

There are 9 baseball cards in a pack. If Jen bought 6 packs of cards, how many cards would she have?

Facts:
_____
_____
_____
_____

A package of gel pens contains 9 pens. How many pens are in 4 packages?

Facts:
_____
_____
_____
_____

There are 9 pieces in a pack of gum. If there are 7 packs of gum, how many pieces are there?

Facts:
_____
_____
_____
_____

© 2013 C. Woodin & Landmark School   241

Word Problems Related to Area: 9× Facts

- Mask the multiplication grid with two index cards to frame the rectangle described by the word problem.
- Use the grid to find the answer.
- Transfer the information to the diagram and label the answer with the appropriate units.

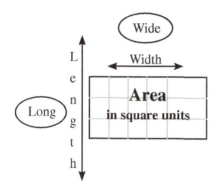

	1	2	3	4	5	6	7	8	9	10
1									9	
2									18	
3									27	
4									36	
5									45	
6									54	
7									63	
8									72	
9	9	18	27	36	45	54	63	72	81	90
10									90	

Problem # 1

The rectangular table is 3 feet long.

The table has an area of 27 square feet.

How wide is the table?

Diagram

Problem # 2

The rectangular rug is 9 feet long.

The area of the rug is 36 square feet.

How wide is the rug?

Diagram

Problem # 3

The garden has an area of 81 square feet.

The garden is 9 feet long.

How wide is the garden?

Diagram

Problem # 4

The wall is 7 feet wide.

It is 9 feet tall.

What is the area of the wall?

Diagram

Word Problems Related to Area
Template: 9× Facts

- Mask the multiplication grid with two index cards to frame the rectangle described by the word problem.
- Use the grid to find the answer.
- Transfer the information to the diagram and label the answer with the appropriate units.

Teachers: customize this template by filling in blanks with appropriate values.

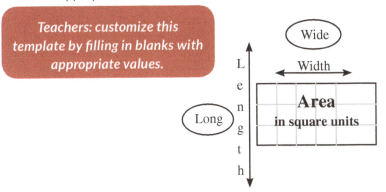

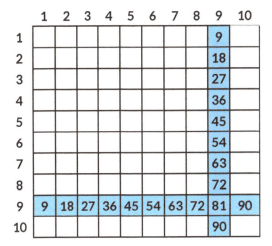

Problem # 1
The rectangular table is 9 feet long.

The table has an area of ___ square feet.

How wide is the table?

Diagram

Problem # 2
The rectangular rug is ___ feet long.

The area of the rug is ___ square feet.

How wide is the rug?

Diagram

Problem # 3
The garden has an area of ___ square feet.

The garden is 9 feet long.

How wide is the garden?

Diagram

Problem # 4
The wall is ___ feet wide.

It is 9 feet tall.

What is the area of the wall?

Diagram

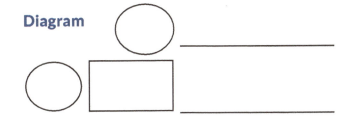

Diagrams That Prompt Related Multiplication and Division Facts

Name _____
Date _____
Day _____

Fill in the diagram and write four related facts.
Each product's digits add to 9!

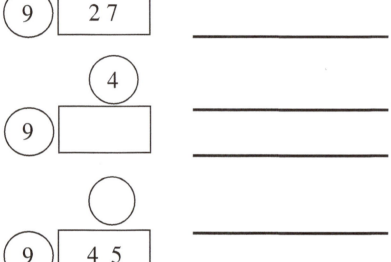

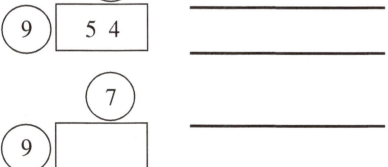

244 © 2013 C. Woodin & Landmark School

9× Fact Mosaic

- Write a product (such as 18) on one side of a dashed grid line and the other part of the fact sentence (2 × 9) on the other side of the dashed line.
- Repeat this process for each of the grid lines.
- Then cut the puzzle along the dashed lines to make nine square pieces and shuffle the pieces.
- Try to put them back together using the fact sentences and products as a guide.
- Trade puzzles with another student and challenge each other!

Name
Date
Day

Baseball Fact Game

9×

OUT = 9, 18, 27
SINGLE = 36, 45
DOUBLE = 54, 63
TRIPLE = 72, 81
HOME RUN = 90

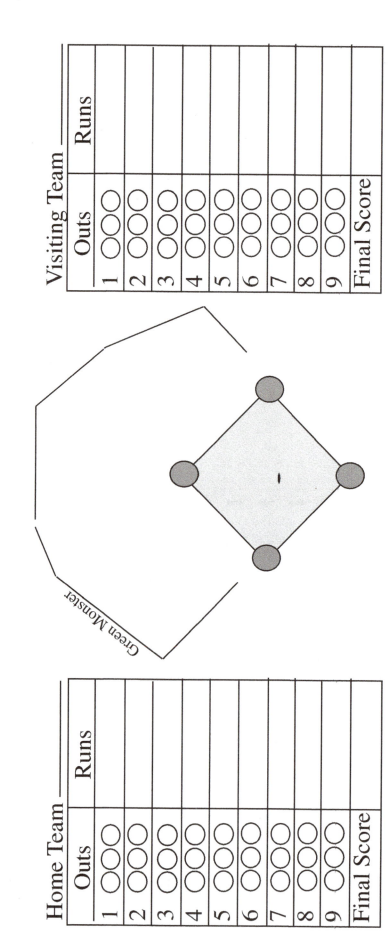

Accuracy Benchmark
Pretest - Untimed

Complete this sheet with 100% accuracy before taking the related timed **Fluency Assessment**.

1) Complete each diagram. Have them scored.
2) Correct diagrams if needed.
3) Write a multiplication fact and a division fact for each.
4) Archive this in your Fact Notebook as a record.

Diagram Accuracy: ___/10

Sentence Accuracy: ___/20

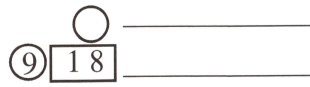

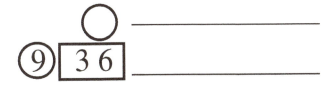

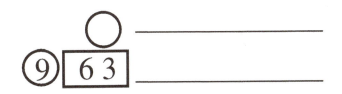

© 2013 C. Woodin & Landmark School

Fluency Assessment - Timed

Name _____
Date _____
Day _____

Administer this test after the student scores 100% accuracy on the related **Accuracy Benchmark Pretest**.

1) Complete each diagram. Note time and accuracy.
2) Correct diagrams as needed.
3) Write a multiplication fact and a division fact for each. Note time and accuracy.
4) Archive this in your Fact Notebook as a record.

Diagram Accuracy: ___/10 Time: _____
Sentences Accuracy: ___/20 Time: _____

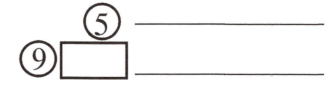

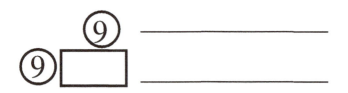

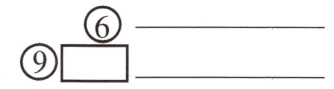

248   © 2013 C. Woodin & Landmark School

Vertical 9× Fact Practice

Name _____
Date _____
Day _____

Timed quiz
___ seconds

/10

× | 1
  | 9

× | 6
  | 9

× | 2
  | 9

× | 7
  | 9

× | 3
  | 9

× | 8
  | 9

× | 4
  | 9

× | 9
  | 9

× | 5
  | 9

× | 1 0
  | 9

© 2013 C. Woodin & Landmark School   249

Multiplying 9 by Magnitudes of 10: Form 9A

This fact sheet is to be done before **9x 3-Digit Multiplication Form 9A**.

 Name
 Date
 Day

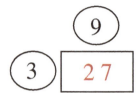

× **Fact**

9 × 3 =
———————————
x 10

9 × 30 =
———————————
x 100

9 × 300 =
———————————

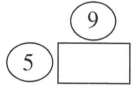

× **Fact**

9 × ___ =
———————————
x 10

9 × ___ =
———————————
x 100

___ =
———————————

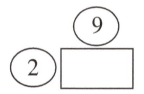

× **Fact**

9 × ___ =
———————————
x 10

9 x ___ =
———————————
x 100

___ =
———————————

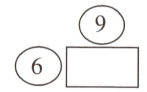

× **Fact**

9 × ___ =
———————————
x 10

___ =
———————————
x 100

___ =
———————————

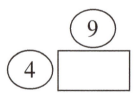

× **Fact**

9 × ___ =
———————————
x 10

___ =
———————————
x 100

___ =
———————————

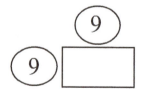

× **Fact**

9 × ___ =
———————————
x 10

___ =
———————————
x 100

___ =
———————————

9 x 3-Digit Multiplication Form 9A

Facts

 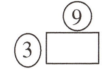 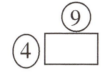

Standard Algorithm

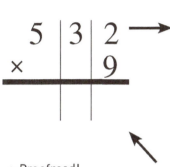

- Proofread!
- Add the digits in the product.
- The sum should be a multiple of 9.
  e.g., 4+7+8+8 = 27: 2 + 7 = **9** ✓

Tabular Array Diagram

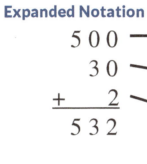

Expanded Notation

```
  500
   30
+   2
  532
```

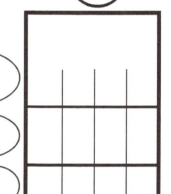

Add these partial products.

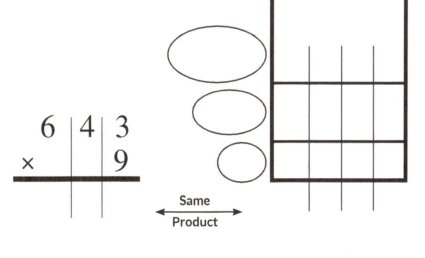

Same Product

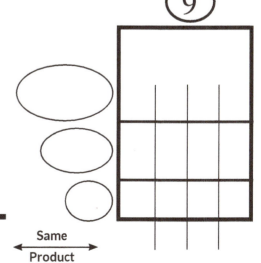

Same Product

© 2013 C. Woodin & Landmark School   251

Multiplying 9 by Magnitudes of 10: Form 9B

This fact sheet is to be done before **9 x 3-Digit Multiplication Form 9B**.

Name
Date
Day

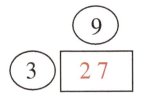

× Fact

9 × 3 =
———————————
x 10

9 × 30 =
———————————
x 100

9 × 300 =
———————————

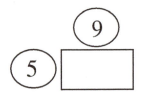

× Fact

9 × =
———————————
x 10

9 × =
———————————
x 100

9 × =
———————————

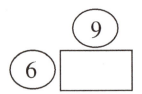

× Fact

9 × 6 =
———————————
x 10

9 × =
———————————
x 100

=
———————————

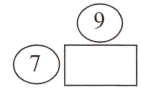

× Fact

9 × =
———————————
x 10

9 × =
———————————
x 100

9 × =
———————————

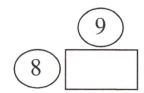

× Fact

9 × =
———————————
x 10

=
———————————
x 100

=
———————————

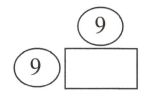

× Fact

2 × =
———————————
x 10

=
———————————
x 100

=
———————————

252   © 2013 C. Woodin & Landmark School

9 x 3-Digit Multiplication Form 9B

Facts

 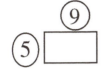 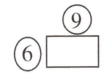 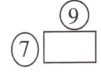 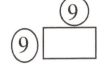

Standard Algorithm   **Tabular Array Diagram**

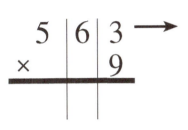   **Expanded Notation**

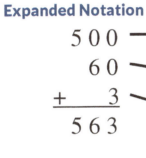

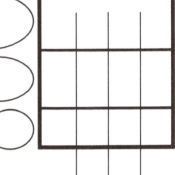

Add these partial products.

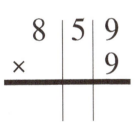 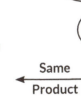

Same Product

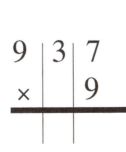

Same Product

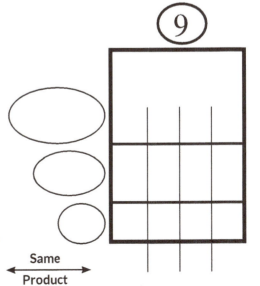

© 2013 C. Woodin & Landmark School

Multiplying 9 by Magnitudes of 10 Template

A skill used to create estimates of multidigit products.

Teachers: customize this template by filling in blanks with appropriate values.

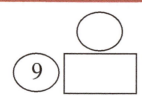

× **Facts** _____

_____

__ × __ 0 = __

9 × __0 0 =

9 0 × __0 =

9 0 × __0 0 =

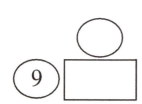

× **Facts** _____

_____

9 × __0 =

9 × __0 0 =

9 0 0 × __0 =

9 0 × __0 0 =

9 × __0 =

9 × __0 0 =

900 × __0 =

9 0 × __0 0 =

× **Facts** _____

_____

254 © 2013 C. Woodin & Landmark School

9× Multidigit Multiplication

× Facts

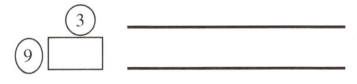

Note: all products must follow the divisibility rule for 9.
The sum of the product's digits should add to 9, or a multiple of 9: 18, 27, 36 ....

Estimate: _____

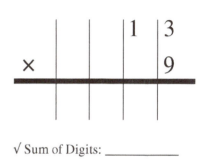

√ Sum of Digits: _____

Estimate: _____

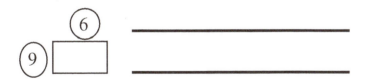

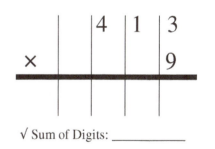

√ Sum of Digits: _____

Estimate: _____

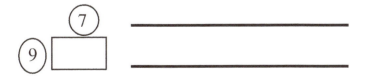

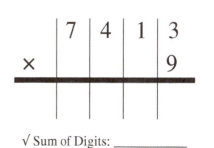

√ Sum of Digits: _____

9x Multidigit Template

Teachers: customize this template by filling in blanks with appropriate values.

× **Facts**

Name _____
Date _____
Day _____

Note: all products must follow the 9 divisibility rule.

The sum of the product's digits should add to 9, or a multiple of 9: 18, 27, 36 ….

Estimate: _____

×

√ Sum of Digits: _____

Estimate: _____

×

√ Sum of Digits: _____

Estimate: _____

×

√ Sum of Digits: _____

256   © 2013 C. Woodin & Landmark School

The 3× Fact Family

Introduce the 3× facts using the divisibility rule to identify multiples of 3 on the 0–100 chart.

Pattern: The 3× products will emerge as a diagonal stripe pattern.

- Each stripe will have multiples whose digits add up to the same sum: either 3, 6, or 9.
- Color the 3× products light blue. The 9× products will already be dark blue.

Divisibility Rule: A number is divisible by 3 if its digits add up to 3, 6, or 9.

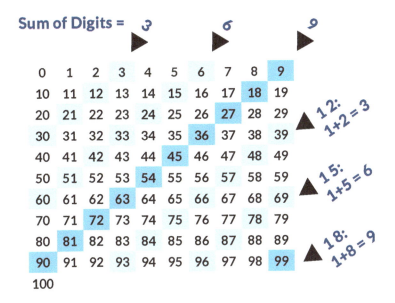

Multiplication Grid with Highlighted 3× Facts

	1	2	3	4	5	6	7	8	9	10
1			3							
2			6							
3	3	6	9	12	15	18	21	24	27	30
4			12							
5			15							
6			18							
7			21							
8			24							
9			27							
10			30							

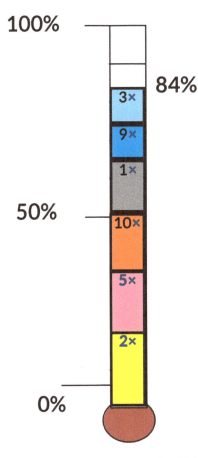

Gain 9 more facts after learning the 3x facts....

84%

After mastering the 3× facts, 84% of the 100 facts have been learned.

Have the student color this additional light blue portion of the big graphic organizer.

© 2013 C. Woodin & Landmark School

The 3 × Fact Family

To teach the 3× facts, exploit the visual pattern and the divisibility rule. The top three rows of the 0–100 chart contain the 3× facts for the numbers 1 through 9. Under close inspection, from the bottom of the diagonal, the digits in the units place present themselves in ascending order along the diagonal stripes. Students can observe this pattern to create the 3× products.

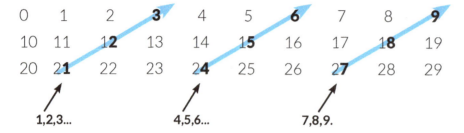

This process is described in a series of activities and worksheets. Also, each previously introduced fact family has included a 3× fact: 2 × 3, 5 × 3, 10 × 3, and 9 × 3. The relevant flash cards have been reprinted in this section for you. Use these cards with students to review these learned facts as a group.

The divisibility rule can also provide cues that will aid in the identification and prediction of products. A series of activities will explain this process and students can use related flash cards to practice it. These cards use two prompts. The decade is provided, as well as the sum of the digits. See the example provided. Because these cards operate in part-to-whole fashion, it takes time for students to formulate the product and fabricate a fact sentence. Use a constant time delay strategy when using these cards with students.

EXAMPLE

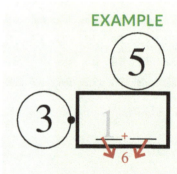

- The sum of the digits is 6.
- There is "1" in the 10's place.
- 6=1+5, therefore the product must be 15.

ADVANCED CONSTANT TIME DELAY STRATEGY

- Hold up a flash card for students to see.
- Ask students to identify the missing product nonverbally by pointing to the product on the 0–100 chart, writing the product on a piece of paper, or displaying the missing ones digit of the product by extending the corresponding number of fingers.
- After all students have responded, say, "Ready!" and then wait four seconds.
- Point to a student who has answered correctly to signal that he or she should recite the entire fact.
- Ask three other students to produce related facts.

Divisibility Rule Poster

A number is **divisible by 3** if the digits add up to 3, 6 or 9.

Examples: 12 → 1 + 2 = <u>3</u>
24 → 2 + 4 = <u>6</u>
459 → 4 + 5 + 9 = <u>18</u> → 1 + 8 = <u>9</u>

If a number is a **multiple** of 3, the digits add up to 3, 6 or 9.

Some multiples of 3: 3 × 4 = 12   3 × 5 = 15   3 × 6 = 18
1+2 = 3   1+5 = 6   1+8 = 9

3 is a **factor** of any number whose digits add up to 3, 6, or 9.

Multiple		Factors
18	=	3 × 6
36	=	3 × 12
15	=	3 × 5
12	=	3 × 4

© 2013 C. Woodin & Landmark School

Divisibility Rule Sheet
Fill in the divisibility rules as you learn them.

Name
Date
Day

A number is **divisible by 3** if . . .

_____

_____

EXAMPLES:

USE THIS DIVISIBILITY POSTER TO START A NEW SECTION OF YOUR FACT NOTEBOOK

Use Divisibility Rules to Identify Multiples of 3

These are car license plates. Multiples of 3 have digits that add to 3, 6, or 9. Sometimes their digits add to multidigit numbers like 12, 33, or 18 whose digits add to 3, 6, or 9 respectively.

- Color multiples of 3 blue.
- Draw an X over numbers not divisible by 3.

132	450	135	420
430	160	234	940
460	222	431	140
300	639	513	131
510	200	917	114
820	780	330	922

© 2013 C. Woodin & Landmark School

Use Divisibility Rules to Identify Multiples of 3

These are car license plates. Multiples of 3 have digits that add to 3, 6, or 9. Sometimes their digits add to multidigit numbers like 12, 33, or 18 whose digits add to 3, 6, or 9 respectively.

- Color multiples of 3 blue.
- Put an "X" over numbers not divisible by 3.

Teachers: customize this template by filling in blanks with appropriate values.

3x Pattern-Based Fact Family

The 3× fact family is typically hard to memorize, but it's easy to *produce* because of an interesting pattern in the facts. Help the students discover the pattern of the first nine multiples of 3.

Ask the students to look at the top three rows of their 0-100 chart, and focus on the light blue diagonal pattern made by the 3× facts.

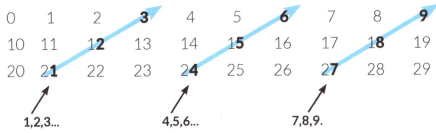

Say, "Put your finger on the 21., then the 12, then the 3. What do you notice about the ones digit as you move up the diagonal?" Write 1,2,3 on the chalkboard from bottom to top. They **go in order!**

Say, "Put your finger on the 24., then the 15, then the 6. What do you notice about the ones digit as you move up *this* diagonal?" Write 4,5,6 in a second column on the chalkboard.

Ask, "Can you predict what will happen in the third column? See if your prediction is true!" After a moment write 7,8,9 in a third column on the chalkboard.

```
   3      6      9
  _2     _5     _8
  _1     _4     _7
```

Say, "Look at your 0-100 chart. What is true about the tens place in the second row?" Confirm that because this row is the tens row, there is a 1 in the tens place for the entire row. Write a 1 in the tens place for each number in your second row.

```
   3      6      9
  1 2    1 5    1 8
  _1     _4     _7
```

Use the same language to complete the third row with 2s in the tens place for the three numbers.

Have students practice this pattern independently on lined paper several times, leading them through each step. This will help familiarize them with the first nine multiples of three. Then use the worksheets that follow.

3x Pattern- Based Fact Family

Circle the multiples of three in this 0-30 chart. Notice the pattern of the digits in the 1's place.

0	1	2	**3**	4	5	**6**	7	8	**9**
10	11	**12**	13	14	**15**	16	17	**18**	19
20	**21**	22	23	**24**	25	26	**27**	28	29

Finish the pattern. The ones digits go in order:

↑1,2,3...   ↑4,5,6...   ↑7,8,9.

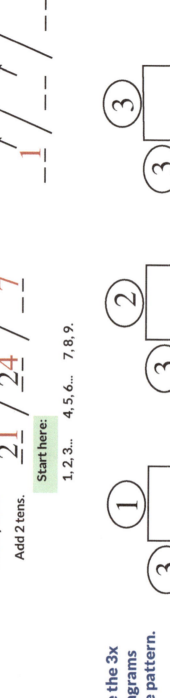

Units Row **3**
Teen Row: **12**   **7**
Add 1 ten.
Twenty Row: **21** **24**
Add 2 tens.

Start here: 1,2,3...   4,5,6...   7,8,9.

Now make the pattern yourself:

1

Now complete the 3x matrix fact diagrams using the same pattern.

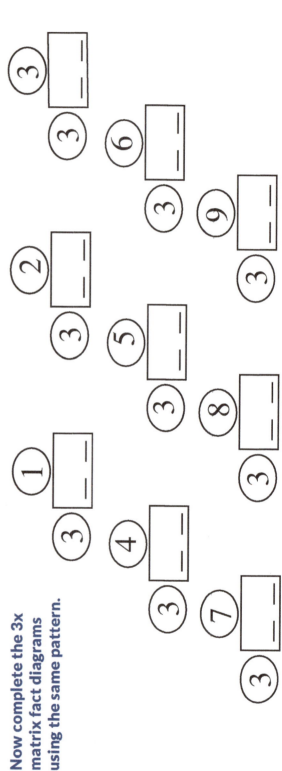

264   © 2013 C. Woodin & Landmark School

3x Pattern- Based Fact Family

Notice how the digits in the ones place go in order (↗↗↗) Write two 3x facts for each diagram.

Circle the multiples of three in this 1-30 chart. Notice the pattern of the digits in the 1's place.

Now complete the 3x matrix fact diagrams using the same pattern.

Write two multiplication facts for each diagram.

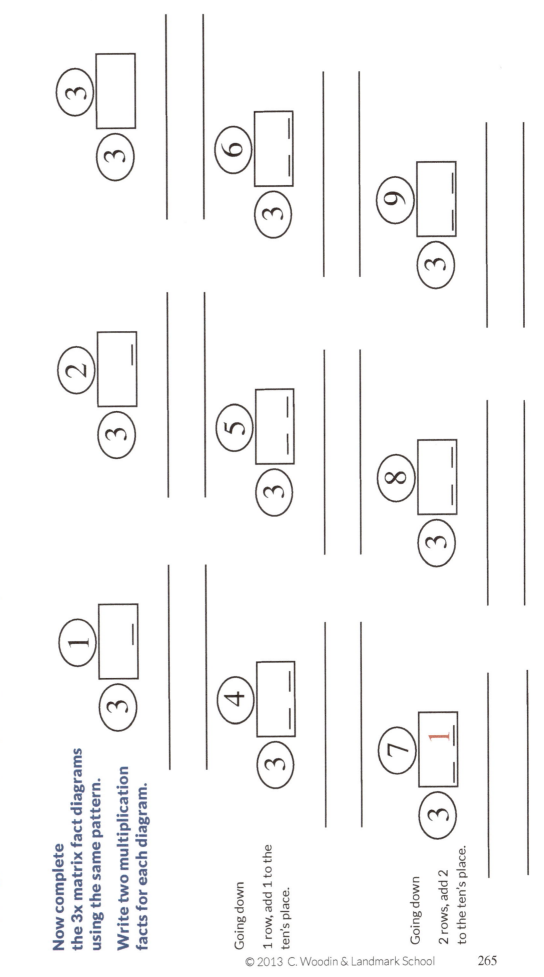

Going down
1 row, add 1 to the ten's place.

Going down
2 rows, add 2 to the ten's place.

© 2013 C. Woodin & Landmark School

Word Problems Related to Area: 3× Facts

- Mask the multiplication grid with two index cards to frame the rectangle described by the word problem.
- Use the grid to find the answer.
- Transfer the information to the diagram and label the answer with the appropriate units.

Name _____
Date _____
Day _____

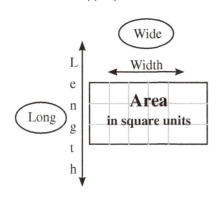

	1	2	3	4	5	6	7	8	9	10
1			3							
2			6							
3	3	6	9	12	15	18	21	24	27	30
4			12							
5			15							
6			18							
7			21							
8			24							
9			27							
10			30							

Problem # 1

The rectangular table is 3 feet long.

The table has an area of 12 square feet.

How wide is the table?

Diagram

Problem # 2

The rectangular rug is 3 feet long.

The area of the rug is 15 square feet.

How wide is the rug?

Diagram

Problem # 3

The garden has an area of 27 square feet.

The garden is 3 feet long.

How wide is the garden?

Diagram

Problem # 4

The wall is 7 feet wide.

It is 3 feet tall.

What is the area of the wall?

Diagram

266 © 2013 C. Woodin & Landmark School

Word Problems Related to Area Template: 3× Facts

- Mask the multiplication grid with two index cards to frame the rectangle described by the word problem.
- Use the grid to find the answer.
- Transfer the information to the diagram and label the answer with the appropriate units.

Teachers: customize this template by filling in blanks with appropriate values.

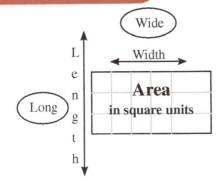

Problem # 1

The rectangular table is 3 feet long.

The table has an area of ____ square feet.

How wide is the table?

Diagram

Problem # 2

The rectangular rug is 3 feet long.

The area of the rug is ____ square feet.

How wide is the rug?

Diagram

Problem # 3

The garden has an area of ____ square feet.

The garden is 3 feet long.

How wide is the garden?

Diagram

Problem # 4

The wall is ____ feet wide.

It is 3 feet tall.

What is the area of the wall?

Diagram

© 2013 C. Woodin & Landmark School   267

3× Flash Cards: Previously Learned Facts:

These 3× flash cards have already been used to prompt the 2×, 5× 9×, and 10× facts. Use these cards to review these learned facts within the context of the 3× fact family.

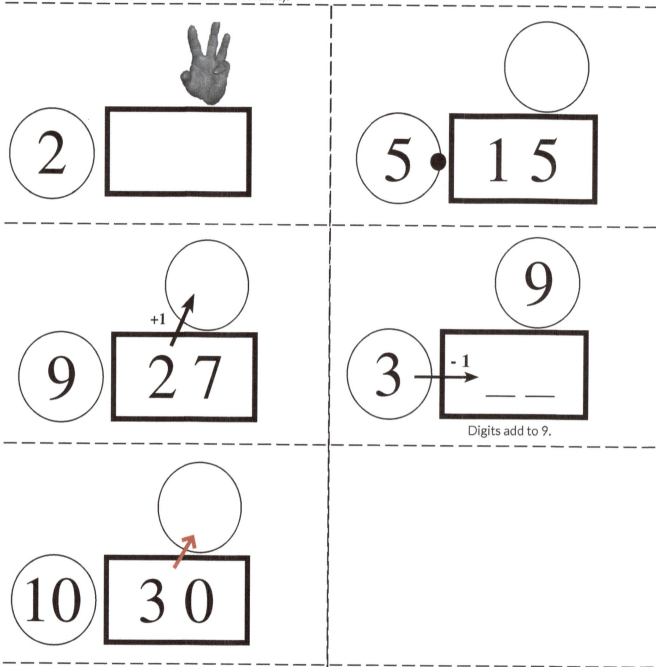

3× Flash Cards: Part-to-Whole

Use these flash cards to prompt the oral expression of the 3× fact family. Students should express entire multiplication or division fact sentences to help commit these facts to auditory memory. The cards present information in a part-to-whole configuration because the 3× products provide few reliable cues to indicate their factors. The red arrows indicate the sums of the digits. This sum is difficult for the student to predict, therefore it is provided. Practice with this method helps to learn the divisibility rule for 3.

- Practice with these flash cards will solidify and validate the divisibility rule.
- Multiples of 3 have digits that add to 3, 6 or 9.
- Students have learned the majority of these facts through exposure to the 2, 5, 10, 1, and 9× facts.
- Practice of previously introduced facts in the context of the 3× fact family will provide additional reinforcement to promote the accuracy and efficiency of students' recall.
- Four new facts (3 × 3, 3 × 4, 3 × 6, 3 × 7) will be learned through the oral recitation process.

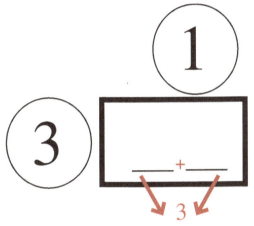

Diagram cues indicate that the sum of the digits is 3.

There is no tens place.

The product must be 3.

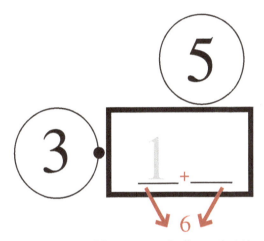

Diagram cues indicate that the sum of the digits is 6.

There is "1" in the tens place.

6 = 1 + 5; therefore, the product must be 15.

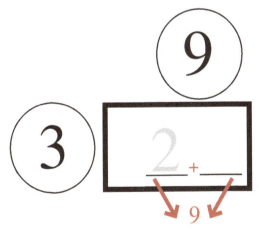

Diagram cues indicate that the sum of the digits is 9.

There is "2" in the 10's place.

9 = 2 + 7, therefore, the product must be 27.

3× Flash Cards: Divisibility Rule Cues

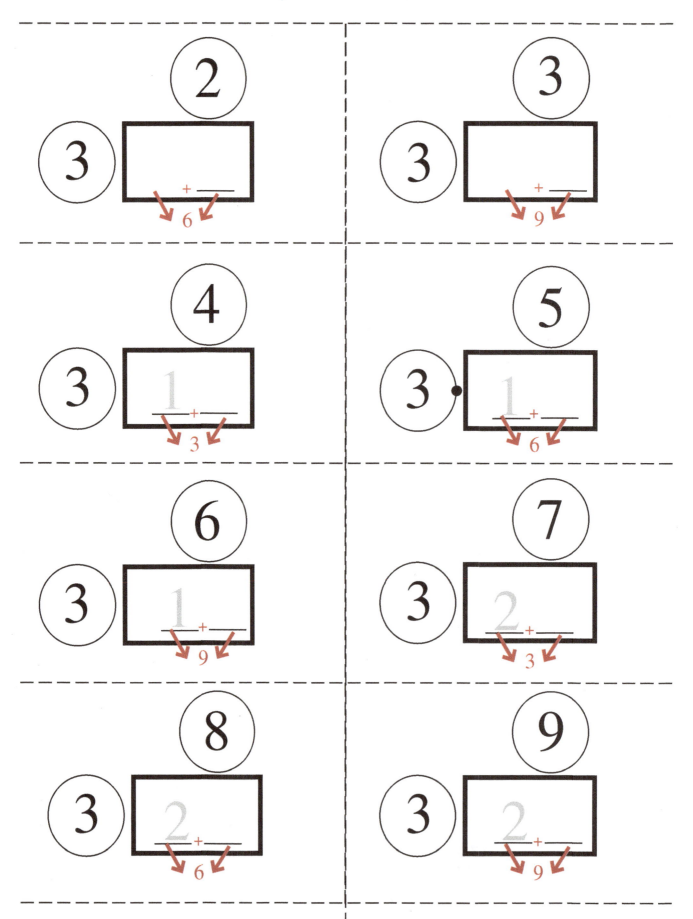

3x Facts Practice

**Complete the 3x matrix fact diagrams using the divisibility rule to help.
Write two multiplication facts for each diagram.**

These products add to 3. →

(3) (1) [_]

These products add to 6. →

(3) (2) [_]

These products add to 9. →

(3) (3) [_]

_____

(3) (4) [_]

(3) (5) [_]

(3) (6) [_]

_____

(3) (7) [_]

(3) (8) [_]

(3) (9) [_]

_____

Accuracy Benchmark Pretest - Untimed

Name _____
Date _____
Day _____

Complete this sheet with 100% accuracy before taking the related timed **Fluency Assessment**.

1) Complete each diagram. Have them scored.
2) Correct diagrams if needed.
3) Write a multiplication fact and a division fact for each.
4) Archive this in your Fact Notebook as a record.

Diagram Accuracy: ____/10
Sentence Accuracy: ____/20

③ | 3 0 | O   _____

③ | 1 5 | O   _____

③ | 9 | O   _____

③ | 1 8 | O   _____

③ | 6 | O   _____

③ | 1 2 | O   _____

③ | 2 4 | O   _____

③ | 2 7 | O   _____

③ | 3 | O   _____

③ | 2 1 | O   _____

272   © 2013 C. Woodin & Landmark School

Fluency Assessment - Timed

Administer this test after the student scores 100% accuracy on the related **Accuracy Benchmark Pretest**.

1) Complete each diagram. Note time and accuracy.
2) Correct diagrams as needed.
3) Write a multiplication fact and a division fact for each.
4) Archive this in your Fact Notebook as a record. Note time and accuracy.

Diagram Accuracy: ___/10   Time: _____

Sentences Accuracy: ___/20   Time: _____

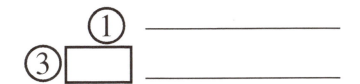   

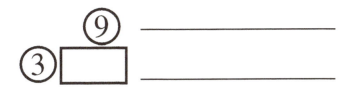   

© 2013 C. Woodin & Landmark School   273

Vertical 3× Fact Practice

Name _____
Date _____
Day _____

Timed quiz
___ seconds

◯/10

× | 3
　| 1

× | 3
　| 6

× | 3
　| 2

× | 3
　| 7

× | 3
　| 3

× | 3
　| 8

× | 3
　| 4

× | 3
　| 9

× | 3
　| 5

× | 1 0
　| 　3

Baseball Fact Game

3×

OUT = 3, 6, 9
SINGLE = 12, 15
DOUBLE = 18, 21
TRIPLE = 24, 27
HOME RUN = 30

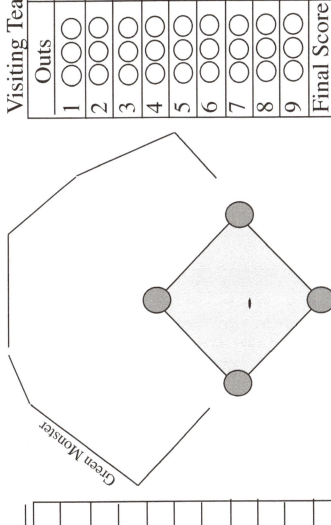

© 2013 C. Woodin & Landmark School

Multiplying 3 by Magnitudes of 10 Template

A skill used to create estimates of multidigit products.

Teachers: customize this template by filling in blanks with appropriate values.

Name _____
Date _____
Day _____

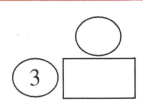

× **Facts:** _____

_____

$3 \times \_0 = \_$ _____

$3 \times \_00 =$ _____

$30 \times \_0 =$ _____

$30 \times \_00 =$ _____

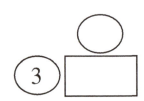

× **Facts:** _____

_____

$3 \times \_0 =$ _____

$3 \times \_00 =$ _____

$300 \times \_0 =$ _____

$30 \times \_00 =$ _____

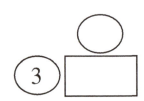

× **Facts:** _____

_____

$3 \times \_0 =$ _____

$3 \times \_00 =$ _____

$300 \times \_0 =$ _____

$30 \times \_00 =$ _____

© 2013 C. Woodin & Landmark School

Multiplying 3 by Magnitudes of 10:

Name
Date
Day

This fact sheet is to be done before 3× 3-Digit Multiplication Form 3A.

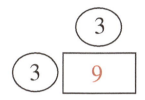

× **Fact**

3 × 3 =
─────────────
x 10

3 × 30 =
─────────────
x 100

3 × 300 =
─────────────

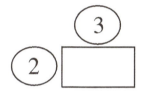

× **Fact**

3 × =
─────────────
x 10

3 × =
─────────────
x 100

3 × =
─────────────

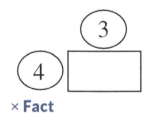

× **Fact**

3 × =
─────────────
x 10

=
─────────────
x 100

=
─────────────

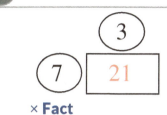

× **Fact**

3 × =
─────────────
x 10

3 × =
─────────────
x 100

3 × =
─────────────

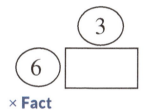

× **Fact**

3 × =
─────────────
x 10

=
─────────────
x 100

=
─────────────

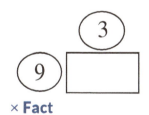

× **Fact**

3 × =
─────────────
x 10

=
─────────────
x 100

=
─────────────

© 2013 C. Woodin & Landmark School

3 x 3-Digit Multiplication: Form 3A

Name
Date
Day

Facts

②×③ ③×③ ④×③ ⑤×③ ⑦×③ ⑨×③

Standard Algorithm

5 | 3 | 2
×   3

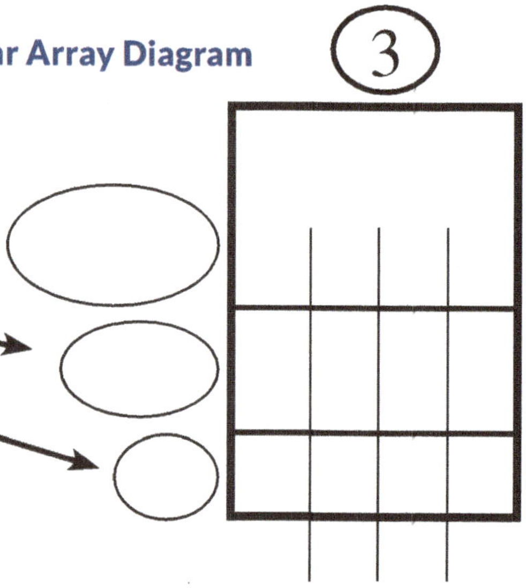

- The product's digits should eventually add to 3, 6, or 9.
- e.g., 1596 : 1+5+9+6= 21
- 2 + 1= 3 √

Expanded Notation

```
  500
   30
+   2
  532
```

Tabular Array Diagram

③

Add these partial products.

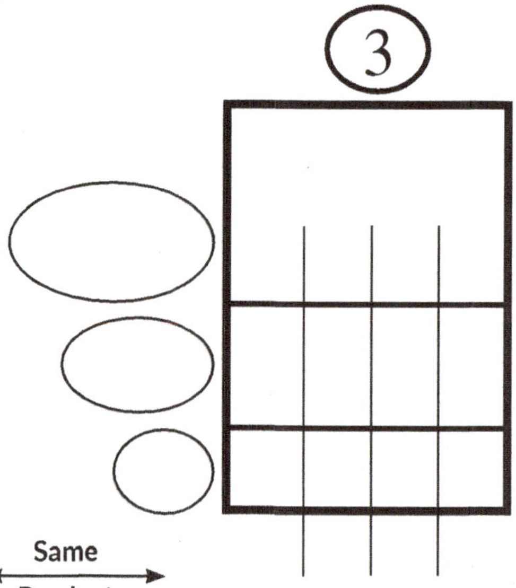

③

4 | 4 | 3
×   3

← Same Product →

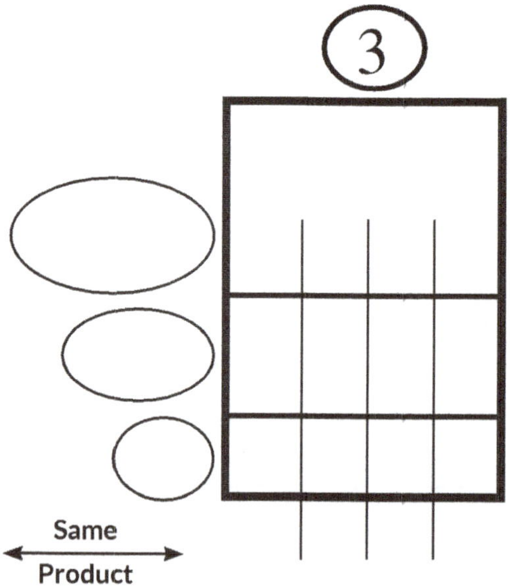

③

9 | 2 | 7
×   3

← Same Product →

③

278   © 2013 C. Woodin & Landmark School

Multiplying 3 by Magnitudes of 10:

This fact sheet is to be done before 3× 3-Digit Multiplication Form 3B.

Name _____
Date _____
Day _____

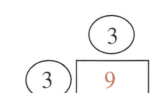

× Fact

3 × 3 =
―――――――――
x 10

3 × 30 =
―――――――――
x 100

3 × 300 =
―――――――――

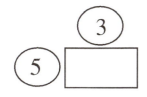

× Fact

3 x   =
―――――――――
x 10

3 x   =
―――――――――
x 100

3 x   =
―――――――――

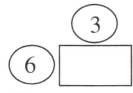

× Fact

3 × 6 =
―――――――――
x 10

3 ×   =
―――――――――
x 100

              =
―――――――――

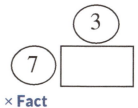

× Fact

3 ×   =
―――――――――
x 10

3 ×   =
―――――――――
x 100

3 ×   =
―――――――――

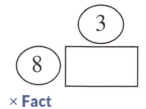

× Fact

3 ×   =
―――――――――
x 10

              =
―――――――――
x 100

              =
―――――――――

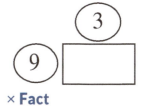

× Fact

3 ×   =
―――――――――
x 10

              =
―――――――――
x 100

              =
―――――――――

© 2013 C. Woodin & Landmark School

3 x 3-Digit Multiplication: Form 3B

Name
Date
Day

Facts

③ ③ | ⑤ ③ | ⑥ ③ | ⑦ ③ | ⑧ ③ | ⑨ ③

Standard Algorithm

```
  5 | 6 | 3   →
×     |   | 3
```

Expanded Notation

```
    5 0 0  →
      6 0  →
  +     3  →
  -------
    5 6 3
```

Tabular Array Diagram

③

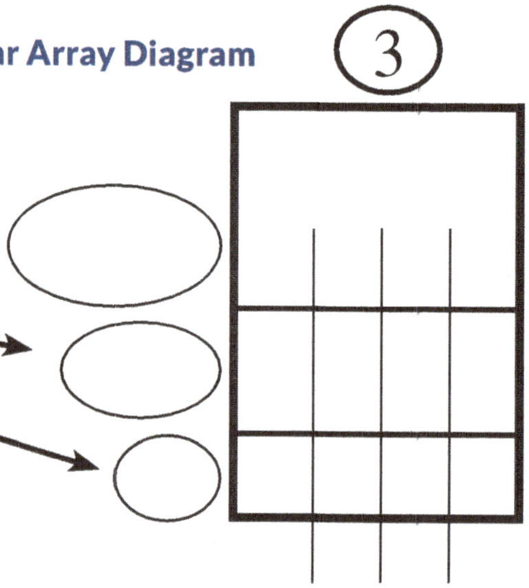

Add these partial products.

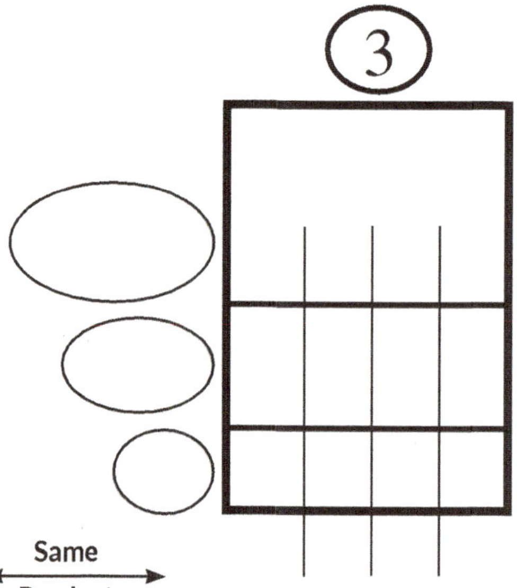

③

```
  8 | 5 | 9
×     |   | 3
```

← Same Product →

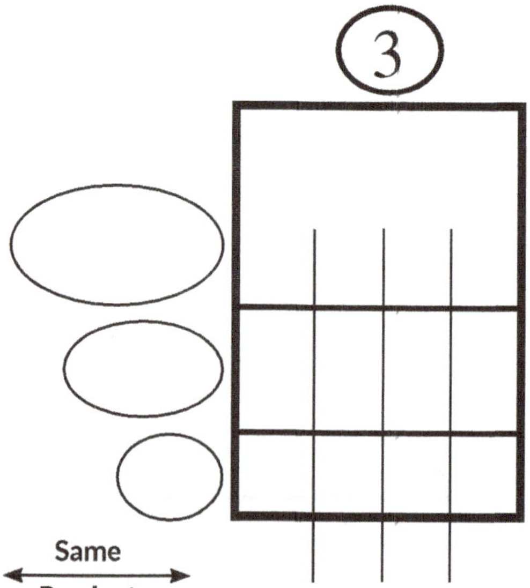

③

```
  9 | 3 | 7
×     |   | 3
```

← Same Product →

③

280 © 2013 C. Woodin & Landmark School

3x Multidigit Multiplication

Facts

The sum of the product's digits must add to **3**, 6, or 9.

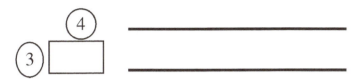

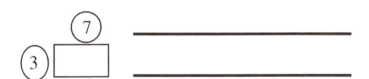

The sum of the product's digits must add to 3, **6**, or 9.

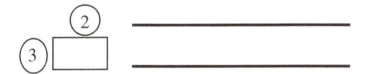

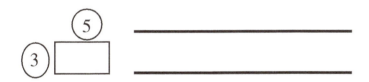

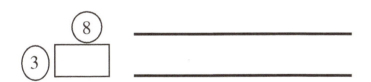

The sum of the product's digits must add to 3, 6, or **9**.

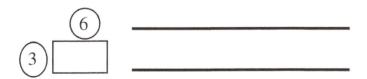

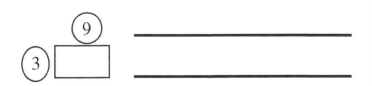

Name _____
Date _____
Day _____

Note: all products must follow the 3 divisibility rule.
The sum of the product's digits must add to 3, 6, or 9.

Estimate: _____

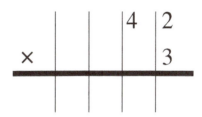

√ Sum of Digits 3, 6, 9: _____

Estimate: _____

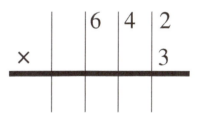

√ Sum of Digits 3, 6, 9: _____

Estimate: _____

√ Sum of Digits 3, 6, 9: _____

© 2013 C. Woodin & Landmark School

3 x Multidigit Template

Teachers: customize this template by filling in blanks with appropriate values.

Name _____
Date _____
Day _____

Facts

The sum of the product's digits must add to **3**, 6, or 9.

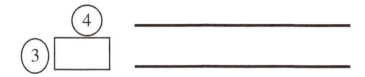

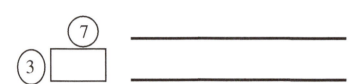

The sum of the product's digits must add to 3, **6**, or 9.

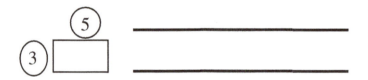

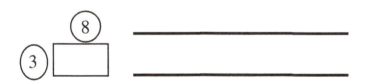

The sum of the product's digits must add to 3, 6, or **9**.

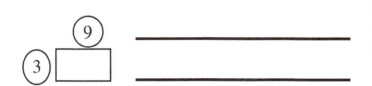

Note: all products must follow the 3 divisibility rule.
The sum of the product's digits must add to 3, 6, or 9.

Estimate: _____

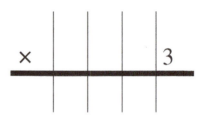

√ Sum of Digits 3, 6, 9: _____

Estimate: _____

√ Sum of Digits 3, 6, 9: _____

Estimate: _____

√ Sum of Digits 3, 6, 9: _____

The 6× Fact Family

Patterning Versus Rote Memorization

Teaching students the patterns associated with the even 6× facts can help create an error-free environment for fact learning. Teach students that 6 multiplied by an even digit always has the same even digit in the ones place of the product. The digit in the tens place of the product will be half of the digit in the ones place of the product.

$$6 \times \underline{2} = 1\underline{2}, \quad 6 \times \underline{4} = 2\underline{4}, \quad 6 \times \underline{6} = 3\underline{6}, \quad \text{and} \quad 6 \times \underline{8} = 4\underline{8}$$

The Let's Read series of books was created as a structured, hierarchical approach to teaching reading and spelling on the basis of patterns in words (Bloomfield and Barnhart 1961). The text presents a page of words that conform to a pattern. Text follows that is heavily laced with these words. After being explicitly shown a linguistic pattern, students are asked to discern the pattern and then use it to help them decode the words in context. When students are systematically provided with these patterns, decoding becomes a success-oriented process for them.

Multiplication and division fact tables should be presented in much the same way as the linguistic patterns in Bloomfield and Barnhart's Let's Read series. Series such as Let's Read (see the example below) explicitly emphasize consistencies inherent in each pattern. A sample lesson that is similar to one in Let's Read follows.

EXAMPLE

Pattern Page			Contextual Page
pat	pit	pet	The fat cat sat on the mat.
sat	sit	set	Pat, can you pet the fat cat?
mat		met	I bet you can.
fat	fit		Pet him Pat.
cat			

Teach multiplication facts in a similar manner. Explicitly teach fact patterns through a multisensory approach, and then have students practice facts in context. Make patterns in multiplication syntax and in each fact family evident. This strategy helps students automatize facts with the fewest number of presentations.

6 x Family

Again, refer back to the 0 -100 chart.

Six Times Family: The 6× products become green as they have already been highlighted in yellow and blue.

Pattern: The 6× products will emerge as a checkerboard diagonal pattern.

Divisibility rule: A number is divisible by 6 if it is divisible by both 2 and 3. (It must be even, and its digits must add to 3, 6, or 9.)

As before, students fill in the Divisibility Rule Sheet, and you post a copy of the Rule Poster. Students fill in the 6× row and column on the multiplication grid in pencil and practice the new facts in a variety of ways.

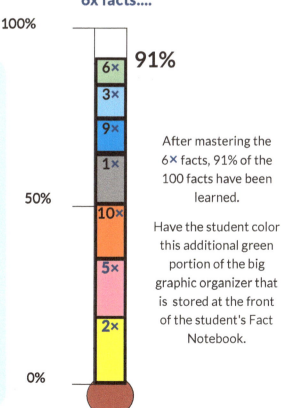

Gain 7 more facts after learning the 6x facts....

After mastering the 6× facts, 91% of the 100 facts have been learned.

Have the student color this additional green portion of the big graphic organizer that is stored at the front of the student's Fact Notebook.

Divisibility Rule Poster

A number is divisible by 6 if it is divisible by BOTH 2 and 3.

Examples: 18 → even? ✓   1 + 8 = 9 ✓
120 → even? ✓   1 + 2 + 0 = 3 ✓
2442 → even? ✓   2 + 4 + 4 + 2 = 12 → 1 + 2 = 3 ✓

If a number is a **multiple** of 6, it is even
and its digits add up to 3, 6, or 9.

Some multiples of 6:   24   54   702

6 is a **factor** of any even number whose
digits add up to 3, 6, or 9.

Multiple		Factors
24	=	6 × 4
30	=	6 × 5
36	=	6 × 6

Divisibility Rule Sheet

Fill in the divisibility rules as you learn them.

A number is **divisible by 6** if . . .

_____

_____

EXAMPLES:

USE THIS DIVISIBILITY POSTER TO START A NEW SECTION OF YOUR FACT NOTEBOOK

Use Divisibility Rules to Identify Multiples of 6

These are car license plates. Multiples of 6 are multiples of 2 and 3.

- Color multiples of 2 yellow - these are even numbers.
- Color multiples of 3 blue. Their digits add to 3, 6, or 9.
- Multiples of 6 will become green- a mix of yellow & blue.
- Draw an X over numbers not divisible by 6.

131	453	130	420
430	160	234	940
460	222	432	140
300	170	503	132
510	900	937	114
810	278	330	922

Use Divisibility Rules to Identify Multiples of 6

These are car license plates. Multiples of 6 are multiples of 2 and 3.

- Color multiples of 2 yellow - these are even numbers.
- Color multiples of 3 blue. Their digits add to 3, 6, or 9.
- Multiples of 6 will become green - a mix of yellow & blue.
- Put an "X" over numbers not divisible by 6.

Teachers: customize this template by filling in blanks with appropriate values.

Word Problems Related to Area: 6× Facts

- Mask the multiplication grid with two index cards to frame the rectangle described by the word problem.
- Use the grid to find the answer.
- Transfer the information to the diagram and label the answer with the appropriate units.

Name
Date
Day

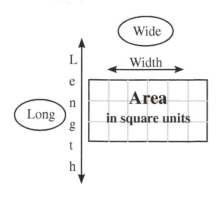

	1	2	3	4	5	6	7	8	9	10
1						6				
2						12				
3						18				
4						24				
5						30				
6	6	12	18	24	30	36	42	48	54	60
7						42				
8						48				
9						54				
10						60				

Problem #1

The rectangular table is 6 feet long.

The table has an area of 12 square feet.

How wide is the table?

Diagram

Problem #2

The rectangular rug is 6 feet long.

The area of the rug is 24 square feet.

How wide is the rug?

Diagram

Problem #3

The garden has an area of 48 square feet.

The garden is 8 feet long.

How wide is the garden?

Diagram

Problem #4

The wall is 6 feet wide.

It is 5 feet tall.

What is the area of the wall?

Diagram

288   © 2013 C. Woodin & Landmark School

Word Problems Related to Area: 6× Facts

- Mask the multiplication grid with two index cards to frame the rectangle described by the word problem.
- Use the grid to find the answer.
- Transfer the information to the diagram and label the answer with the appropriate units.

Teachers: customize this template by filling in blanks with appropriate values.

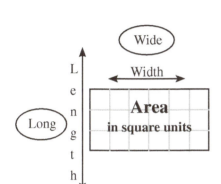

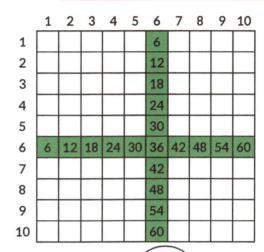

Problem #1

The rectangular table is 6 feet long.

The table has an area of ___ square feet.

How wide is the table?

Diagram

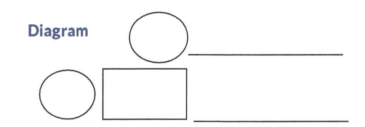

Problem #2

The rectangular rug is 6 feet long.

The area of the rug is ___ square feet.

How wide is the rug?

Diagram

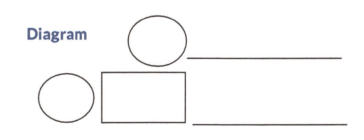

Problem #3

The garden has an area of ___ square feet.

The garden is 6 feet long.

How wide is the garden?

Diagram

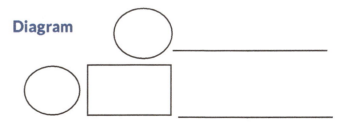

Problem #4

The wall is 6 feet wide.

It is ___ feet tall.

What is the area of the wall?

Diagram

© 2013 C. Woodin & Landmark School

6× Flash Cards:

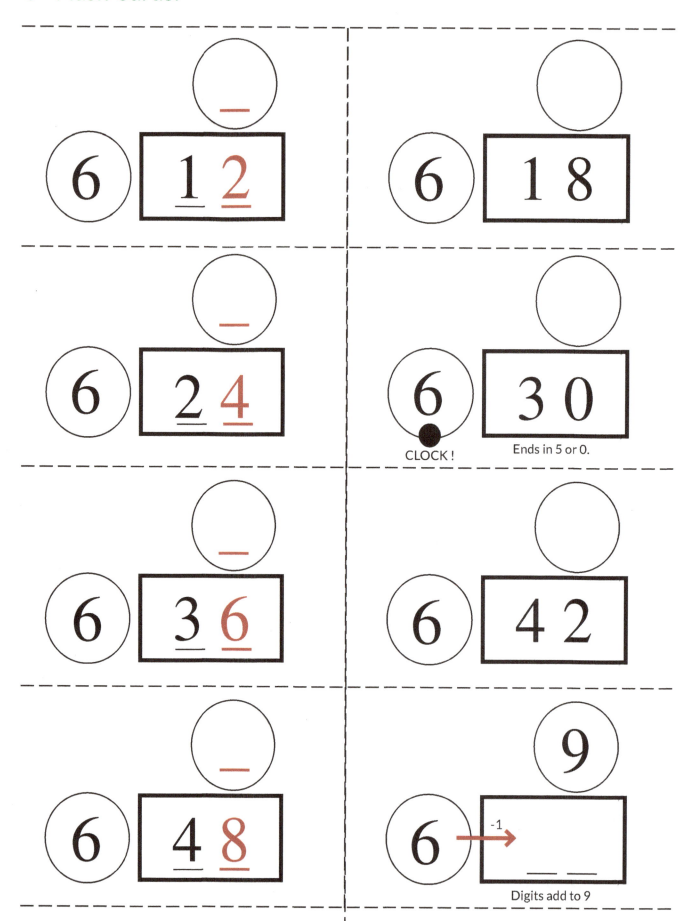

Baseball Fact Game

6×

OUT = 6, 12, 18
SINGLE = 24, 30
DOUBLE = 36, 42
TRIPLE = 48, 54
HOME RUN = 60

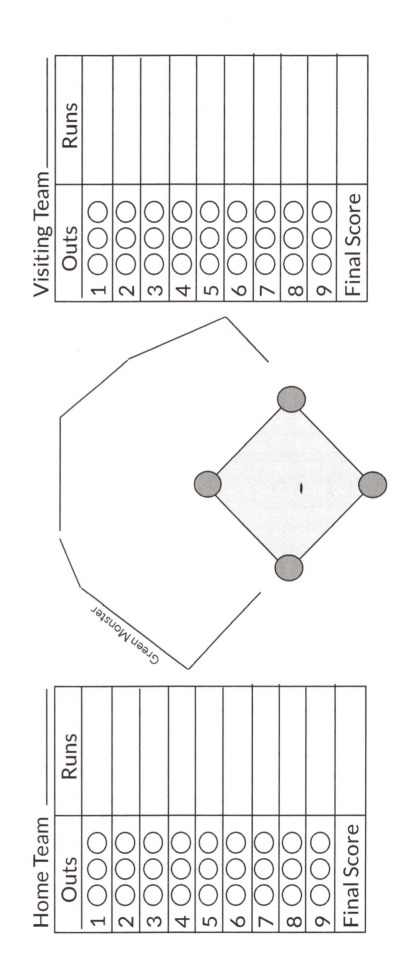

Accuracy Benchmark Pretest - Untimed

Complete this sheet with 100% accuracy before taking the related timed *Fluency Assessment*.

1) Complete each diagram. Have them scored.
2) Correct diagrams if needed.
3) Write a multiplication fact and a division fact for each.
4) Archive this in your Fact Notebook as a record. Retake it to improve.

Name _____
Date _____
Day _____

Diagram Accuracy: ____/10
Sentence Accuracy: ____/20

6) 12 _____

6) 6 _____

6) 36 _____

6) 18 _____

6) 24 _____

6) 30 _____

6) 48 _____

6) 54 _____

6) 60 _____

6) 42 _____

292   © 2013 C. Woodin & Landmark School

6× Fluency Assessment - Timed

Administer this test after the student scores 100% accuracy on the related *Accuracy Benchmark Pretest*.

1) Complete each diagram. Note time and accuracy.

2) Correct diagrams as needed.

3) Write a multiplication fact and a division fact for each. Note time and accuracy.

4) Archive this in your Fact Notebook as a record. Retake it to improve.

Name _____
Date _____
Day _____

Diagram Accuracy: ____/10 Time: _____

Sentences Accuracy: ____/20 Time: _____

(6) [2] _____

(6) [5] _____

(6) [8] _____

(6) [1] _____

(6) [4] _____

(6) [3] _____

(6) [6] _____

(6) [9] _____

(6) [10] _____

(6) [7] _____

© 2013 C. Woodin & Landmark School

6× Vertical Fact Practice

Name: _____
Date: _____
Day: _____

Timed quiz
____ seconds

◯/10

```
    | 1            | 6
  x | 6          x | 6
----+---        ----+---
    |              |

    | 2            | 7
  x | 6          x | 6
----+---        ----+---
    |              |

    | 3            | 8
  x | 6          x | 6
----+---        ----+---
    |              |

    | 4            | 9
  x | 6          x | 6
----+---        ----+---
    |              |

    | 5            |1 0
  x | 6          x | 6
----+---        ----+---
    |              |
```

Multiplying 6 by Magnitudes of 10: Form 6A

This fact sheet is to be done before 6x 3-Digit Multiplication Form 6A.

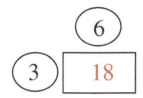

× Fact

6 × 3 =
───────
x 10

6 × 3 0 =
───────
x 100

6 × 3 0 0 =
───────

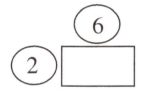

× Fact

6 ×   =
───────
x 10

6 ×   =
───────
x 100

6 ×   =
───────

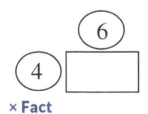

× Fact

6 ×   =
───────
x 10

6 ×   =
───────
x 100

      =
───────

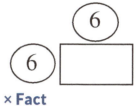

× Fact

6 x   =
───────
x 10

6 x   =
───────
x 100

6 x   =
───────

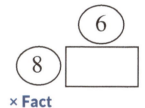

× Fact

6 x   =
───────
x 10

      =
───────
x 100

      =
───────

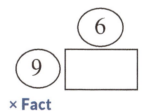

× Fact

6 ×   =
───────
x 10

      =
───────
x 100

      =
───────

© 2013 C. Woodin & Landmark School

6 x 3-Digit Multiplication Form 6A

Name
Date
Day

Facts

② ⑥ ☐   ③ ⑥ ☐   ④ ⑥ ☐   ⑥ ⑥ ☐   ⑧ ⑥ ☐   ⑨ ⑥ ☐

Standard Algorithm

```
  6 | 4 | 2   →
×     |   | 6
```

↑ The product should be an even number, and the digits should eventually add to 3, 6, or 9.

e.g., 3852 ends with 2 (even #)

3+8+5+2= 18
      1 + 8 = 9 √

```
  8 | 6 | 4
×     |   | 6
```

Tabular Array Diagram

⑥

Expanded Notation

```
    6 0 0  →
       4 0 →
  +      2
    6 4 2 →
```

Add these partial products.

⑥

← Same Product →

```
  4 | 2 | 6
×     |   | 6
```

⑥

← Same Product →

296 © 2013 C. Woodin & Landmark School

Multiplying 6 by Magnitudes of 10: Form 6B

This fact sheet is to be done before 6x 3-Digit Multiplication Template 6B.

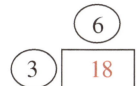

× Fact

6 × 3 =
―――――――
x 10

6 × 30 =
―――――――
x 100

6 × 300 =
―――――――

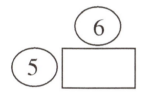

× Fact

6 × =
―――――
x 10

6 × =
―――――
x 100

6 × =
―――――

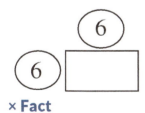

× Fact

6 × 6 =
―――――――
x 10

6 × =
―――――
x 100

=

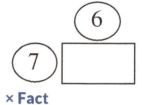

× Fact

6 × =
―――――
x 10

6 × =
―――――
x 100

6 × =
―――――

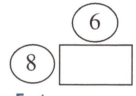

× Fact

6 × =
―――――
x 10

=
―――――
x 100

=
―――――

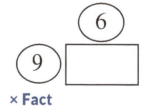

× Fact

6 × =
―――――
x 10

=
―――――
x 100

=
―――――

© 2013 C. Woodin & Landmark School

6 x 3-Digit Multiplication Template: Form 6B

Facts

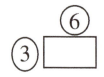 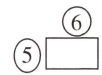 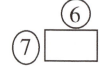 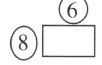

Standard Algorithm

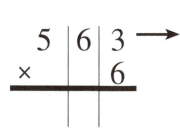

Expanded Notation

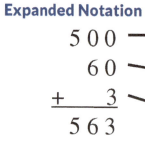

Tabular Array Diagram

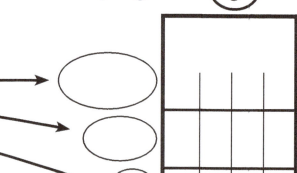

Add these partial products.

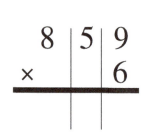

Same Product

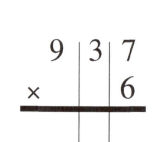

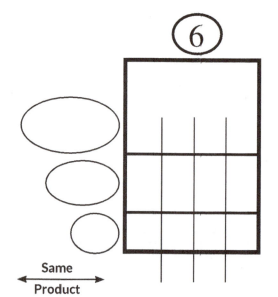

Same Product

Multiplying 6 by Magnitudes of 10

Use this skill to create estimates of multidigit products.

Teachers: customize this template by filling in blanks with appropriate values.

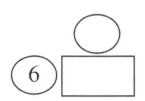

× **Facts:** _____

6 × __0 = __

6 × __00 =

60 × __0 =

60 × __00 =

× **Facts:** _____

6 × __0 =

6 × __00 =

600 × __0 =

60 × __00 =

× **Facts:** _____

6 × __0 =

6 × __00 =

600 × __0 =

60 × __00 =

© 2013 C. Woodin & Landmark School

6x Multidigit Multiplication

Note: all products must follow the 6 divisibility rule. The sum of the product's digits must add to 3, 6, or 9, and must have an even digit in the one's place.

Facts

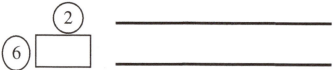

Estimate: _____

√ Even #!

√ Sum of Digits: _____

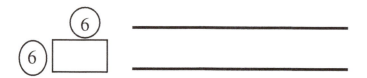

Estimate: _____

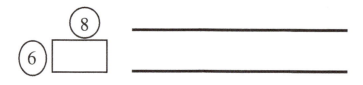

√ Even #!

√ Sum of Digits: _____

Estimate: _____

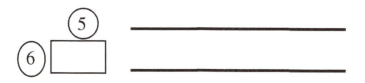

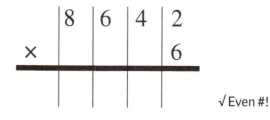

√ Even #!

√ Sum of Digits: _____

6x Multidigit Multiplication Template

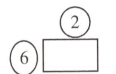

Teachers: customize this template by filling in blanks with appropriate values.

Note: all products must follow the 6× divisibility rule. The sum of the product's digits must add to 3, 6, or 9, and must have an even digit in the one's place.

Facts

6 × 2 = _____

6 × 4 = _____

Estimate: _____

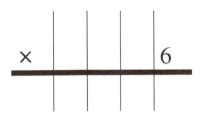

√ Even #!

√ Sum of Digits: _____

6 × 6 = _____

6 × 8 = _____

Estimate: _____

√ Even #!

√ Sum of Digits: _____

6 × 9 = _____

6 × 5 = _____

Estimate: _____

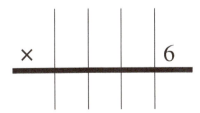

√ Even #!

6 × 3 = _____

√ Sum of Digits: _____

© 2013 C. Woodin & Landmark School   301

The Perfect Squares

After students have mastered the 6× fact family, it is time for them to learn facts related to perfect squares. These facts are members of many previously learned fact families. Many will already be colored on the multiplication grid. The perfect squares that students have not yet learned—16, 49, and 64—will not be colored. These add an additional three facts (3 percent), for a total of 94 percent of the one hundred facts on the grid. Rather than coloring these facts, locate the square products, including 16, 49, and 64, and trace each of the square grid borders of these square products with a grey pencil. This will create a grey diagonal pattern on the 10 × 10 Multiplication Grid.

Use the multiplication grid to demonstrate the visual qualities of this unique fact family. The area models of these facts are, by definition, squares. Use two pieces of paper to mask the right and lower portions of the multiplication grid to isolate the square areas of these facts. These squares will have square roots as their factors.

EXAMPLE

For example, start by masking all of the grid except for the upper left square corner of the multiplication grid measuring 2 × 2. The square has an area of four square units (the product of 2 × 2).

The perfect square of 4 is defined by its root (2).

Move the lower sheet of masking paper down one row and move the right sheet one column to the right to expose the next perfect square of nine square units. This perfect square area will be three units wide and three units high.

Use this technique to unmask the ten perfect squares of the multiplication table. Extend this visual prompt to the flash cards that show these images. These flash cards have an accented fifth gridline to help students discern each dimension of the squares.

Use these flash cards to prompt the facts relating to the perfect squares. This model can be extended to teach the terms square and square root.

The Perfect Squares

Gain 3 more facts after learning the perfect squares.

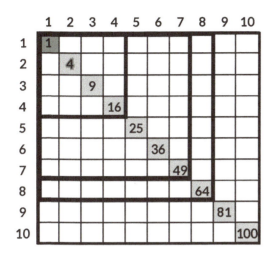

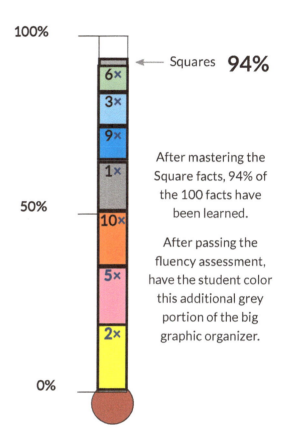

Squares **94%**

After mastering the Square facts, 94% of the 100 facts have been learned.

After passing the fluency assessment, have the student color this additional grey portion of the big graphic organizer.

TEACHING THE PERFECT SQUARES

- This is the perfect opportunity to explore the concepts of squares and square roots.
- Introduce the square notation e.g., $5^2 = 25$.
- Introduce the ideas that the lengths of the sides of squares are called square roots.
- Introduce the square root notation e.g., $\sqrt{25} = 5$.
- Using the perfect square flash cards, ask students to point to the card that has a square root of 6.
- Ask students to find the card that represents 10 squared.

© 2013 C. Woodin & Landmark School

Word Problems Related to Area: Perfect Squares

- Mask the multiplication grid with two index cards to frame the rectangle described by the word problem.
- Use the grid to find the answer.
- Transfer the information to the diagram and label the answer with the appropriate units.

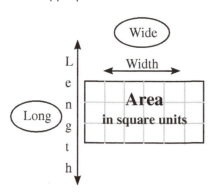

Problem #1

The checkerboard is 8 spaces long.

The checkerboard has an area of 64 square spaces.

How many spaces wide is the checkerboard?

Diagram

Problem #2

The square tic-tac-toe grid is 3 spaces wide.

The tic-tac-toe grid is 3 spaces long.

What is the area of the tic-tac-toe grid?

Diagram

Problem #3

The garden has an area of 64 square feet.

The garden is 8 feet long.

How wide is the garden?

Diagram

Problem #4

The square floor is 6 feet wide.

What is the area of the floor?

Diagram

Word Problems Related to Area: Perfect Squares

- Mask the multiplication grid with two index cards to frame the rectangle described by the word problem.
- Use the grid to find the answer.
- Transfer the information to the diagram and label the answer with the appropriate units.

Teachers: customize this template by filling in blanks with appropriate values.

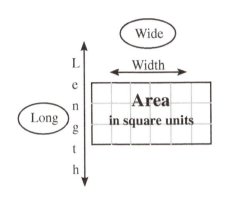

Problem #1

The square table top is ___ inches long.

The table has an area of _____ square inches.

How many inches wide is the table top?

Diagram

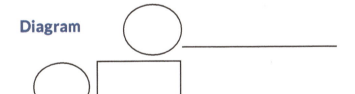

Problem #2

A square tile is _____ cm wide.

It is _____ cm long.

What is the area of the tile?

Diagram

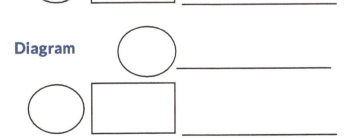

Problem #3

The square garden has an area of _____ square feet.

The garden is ____ feet long.

How wide is the garden?

Diagram

Problem #4

The square floor is _____ tiles wide.

What is the area of the floor?

Diagram

© 2013 C. Woodin & Landmark School

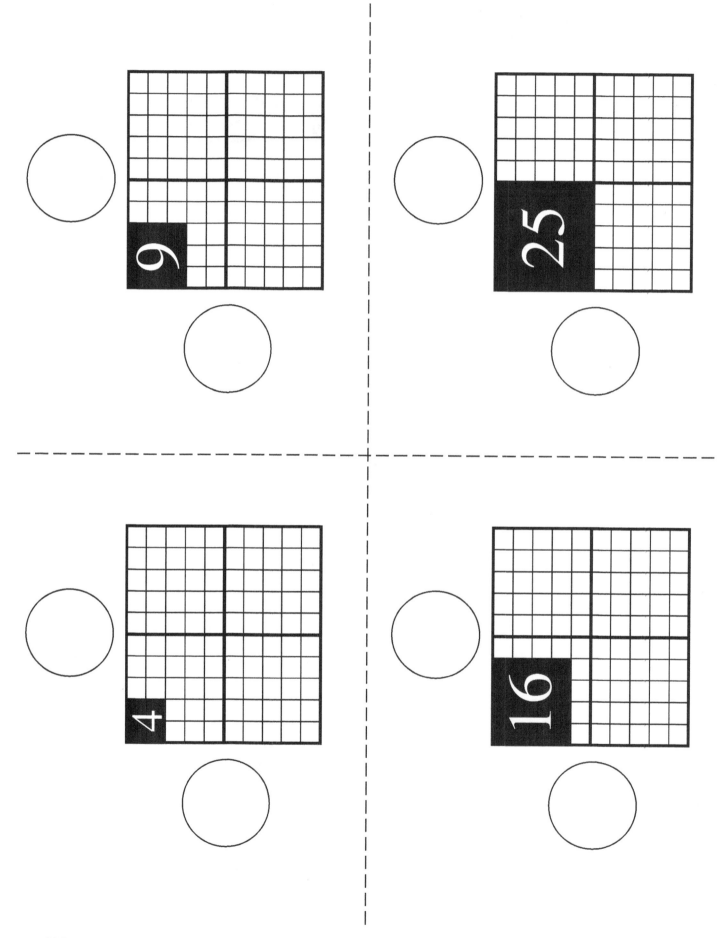

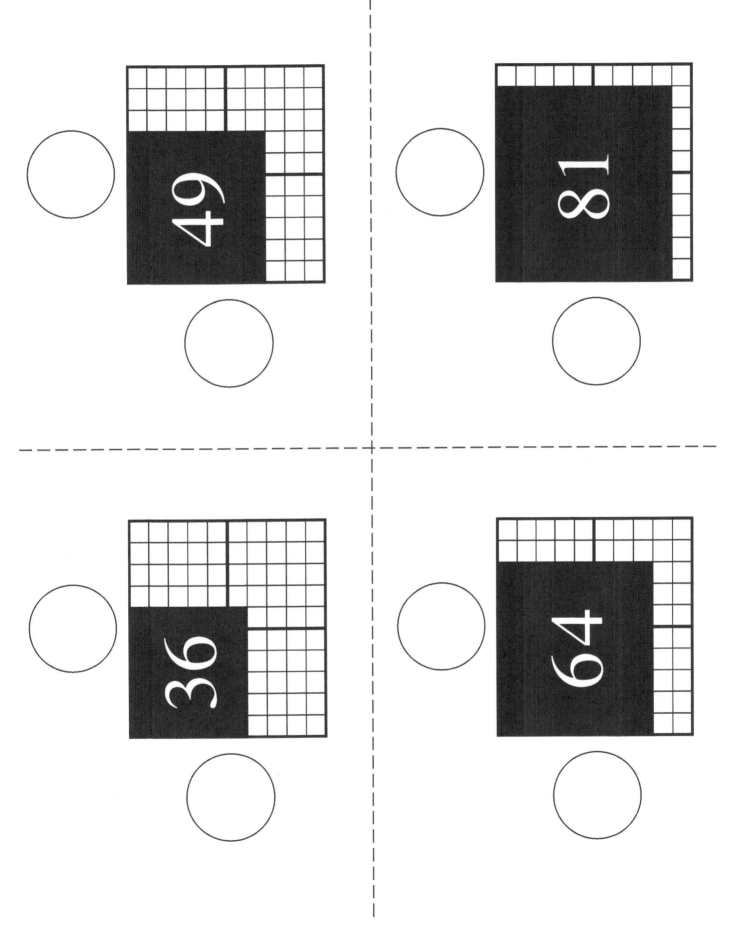

Accuracy Benchmark Pretest - Untimed

Complete this sheet with 100% accuracy before taking the related timed *Fluency Assessment*.

Name _____
Date _____
Day _____

1) Complete each diagram. Have them scored.
2) Correct diagrams if needed.
3) Write a multiplication fact and a division fact for each.
4) Archive this in your Fact Notebook as a record.

Diagram Accuracy: ____/10

Sentence Accuracy: ____/20

9) 81

2) 4

6) 36

5) 25

10) 100

8) 64

1) 1

7) 49

3) 9

4) 16

308   © 2013 C. Woodin & Landmark School

Fluency Assessment - Timed

Administer this test after the student scores 100% accuracy on the related *Accuracy Benchmark Pretest*.

1) Complete each diagram. Note time and accuracy.
2) Correct diagrams as needed.
3) Write a multiplication fact and a division fact for each. Note time and accuracy.
4) Archive this in your Fact Notebook as a record. Retake it to improve.

Name _____
Date _____
Day _____

Diagram Accuracy: _____/10 Time: _____

Sentences Accuracy: _____/20 Time: _____

① 1 ①
1 ☐ _____

⑤ 5 ⑤
5 ☐ _____

⑨ 9
9 ☐ _____

② 2
2 ☐ _____

⑥ 6
6 ☐ _____

③ 3
3 ☐ _____

⑩ 10
10 ☐ _____

④ 4
4 ☐ _____

⑧ 8
8 ☐ _____

⑦ 7
7 ☐ _____

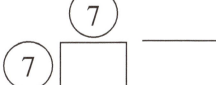

© 2013 C. Woodin & Landmark School

Vertical Fact Practice With Squares

Name _____
Date _____
Day _____

Timed quiz
_____ seconds

◯/10

```
    | 1          | 6
  x | 1        x | 6
----+---      ----+---
    |            |
```

```
    | 2          | 7
  x | 2        x | 7
----+---      ----+---
    |            |
```

```
    | 3          | 8
  x | 3        x | 8
----+---      ----+---
    |            |
```

```
    | 4          | 9
  x | 4        x | 9
----+---      ----+---
    |            |
```

```
    | 5
  x | 5
----+---
    |
```

10 x 10 = _____

The 4× Fact Family

The divisibility rule for the 4× family is more complex than some. The rule is useful for checking the accuracy of products, and it can also be used in reverse to create 4× facts from learned 2× facts. The multiples, however, are difficult to distinguish from the 2× facts when highlighted on the 0–100 chart. For this reason, the usual 0–100 chart shading activity is not used for this fact family. Worksheets for the 4× family should be stored in a new yellow-tabbed section of the Fact Notebook binder.

Though the ultimate goal for students is to recite facts related to the 4× family in a fluent manner from auditory memory, it is important for them to be able to generate these facts on an independent basis in case memory fails. The 4× facts are easily calculated by doubling the automatized 2× facts. There are exercises in this section that provide visual support to guide students to perform this calculation and then scaffold the production of a 4× fact. Remember, the ultimate goal is fact fluency. After a student has computed a 4× fact, it important to have him or her recite the entire fact or, even better, recite a related division fact to help establish the fact in auditory memory for later recall.

The majority of these 4× facts should be familiar as students have learned them through the course of learning the 2×, 5×, 10×, 9×, 3×, and 6× fact families. Reuse flash cards from these fact families to review the 4× facts and draw on students' existing knowledge base. After using the older flash cards to draw upon background knowledge, teach the 2× doubling procedure to compute all of the 4× facts. There are two methods of presentation. The first model uses vertical addition of the subproducts, in a matrix model, to help students with working memory constraints. The horizontal methods uses parentheses. Both the horizontal method involving parentheses or the initial vertical matrix model work in a similar way, though one will probably best meet the needs of an individual student. **Try one method, if it works well, there is no need to introduce the other.**

Finally, students will use new 4× flash cards that include previously learned facts, but that also utilize the distributive property to create the 4× facts by adding two 2× facts.

Rehearse these facts in their entirety by using the familiar drill-and-practice games and activities that the students practiced with earlier fact families.

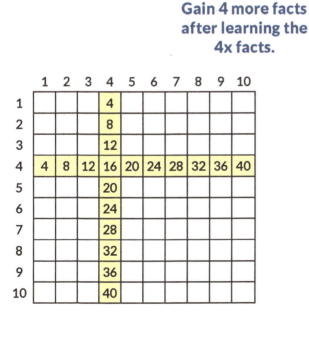

Gain 4 more facts after learning the 4x facts.

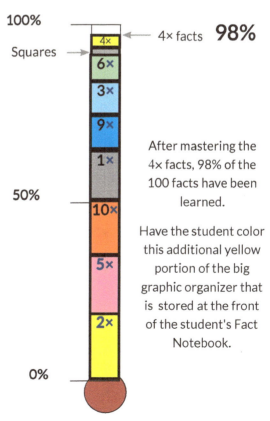

After mastering the 4x facts, 98% of the 100 facts have been learned.

Have the student color this additional yellow portion of the big graphic organizer that is stored at the front of the student's Fact Notebook.

Divisibility Rule Poster

DIVISIBLE BY 4

A number is **divisible by 4** if dividing the last two digits by 2 results in an even quotient.

Example: Is 128 divisible by 4?

Step 1: Underline, or write down the last two digits: 1 2 8.

Step 2: Divide them by 2. (Cut 28 in half.)

Step 3: If the quotient is even, the number is divisible by 4.

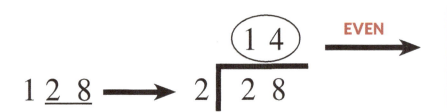

EVEN → **YES** This quotient (14) is even. 128 is divisible by 4!

ODD → **NO** This quotient (13) is odd. 126 is not divisible by 4.

Divisibility Rule Sheet

Fill in the divisibility rules as you learn them.

A number is **divisible by 4** if . . .

_____

_____

Example: Is 128 divisible by 4?

Step 1: →
Underline, or write down the last two digits: 1 4 0.

Step 2: →
Divide them by 2. (Cut 40 in half.)

Step 3:
If the quotient is even, the number is divisible by 4.
In this case- Yes!

EXAMPLES:

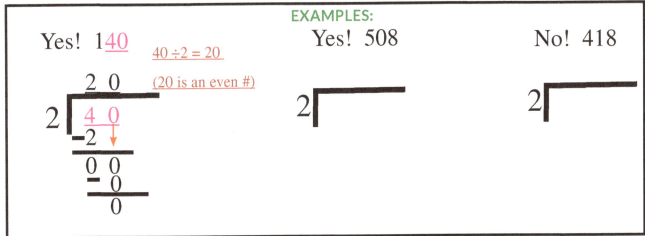

Use Divisibility Rules to Identify Multiples of 4

These are car license plates.
Multiples of 4 are also multiples of 2.
- Color multiples of 2 yellow - these are even numbers.
- Underline the ten's and one's place (e.g., 1<u>40</u>).
- Divide the underlined part of the number by 2 (cut it in half).
- If your quotient (answer) is even, the number is divisible by 4! e.g., 40÷2 = 20, an even number!
- Draw a √ next to numbers divisible by 4. Cross out (X) all others.

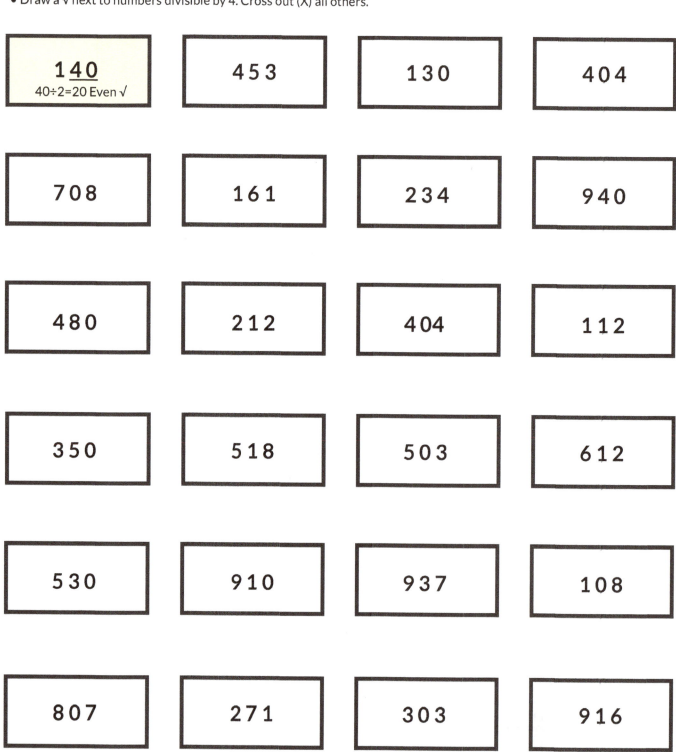

1<u>40</u> 40÷2=20 Even √	453	130	404
708	161	234	940
480	212	404	112
350	518	503	612
530	910	937	108
807	271	303	916

314 © 2013 C. Woodin & Landmark School

Use Divisibility Rules to Identify Multiples of 4

These are car license plates.
Multiples of 4 are also multiples of 2.
- Color multiples of 2 yellow - these are even numbers.
- Underline the ten's and one's place (e.g., 1<u>40</u>).
- Divide the underlined part of the number by 2 (cut it in half).
- If your quotient (answer) is even, the number is divisible by 4! e.g., 40÷2 = 20, an even number!
- Draw a √ next to numbers divisible by 4. Cross out (X) all others.

Teachers: customize this template by filling in blanks with appropriate values.

Word Problems Related to Area: 4× Facts

- Mask the multiplication grid with two index cards to frame the rectangle described by the word problem.
- Use the grid to find the answer.
- Transfer the information to the diagram and label the answer with the appropriate units.

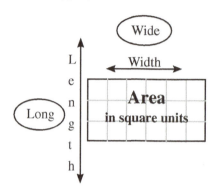

Problem # 1
The board is 4 inches long.

The board has an area of 40 square inches.

How wide is the board?

Diagram

Problem # 2
The rectangular bookmark is 4 inches long.

The area of the bookmark is 32 square inches.

How wide is the bookmark?

Diagram

Problem # 3
The card has an area of 12 square inches.

The card is 4 inches long.

How wide is the card?

Diagram

Problem # 4
The rug is 4 feet wide.

It is 9 feet long.

What is the area of the rug?

Diagram

316 © 2013 C. Woodin & Landmark School

Word Problems Related to Area: 4× Facts

- Mask the multiplication grid with two index cards to frame the rectangle described by the word problem.
- Use the grid to find the answer.
- Transfer the information to the diagram and label the answer with the appropriate units.

Teachers: customize this template by filling in blanks with appropriate values.

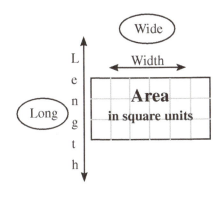

	1	2	3	4	5	6	7	8	9	10
1				4						
2				8						
3				12						
4	4	8	12	16	20	24	28	32	36	40
5				20						
6				24						
7				28						
8				32						
9				36						
10				40						

Problem # 1

The board is 4 inches long.

The board has an area of ____ square inches.

How wide is the board?

Diagram

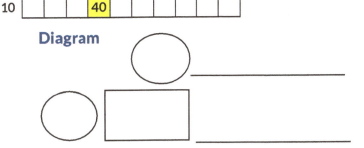

Problem # 2

The rectangular bookmark is 4 inches long.

The area of the bookmark is ____ square inches.

How wide is the bookmark?

Diagram

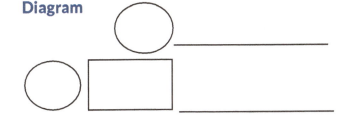

Problem # 3

The card has an area of ____ square inches.

The card is 4 inches long.

How wide is the card?

Diagram

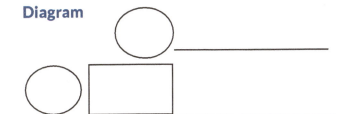

Problem # 4

The rug is 4 feet wide.

It is ____ feet long.

What is the area of the rug?

Diagram

© 2013 C. Woodin & Landmark School

Composite 4× Multiplication and Division Facts

Most of the 4× facts have been learned by this point, but it is important for students to be able to generate these facts on an independent basis in case memory fails. The 4× facts are easily calculated by doubling the automatized 2× facts. The first model presented here uses vertical addition of the subproducts to help students with working memory constraints. Use the distributive property to create the 4× facts with a composite matrix diagram.

Students will multiply 7 × 4 by breaking the 4 into the sum of two smaller numbers:

The property involved is called the distributive property because you are distributing a factor (7) over two or more terms (2 + 2). For any real numbers, a, b and c: $a \times (b + c) = ab + ac$.

Once the 4 has been broken into 2 + 2, students will use their learned 2× facts to solve the problem. Multiply the top factor, in this case 7, by each of the 2s as shown in the composite matrix diagram below.

Add the two products e.g., 7 × 2 = 14 twice: 14 + 14 = 28, so 7 × 4 = 28.

Remember, after a student has computed a 4× fact, it important to have him or her recite the entire fact or, even better, recite a related division fact to help establish the fact in auditory memory for later recall.

$$7 \times 4 = 28$$
$$28 \div 7 = 4$$

$$4 \times 7 = 28$$
$$28 \div 4 = 7$$

Composite 4× Multiplication and Division Facts

Create 4× facts using the Distributive Property, then write the related × and ÷ facts.

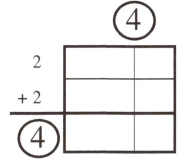
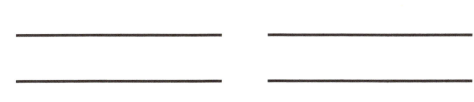

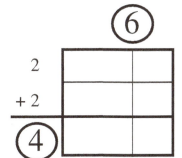

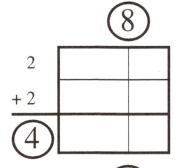
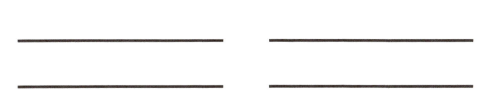

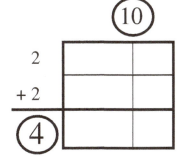
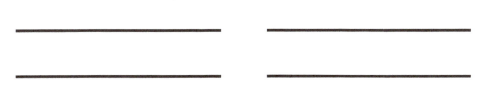

Composite 4× Multiplication and Division Facts

Name _____
Date _____
Day _____

Create 4× facts using the Distributive Property, then write the related × and ÷ facts.

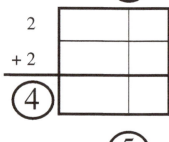

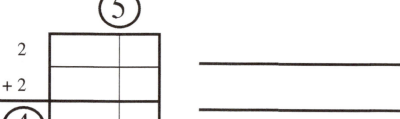

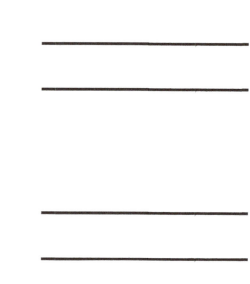

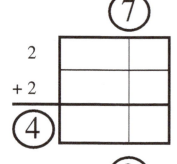

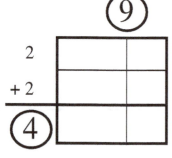

4× Facts:
Students should identify and name the missing component of each diagram, then verbalize four related facts.

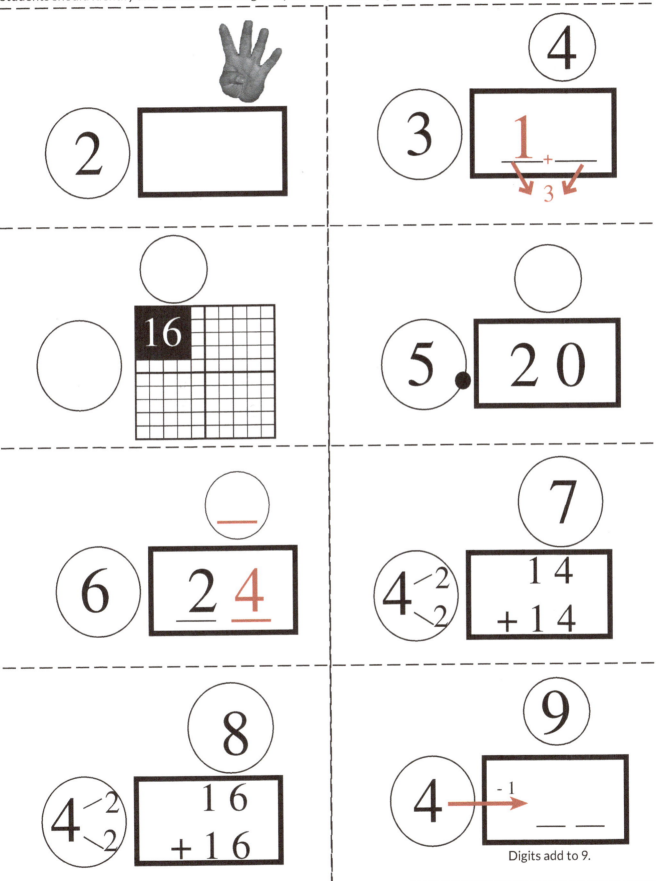

Multiplying by 4 Using the Distributive Property, Horizontally

Again write 4× facts using the distributive property, but this time the process will be done horizontally. Complete the diagram, then write related × and ÷ facts.

Multiply 5 × 4 by breaking the 4 into the sum of two smaller numbers: 4 = (2 + 2).

Once the 4 has been broken into (2 + 2), students use familiar 2× facts to solve the problem. Multiply the left factor, in this case 5, by each of the 2s as shown with the arrows below.

Add the two subproducts e.g., 10 + 10 = 20, so 5 × 4 = 20.

Remember, after a student has computed a 4× fact, it important to have him or her recite the entire fact or, even better, recite a related division fact to help establish the fact in auditory memory for later recall.

DIAGRAM

Use the distributive property to complete the matrix diagram of the 4× fact, then write the related fact sentences.

5 (4)

5 (2 + 2) = 10 + 10

	4
5	20

5 × 4 = 20
20 ÷ 4 = 5

4 × 5 = 20
20 ÷ 5 = 4

Multiplying by 4 Using the Distributive Property.

Name _____
Date _____
Day _____

Rewrite 4 as (2 + 2), multiply the factor by each term, then add these products to calculate the 4× fact.

Complete the diagram, then write related × and ÷ facts.

2 (4)
2 (2 + 2) = __4__ + __4__

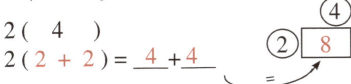

3 (4)
3 (+) = ___ + ___

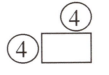

4 (4)
4 (+) = ___ + ___

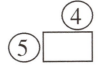

5 (4)
5 (+) = ___ + ___

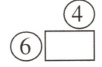

6 (4)
6 (+) = ___ + ___

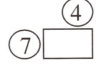

7 (4)
7 (+) = ___ + ___

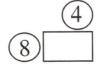

8 (4)
8 (+) = ___ + ___

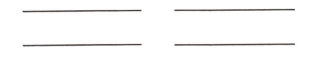

9 (4)
9 (+) = ___ + ___

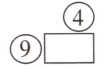

10 (4)
10 (+) = ___ + ___

© 2013 C. Woodin & Landmark School

Accuracy Benchmark Pretest - Untimed

Name _____
Date _____
Day _____

Complete this sheet with 100% accuracy before taking the related timed **Fluency Assessment**.

1) Complete each diagram. Have them scored.
2) Correct diagrams if needed.
3) Write a multiplication fact and a division fact for each.
4) Archive this in your Fact Notebook as a record.

Diagram Accuracy: ____/10
Sentences Accuracy: ____/20

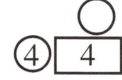

Fluency Assessment - Timed

Administer this test after the student scores 100% accuracy on the related **Accuracy Benchmark Pretest**.

1) Complete each diagram. Note time and accuracy.

2) Correct diagrams as needed.

3) Write a multiplication fact and a division fact for each. Note time and accuracy.

4) Archive this in your Fact Notebook as a record. Retake it to improve.

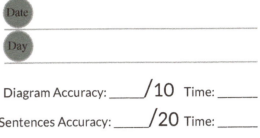

Diagram Accuracy: ____/10   Time: _____

Sentences Accuracy: ____/20   Time: _____

Fold-em Fact Practice Sheet

2 × 3 =		6
3 × 3 =		9
4 × 3 =		12
5 × 3 =		15
6 × 3 =		18
7 × 3 =		21
8 × 3 =		24
9 × 3 =		27
10 × 3 =		30

Fold here.

2 × 4 =		8
3 × 4 =		12
4 × 4 =		16
5 × 4 =		20
6 × 4 =		24
7 × 4 =		28
8 × 4 =		32
9 × 4 =		36
10 × 4 =		40

Fold here.

Fold the paper on the two dotted lines. Read each fact and then try to answer it. Open the fold to check each answer. If you were wrong, read the fact, then say a related multiplication or division fact using the same three numbers.
E.G., 2 x 3 = 6 so 3 x 2 = 6 or 6÷2 =3.
For another challenge, look at the answer side of the paper fold. Try to predict the correct fact sentence from the product.
E.g., Look at the product 6. Try to predict the 2 x 3 on the other side of the fold.

326 © 2013 C. Woodin & Landmark School

Multiplying 4 by Magnitudes of 10: Form 4A

This fact sheet is to be done before **4x 3-Digit Multiplication Form 4A**.

Name _____
Date _____
Day _____

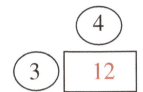

× Fact

4 × 3 = _____
   x 10

4 × 30 = _____
   x 100

4 × 300 = _____

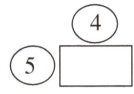

× Fact

4 × ___ = _____
   x 10

4 × ___ = _____
   x 100

4 × ___ = _____

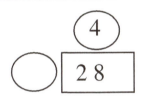

× Fact

4 × ___ = _____
   x 10

4 × ___ = _____
   x 100

4 × ___ = _____

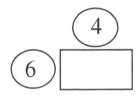

× Fact

4 × ___ = _____
   x 10

___ = _____
   x 100

___ = _____

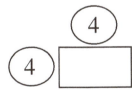

× Fact

4 × ___ = _____
   x 10

___ = _____
   x 100

___ = _____

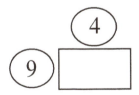

× Fact

4 × ___ = _____
   x 10

___ = _____
   x 100

___ = _____

© 2013 C. Woodin & Landmark School

4 x 3-Digit Multiplication: Form 4A

Name
Date
Day

Facts

3 × 4 ☐   4 × 4 ☐   5 × 4 ☐   6 × 4 ☐   7 × 4 ☐   9 × 4 ☐

Standard Algorithm

5 | 3 | 2
× | | 4

→ **Expanded Notation**

5 0 0
  3 0
+   2
─────
5 3 2

Tabular Array Diagram

④

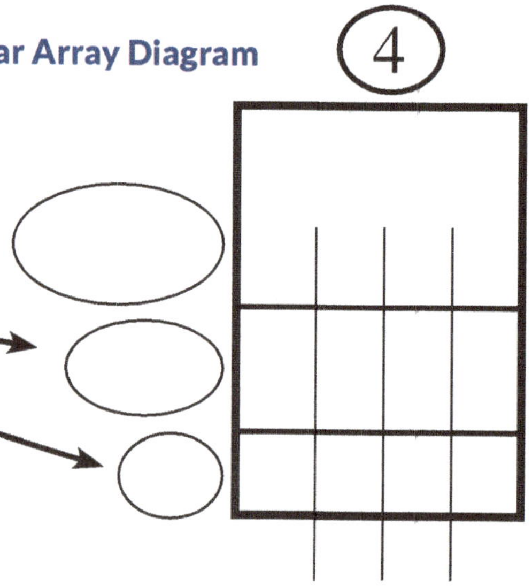

Add these partial products.

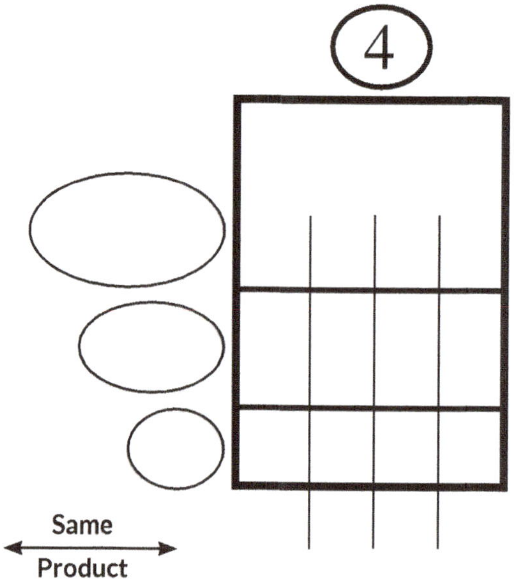

6 | 4 | 3
× | | 4

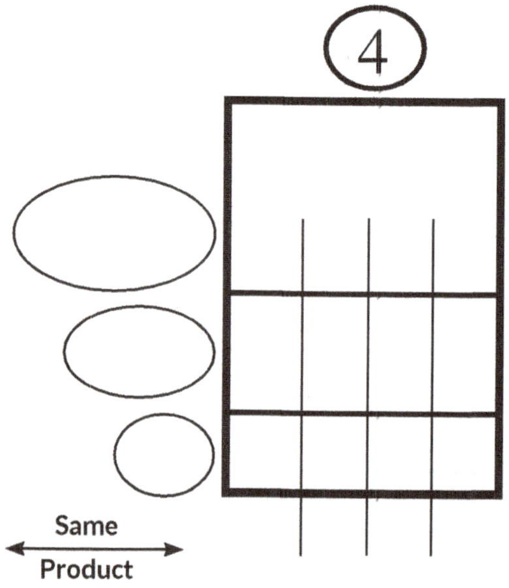

④

← Same Product →

9 | 2 | 7
× | | 4

④

← Same Product →

328 © 2013 C. Woodin & Landmark School

Multiplying 4 by Magnitudes of 10: Form 4B

This fact sheet is to be done before 4x 3-Digit **Multiplication** Form **4B**.

Name _____
Date _____
Day _____

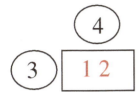

× **Fact**

4 × 3 = _____
   x 10

4 × 30 = _____
   x 100

4 × 300 = _____

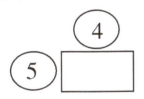

× **Fact**

4 × 5 = _____
   x 10

4 × ___ = _____
   x 100

4 × ___ = _____

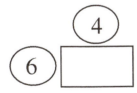

× **Fact**

4 × 6 = _____
   x 10

4 × ___ = _____
   x 100

___ = _____

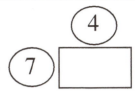

× **Fact**

4 × 7 = _____
   x 10

5 × ___ = _____
   x 100

5 × ___ = _____

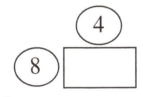

× **Fact**

4 × ___ = _____
   x 10

___ = _____
   x 100

___ = _____

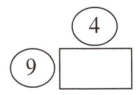

× **Fact**

4 × ___ = _____
   x 10

___ = _____
   x 100

___ = _____

© 2013 C. Woodin & Landmark School

4 x 3-Digit Multiplication: Form 4B

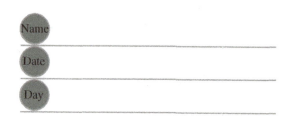

Facts

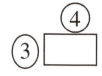 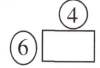 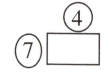 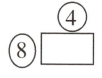 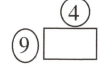

Standard Algorithm

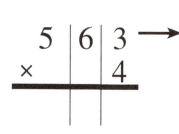

Tabular Array Diagram

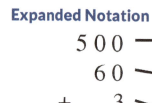

Expanded Notation

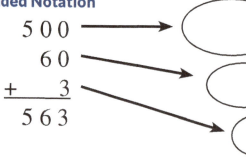

Add these partial products.

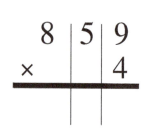

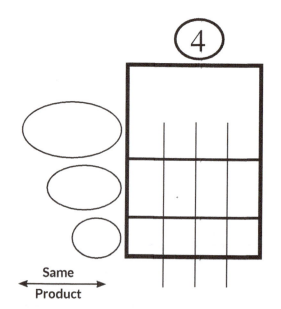

Same Product

The 7× Fact Family

Create Composite Facts From Combinations of Learned Facts

Certain numbers have multiples that do not present a readily discernible pattern to exploit in the pursuit of fact learning. The 7× fact family is an example of a fact family without a practical divisibility rule. Seven, however, is the sum of 5 and 2. Stick out seven fingers—five fingers from one hand as well as two fingers from the other.

At this point in the fact learning process, students should have a robust understanding of the 2× and 5× fact families. The distributive property of multiplication will be used to generate the 7× facts from these well-developed pools of factual information. Once the 7× facts are generated through some simple computation, students must rehearse them in their entirety to commit them to auditory memory. Though nine of the ten 7× facts have been rehearsed within the context of learning the previous fact families, it is useful to understand this application of the distributive property.

There are only two unfamiliar facts—or rather, two forms of the same fact—to be learned that students have not recited through the process of learning the previous fact families: 7 × 8 = 56 and 8 × 7 = 56. The (insidious) last fact may be presented by using an interesting visual device specific to this fact.

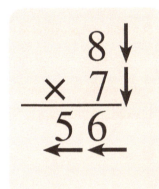

Writing the fact in its vertical presentation reveals the digits 8, 7, 6, and 5 in descending order when viewed from the top to the bottom left. Not very scientific, but it's the last fact, so have fun with it!

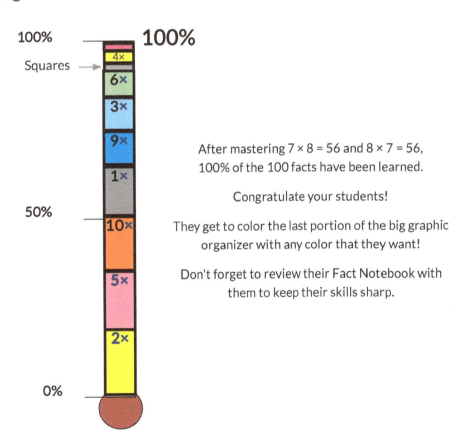

Gain the last 2 facts after learning 7× 8 = 56!

After mastering 7 × 8 = 56 and 8 × 7 = 56, 100% of the 100 facts have been learned.

Congratulate your students!

They get to color the last portion of the big graphic organizer with any color that they want!

Don't forget to review their Fact Notebook with them to keep their skills sharp.

Composite 7× Multiplication and Division Facts

Use the distributive property to create the 7× facts with a composite matrix diagram, as you did with the 4× facts.

This model uses vertical addition of the subproducts to help students with working memory constraints. Both the horizontal method (following) involving parentheses or this vertical matrix model work in a similar way, though one will probably best meet the needs of an individual student. Try one method, if it works well, there is no need to introduce the other.

Here, the student will multiply 7 × 6 by breaking the 7 into the sum of two smaller numbers: 5 and 2.

EXAMPLE

Sometimes it is useful to use a familiar semantic-based example to illustrate this process.

To find the number of days in 6 weeks, multiply 6 × 7.

7-day weeks are a combination of weekdays and weekends.

Break each 7-day week into 5 weekdays and 2 weekend days: **7 = (5 + 2)**.

Compute 6 weeks of weekdays:	**5 × 6 = 30**
Compute 6 weeks of weekend days:	**2 × 6 = 12**
The sum will be the number of days in 6 weeks:	**7 × 6 = 42**

5 × 6 = 30 weekdays

2 × 6 = 12 weekend days

7 × 6 = 42 days in 6 weeks

Once the 7 has been broken into (5 + 2), use learned 2 × and 5 × facts to calculate the 7 × fact. Multiply the top factor, in this case 6 by 5 and 2 as shown in the composite matrix diagram.

Add these partial products to find 6 × 7 = 42.

Related 7 × Facts:

7 × 6 = 42

42 ÷ 7 = 6

6 × 7 = 42

42 ÷ 6 = 7

Show students how to construct the 7× facts by using the red margin line found on lined notebook paper to create their own template. 7 × 8 = 56 is shown.

This strategy can be used for any fact!

Composite 7× Multiplication and Division Facts

Create 7× facts using the distributive property, then write the related × and ÷ facts.

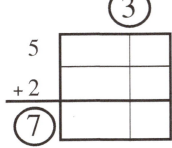

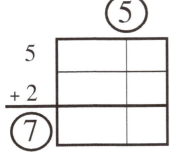

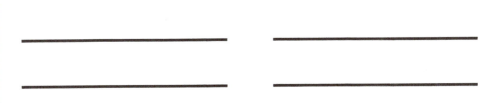

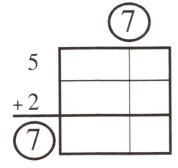

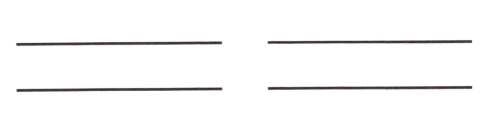

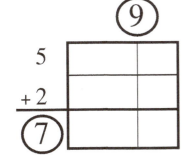

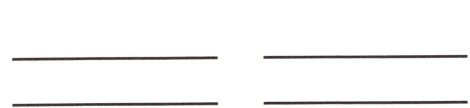

Composite 7× Multiplication and Division Facts

Create 7× facts using the Distributive Property, then write the related × and ÷ facts.

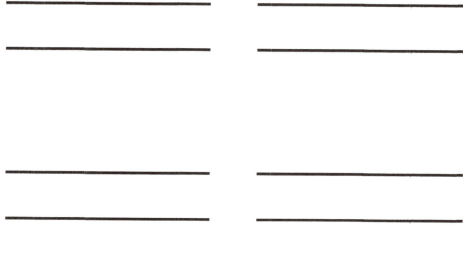

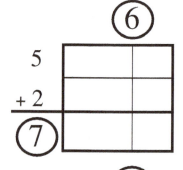

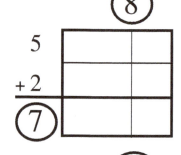

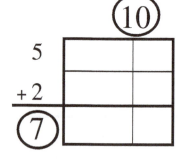

Composite 7x Multiplication and Division Facts

Name _____
Date _____
Day _____

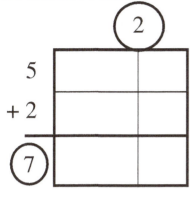

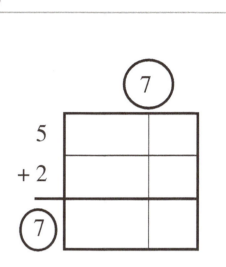

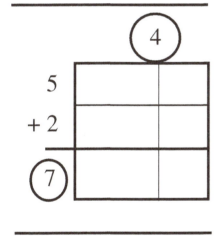

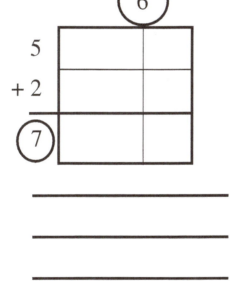

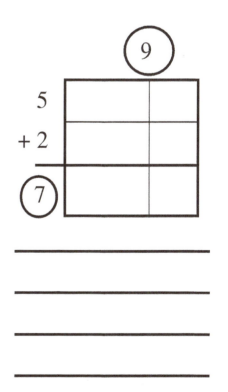

© 2013 C. Woodin & Landmark School   335

Multiplying by 7 Using the Distributive Property, Horizontally

As an alternative to the vertical composite diagram, you may choose to use a horizontal presentation. As before, explain to the students that they will learn how to multiply 5 × 7 by breaking the 7 into the sum of two smaller numbers: 7 = (5 + 2). For example, a 7 day week can be broken into 5 work days and 2 weekend days. If a man walks 4 miles every day for a week, the total could be found by multiplying 4 by 7 days: 4(7) = 28, or by splitting the week apart into weekdays and weekend days and distributing the factor 4 over both 5 and 2: 4(5+2)= 20 + 8 = 28.

Ask a student to extend 7 fingers. This usually results in the student extending five fingers from one hand and two from the other. The seven has been made by combining fingers on two hands.

Ask, "How did you make seven?"

The student should answer, "Five plus two is seven."

Once the 7 has been broken into (5 + 2), use familiar 2× and 5× facts to calculate the 7× fact.

For example, in the problem 4 × 7, multiply the left factor, in this case 4, by both 5 and 2 as indicated by the arrows below.

Add the two products e.g., 20 + 8 = 28, so 4 × 7 = 28.

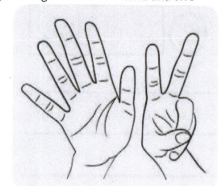

DIAGRAM

Write 7 × facts using the distributive property.

Complete the diagram, then write related × and ÷ facts.

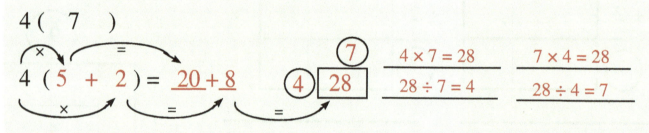

Multiplying by 7 Using the Distributive Property.

Rewrite 7 as (5 + 2), multiply the factor by each term, then add these products to calculate the 7× fact.

Complete the diagram, then write related × and ÷ facts.

2 (7)
2 (5 + 2) = _10_ + _4_

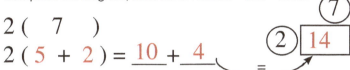

3 (7)
3 (+   ) = ___ + ___

4 (7)
4 (+   ) = ___ + ___

5 (7)
5 (+   ) = ___ + ___

6 (7)
6 (+   ) = ___ + ___

7 (7)
7 (+   ) = ___ + ___

8 (7)
8 (+   ) = ___ + ___

9 (7)
9 (+   ) = ___ + ___

10 (7)
10 (+   ) = ___ + ___

© 2013 C. Woodin & Landmark School

Bubbles!!

Use the distributive property to multiply by 7:

$2\times + 5\times = 7\times$

Blow some bubbles. Each bubble will be worth 7 points!

Find the 7× value by combining learned 5× and 2× facts:

Multiply each bubble by 2 points.

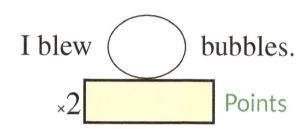

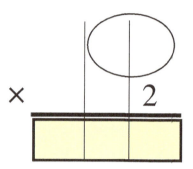

Now, multiply the same number of bubbles by 5 points.

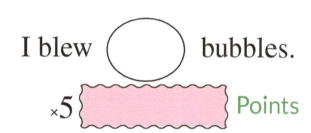

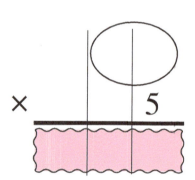

Add the two products to get a 7× point score.

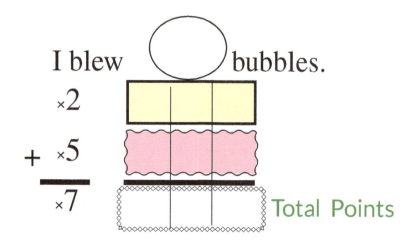

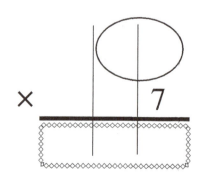

338   © 2013 C. Woodin & Landmark School

Ladder Charts: A Function of the Distributive Property and the Fibonacci Sequence

Once students understand the basic concepts of multiplication and the divisibility rules for 2×, 3×, 5×, 9×, and 10× facts, they can use a Ladder Chart to generate multiplication facts (Woodin 1995). Ladder Charts are a fast, accurate means to produce multiplication products, and they have the added benefit of self-checking mechanisms (students can employ divisibility rules for 2×, 3×, 5×, 9×, and 10× facts as they complete the chart). The Ladder Chart provides necessary structure to create facts, as well as a tabular format that provides easy access to the organized listing of the facts. Later, while studying long division, Ladder Charts will be used to generate multiples of divisors. These charts greatly facilitate the long division procedure because they provide accurate multiples of divisors, even if the divisors are multidigit numbers.

Using only the process of adding two numbers at a time, students create a chart that provides six of the nine multiples of a divisor that are usable in long division problems. The Ladder Charts shown provide six usable multiples of 5, 7, and 36, as well as ten times the divisor for checking purposes.

THREE COMPLETED LADDER CHARTS.

1	5	1	7	1	36
1	5	1	7	1	36
2	10	2	14	2	72
3	15	3	21	3	108
5	25	5	35	5	180
8	40	8	56	8	288
1	5	1	7	1	36
9	45	9	63	9	324
10	50	10	70	10	360

Initially, demonstrate the Ladder Chart with manipulatives on enlarged versions of the charts drawn on the board. Do not fill in the numbers in advance, instead, let them develop as you narrate (see below). Combine groups of one type of coin or other items that have a consistent number of parts (egg cartons, hands, six pack plastic rings) to illustrate multiplication as the process of adding a defined quantity to itself a specified number of times.

EXAMPLE

- Use nickels to demonstrate how the Ladder Chart works. Place enlarged photocopies of nickels as you speak.
- Say, "One nickel plus one nickel equals...." (Students respond: two nickels) Say, "One nickels is five cents." Write 5s next to the 1s in the chart. Say, "Five cents plus five cents equals..." (Ten cents).
- Next say, "One nickel plus two nickels equals..." (Three nickels). Say, "Five cents plus ten cents equals..." (Fifteen cents).

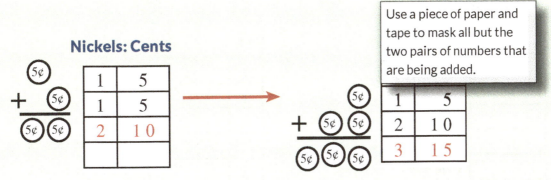

Continue the addition in the chart to produce a series of factors and related multiples inspired by the Fibonacci sequence.

When students are completing the chart, they may find it useful to use an index card to mask the upper numbers that are not being combined to produce the next multiple. Multiples are produced by adding the two previous factors' multiples.

EXAMPLE

Use an index card to mask all but the two pairs of numbers that are being added.

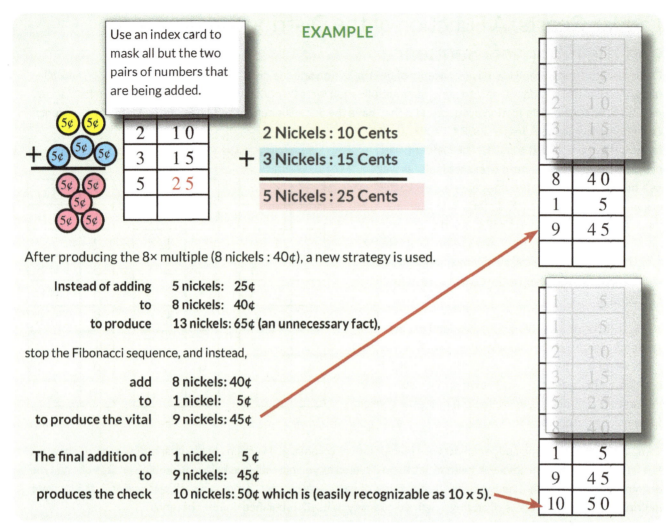

2 Nickels : 10 Cents
+ 3 Nickels : 15 Cents
_____
5 Nickels : 25 Cents

After producing the 8× multiple (8 nickels : 40¢), a new strategy is used.

Instead of adding	5 nickels:	25¢
to	8 nickels:	40¢
to produce	13 nickels:	65¢ (an unnecessary fact),

stop the Fibonacci sequence, and instead,

add	8 nickels:	40¢
to	1 nickel:	5¢
to produce the vital	9 nickels:	45¢

The final addition of	1 nickel:	5¢
to	9 nickels:	45¢
produces the check	10 nickels:	50¢ which is (easily recognizable as 10 x 5).

Ladder Charts have the added benefit of self-checking mechanisms, as the multiples of 2, 3, 5, 9, and 10 are readily checked by divisibility rules. Using these rules, students can check their addition five times on each chart.

When introducing Ladder Charts, do multiple examples of semantic-based Ladder Charts on the board, narrating the process, and using divisibility rules to check as you go. Go back to your reference banks to find examples of durable groups and their associated parts. The goal is for the students to understand how the chart is created.

EXAMPLES

Group name: Parts:
6-Packs   Cans

1	6
1	6
2	
3	
5	
8	
1	6
9	
10	

√ Ends with an even number.
√ Digits add to 3, 6, or 9
√ Ends with 5 or zero.
√ Ends with an even number.
√ 1 x the number.
√ Digits add to 9!
√ Original number with a "0". placeholder in the one's place.

Dozens: eggs

1	12
1	
2	
3	
5	
8	
1	
9	
10	

√ Ends with an even number.
√ Digits add to 3, 6, or 9
√ Ends with 5 or zero.
√ Ends with an even number.
√ 1 x the number.
√ Digits add to 9!
√ Original number with a "0". placeholder in the one's place.

The ladder chart offers a system for finding all multiples of the divisor that are necessary for long division. By using the multipliers of 1, 2, 3, 5, 8, and 9 and their accompanying products, students can add combinations of these facts to construct the missing facts. We call these "Step Ladders".

Although intially Ladder Charts and Step Ladders are provided to students, eventually they should create them on their own, using the red margin line on lined paper. When students begin to create their own Ladders it demonstrates that they have internalized the concept of the distributive property (to find 6 fourteens, one can combine 2 fourteens and 4 fourteens) and the utility behind this. This empowers the student to be self-reliant. After understanding and creating the established pattern of the Ladder Chart, they can fabricate targeted facts as needed.

1		7
1		7
2	1	4
3	2	1
5	3	5
8	5	6
1		7
9	6	3
10	7	0

2	1	4
2	1	4
4	2	8
6	4	2
10	7	0

4	2	8
3	2	1
7	4	9
10	7	0

EXAMPLE
A student wants to know 7 × 6.

A) Have the student write the incomplete fact (e.g., 7 × 6 = _____) to create a structure to draw from.

B) Have the student write a 7 to the left of the margin line, and above it, two numbers that have a sum of seven. Use familiar fact families when possible: Here use 2, and 5.

C) Above and to the right of the margin, write the other factor (e.g., ×6).

D) Fill in the known subproducts (5 × 6 = <u>30</u> and 2 × 6 = <u>12</u>.)

E) Add the subproducts.

A)
$7 \times 6 =$ _____

B)
5	
2	
7	

C)
$7 \times 6 =$ _____
	× 6
5	
2	
7	

D)
$7 \times 6 =$ _____
	× 6
5	30
2	12
E) | 7 | 42 |

After a student creates a fact from subproducts have them complete the intial fact they had written (Step A), then verbalize it in two forms (e.g, 7×6 = 42, then 42 ÷ 7 = 6).

Later, when introducing long division, initially create division problems with digits in their quotients that match the factors in a basic Ladder Chart. This allows students to focus on the process of long division, rather than expending mental energy on factors and multiples. Additionally, the multiples are more likely to be accurate due to the built in checks.

The Ladder Chart is usually accessible to students with poor fact-retrieval skills. Many of these students have learned to find products of divisors in a similar manner, by adding the divisor to itself a number of times. When you detect these multidigit addition problems in the margins of division problems, you have discovered a child who will benefit greatly from the use of Ladder Charts.

On following pages, students will practice 4× and 7× fact families with Ladder Charts. Again, the goal is for students eventually to create their own Ladder Charts, in the margin of their paper.

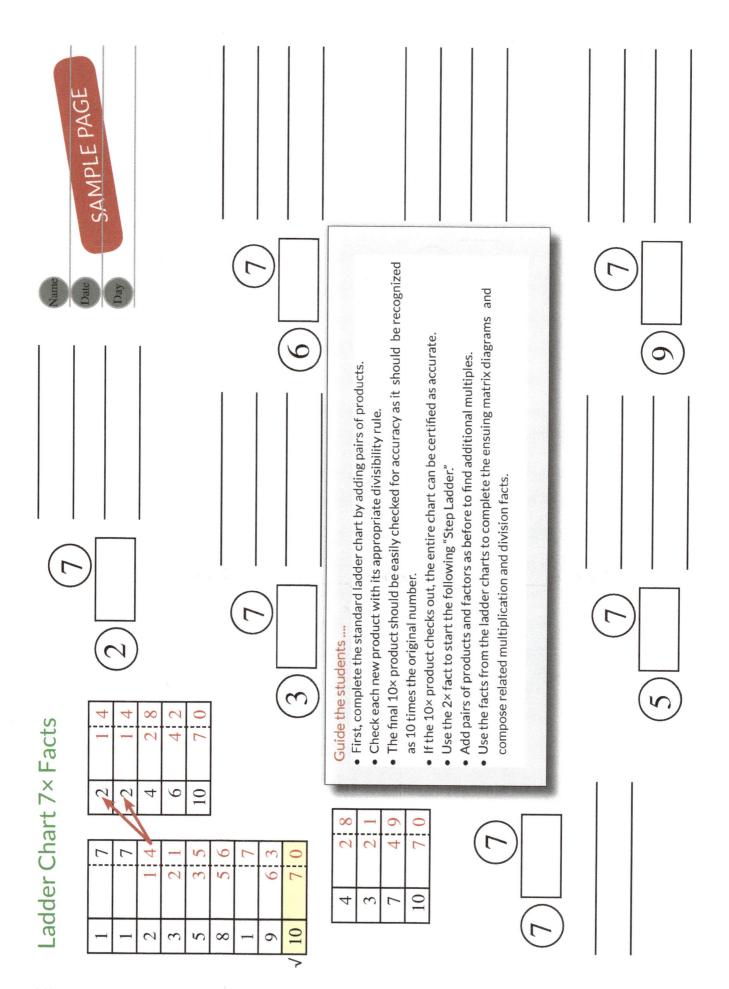

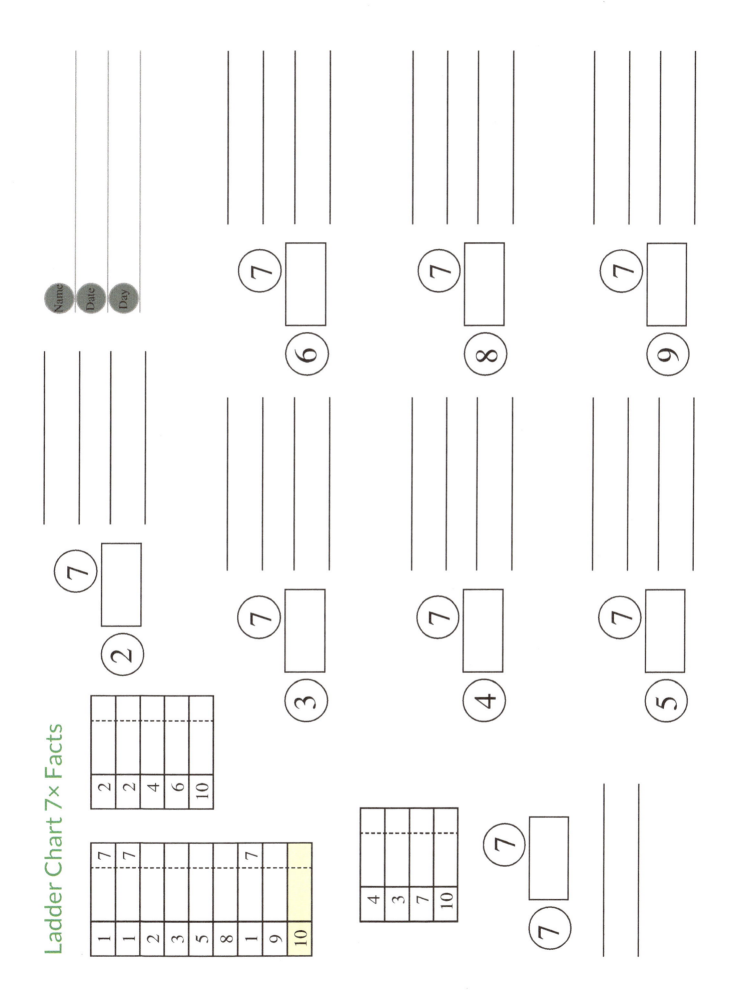

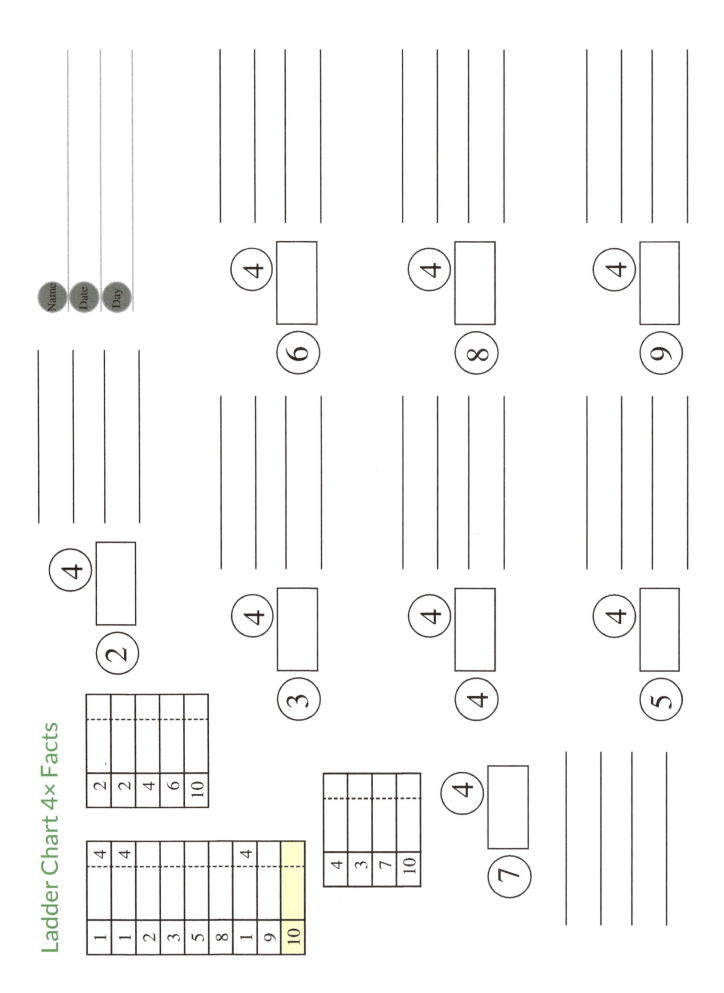

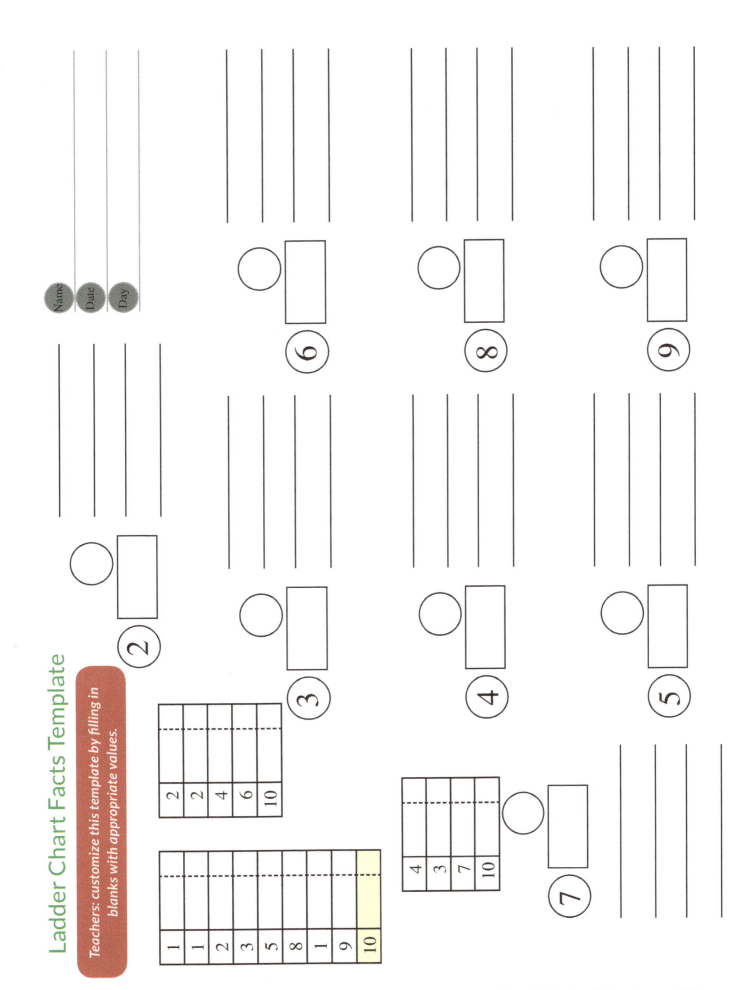

Accuracy Benchmark Pretest - Untimed

Name _____
Date _____
Day _____

Complete this sheet with 100% accuracy before taking the related timed **Fluency Assessment**.

1) Complete each diagram. Have them scored.
2) Correct diagrams if needed.
3) Write a multiplication fact and a division fact for each. and accuracy.
4) Archive this in your Fact Notebook as a record.

Diagram Accuracy: ____/10
Sentences Accuracy: ____/20

⑦|14| _____   ⑦|70| _____

⑦|35| _____   ⑦|63| _____

⑦|7| _____   ⑦|49| _____

⑦|21| _____   ⑦|28| _____

⑦|42| _____   ⑦|56| _____

Fluency Assessment - Timed

Administer this test after the student scores 100% accuracy on the related <u>Accuracy Benchmark Pretest.</u>

1) Complete each diagram. Note time and accuracy.
2) Correct diagrams as needed.
3) Write a multiplication fact and a division fact for each. Note time and accuracy. and accuracy.
4) Archive this in your Fact Notebook as a record. Retake it to improve.

Name _____
Date _____
Day _____

Diagram Accuracy: ____/10 Time: ____
Sentences Accuracy: ____/20 Time: ____

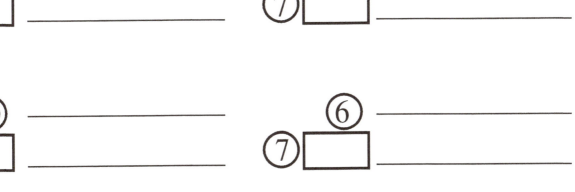
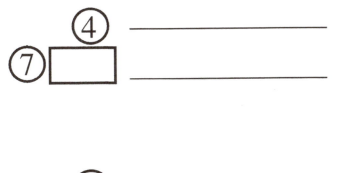
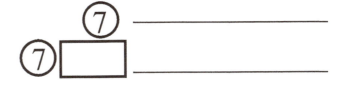

© 2013 C. Woodin & Landmark School

Fold-em Fact Practice Sheet

Fold the paper on the two dotted lines. Read each fact and then try to answer it. Open the fold to check each answer. If you were wrong, read the fact, then say a related multiplication or division fact using the same three numbers.
E.G., 2 x 6 = 12 so 6 x 2 = 12 or 12÷2 = 6.

For another challenge, look at the answer side of the paper fold. Try to predict the correct fact sentence from the product.
E.g., Look at the product 12. Try to predict the 2 x 6 on the other side of the fold.

2 x 6 =	12
3 x 6 =	18
4 x 6 =	24
5 x 6 =	30
6 x 6 =	36
7 x 6 =	42
8 x 6 =	48
9 x 6 =	54
10 x 6 =	60

10 x 7 =	70
9 x 7 =	63
8 x 7 =	56
7 x 7 =	49
6 x 7 =	42
5 x 7 =	35
4 x 7 =	28
3 x 7 =	21
2 x 7 =	14

Multiplying 7 by Magnitudes of 10: Form 7A

This fact sheet is to be done before **7x 3-Digit Multiplication Form 7A**.

Name _____
Date _____
Day _____

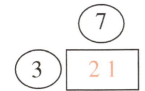

× Fact

7 × 3 = _____
　　　x 10

7 × 30 = _____
　　　x 100

7 × 300 = _____

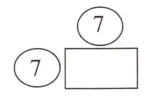

× Fact

7 × ____ = _____
　　　x 10

7 × ____ = _____
　　　x 100

7 × ____ = _____

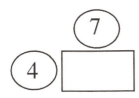

× Fact

7 × ____ = _____
　　　x 10

____ = _____
　　　x 100

____ = _____

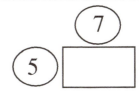

× Fact

7 × ____ = _____
　　　x 10

7 × ____ = _____
　　　x 100

7 × ____ = _____

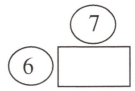

× Fact

7 × ____ = _____
　　　x 10

____ = _____
　　　x 100

____ = _____

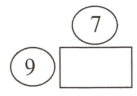

× Fact

7 × ____ = _____
　　　x 10

____ = _____
　　　x 100

____ = _____

7 x 3-Digit Multiplication: Form 7A

Name
Date
Day

Facts

③ × ⑦ □   ④ × ⑦ □   ⑤ × ⑦ □   ⑥ × ⑦ □   ⑦ × ⑦ □   ⑨ × ⑦ □

Standard Algorithm

Tabular Array Diagram

$$\begin{array}{r} 5\,3\,1 \\ \times 7 \\ \hline \end{array}$$

→ **Expanded Notation**

$$\begin{array}{r} 500 \\ 30 \\ +1 \\ \hline 531 \end{array}$$

Add these partial products.

$$\begin{array}{r} 6\,4\,3 \\ \times 7 \\ \hline \end{array}$$

←Same Product→

$$\begin{array}{r} 9\,5\,7 \\ \times 7 \\ \hline \end{array}$$

←Same Product→

350 © 2013 C. Woodin & Landmark School

Multiplying 7 by Magnitudes of 10: Form 7B

This fact sheet is to be done before **Multiplication Form 7B**.

Name _____
Date _____
Day _____

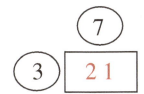

× **Fact**

7 × 3 = _____
         x 10

7 × 30 = _____
          x 100

7 × 300 = _____

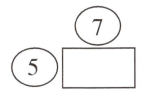

× **Fact**

7 × ___ = _____
          x 10

7 × ___ = _____
          x 100

7 × ___ = _____

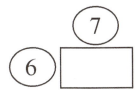

× **Fact**

7 × 6 = _____
         x 10

7 × ___ = _____
          x 100

= _____

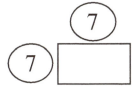

× **Fact**

7 × ___ = _____
          x 10

7 × ___ = _____
          x 100

7 × ___ = _____

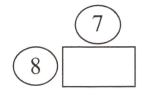

× **Fact**

7 × ___ = _____
          x 10

= _____
x 100

= _____

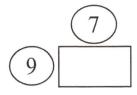

× **Fact**

7 × ___ = _____
          x 10

= _____
x 100

= _____

7 x 3-Digit Multiplication: Form 7B

Name

Date

Day

Facts

7	7	7	7	7	7
3 ☐	5 ☐	6 ☐	7 ☐	8 ☐	9 ☐

Standard Algorithm

$$\begin{array}{r} 5\,|\,6\,|\,3 \\ \times \quad\;\; 7 \\ \hline \end{array}$$

→ **Expanded Notation**

$$\begin{array}{r} 500 \\ 60 \\ +\;\; 3 \\ \hline 563 \end{array}$$

Tabular Array Diagram

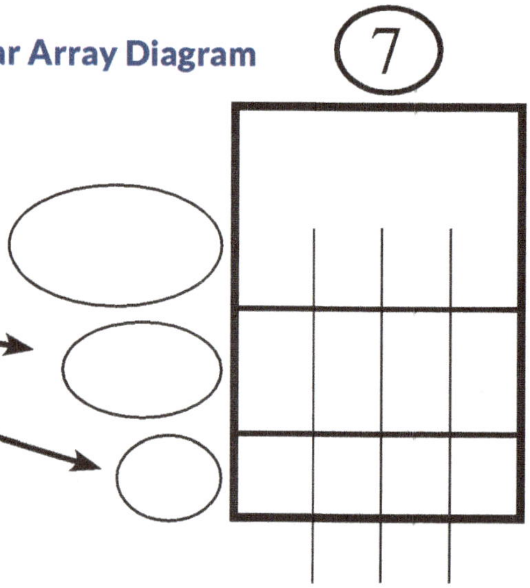

Add these partial products.

$$\begin{array}{r} 8\,|\,5\,|\,9 \\ \times \quad\;\; 7 \\ \hline \end{array}$$

Same ↔ Product

$$\begin{array}{r} 9\,|\,3\,|\,7 \\ \times \quad\;\; 7 \\ \hline \end{array}$$

Same ↔ Product

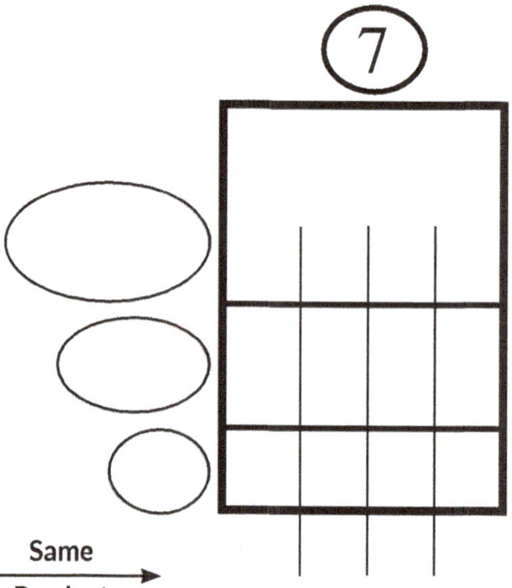

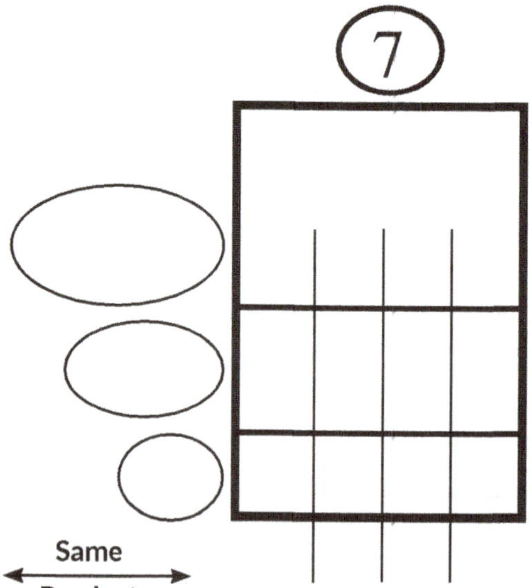

The 8× Fact Family

Review and Automatize the 8x Facts Through Rehearsal

Learning of the 8× facts as a group can be achieved through the rehearsal of the 8× facts as they were presented in the context of previously learned fact families. For example, the 2× facts were expressed multiple ways using the commutative property (2 × 8 = 16, 8 × 2 = 16), so the 8× facts within the 2× fact family have already been practiced. Students increase fluency through the use of the 8× facts within multidigit multiplication problems. Drill and practice with the flash cards from previously learned facts that have a factor of 8 will activate students' background knowledge and increase familiarity with these facts. The Fold 'Em Fact Practice Sheet also provides a way to review the 8× facts.

A composite flash card set follows, along with additional worksheets involving the expression of the 8× facts.

8× Facts: Cut out these previously learned flash cards on the dotted lines. Students should identify and name missing component of each diagram, then verbalize four related facts.

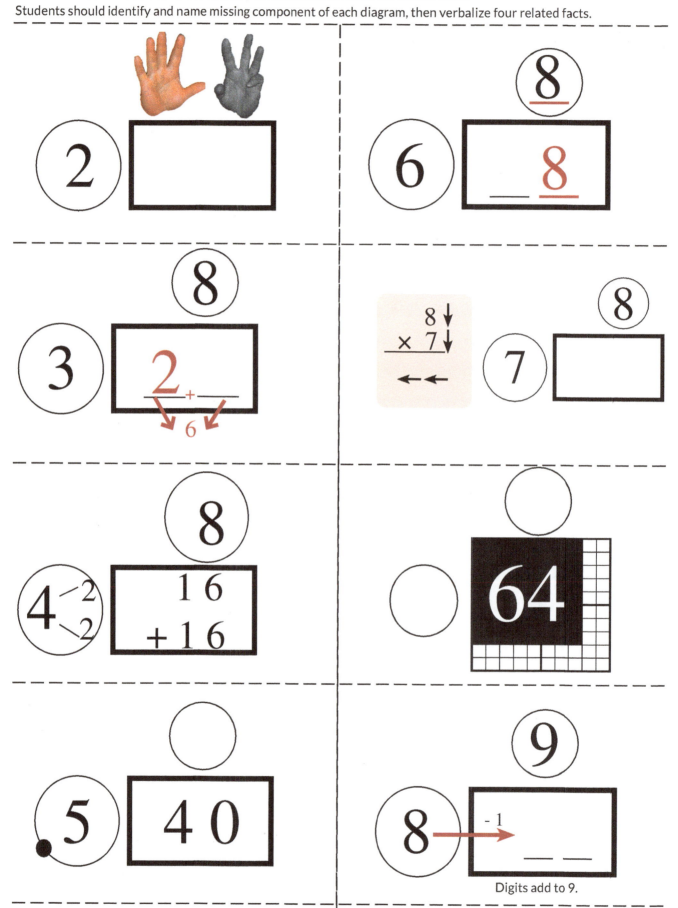

Digits add to 9.

Fold-em Fact Practice Sheet

Fold the paper on the two dotted lines. Read each fact and then try to answer it. Open the fold to check each answer. If you were wrong, read the fact, then say a related multiplication or division fact using the same three numbers. E.G., 2 x 8 = 16 so 8x2 =16 or 16÷2 =8.

For another challenge, look at the answer side of the paper fold. Try to predict the correct fact sentence from the product. E.g., Look at the product 16. Try to predict the 2 x 8 on the other side of the fold.

2 × 8 =	16	10 × 9 =	90
3 × 8 =	24	9 × 9 =	81
4 × 8 =	32	8 × 9 =	72
5 × 8 =	40	7 × 9 =	63
6 × 8 =	48	6 × 9 =	54
7 × 8 =	56	5 × 9 =	45
8 x 8 =	64	4 × 9 =	36
9 × 8 =	72	3 × 9 =	27
10 × 8 =	80	2 × 9 =	18

Fold here.

© 2013 C. Woodin & Landmark School

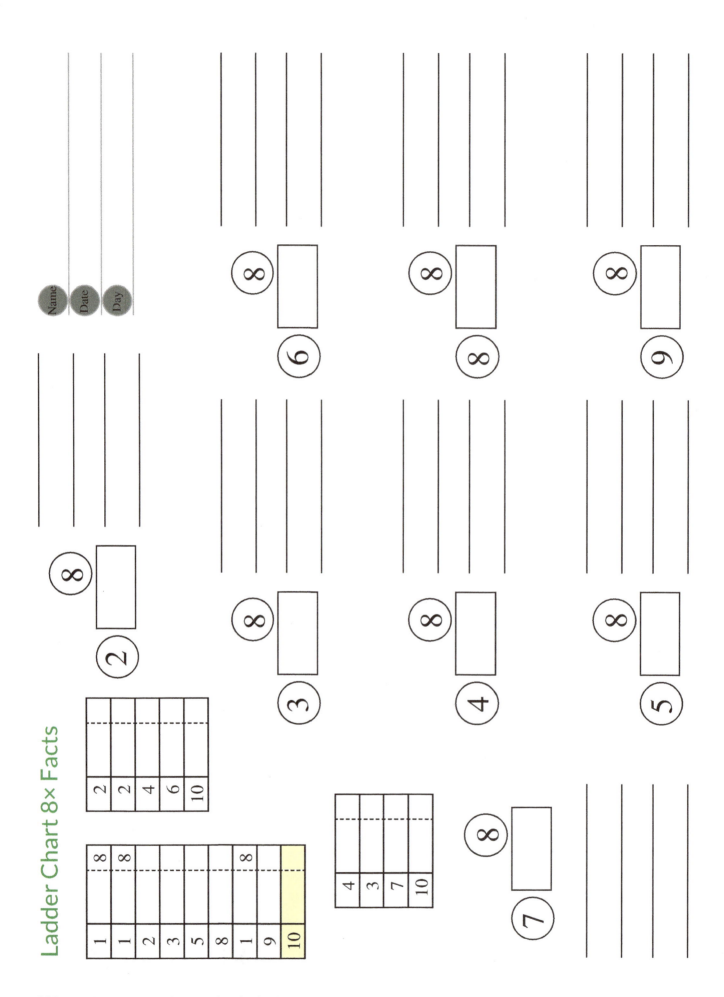

Accuracy Benchmark Pretest - Untimed

Complete this sheet with 100% accuracy before taking the related timed **Fluency Assessment**.

1) Complete each diagram. Have them scored.
2) Correct diagrams if needed.
3) Write a multiplication fact and a division fact for each.
4) Archive this in the students Fact Notebook as a record.

Diagram Accuracy: _____/10

Sentences Accuracy: _____/20

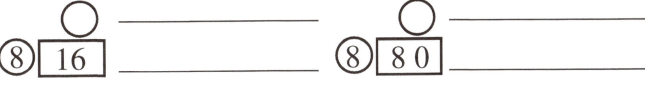

Fluency Assessment - Timed

Administer this test after the student scores 100% accuracy on the related **Accuracy Benchmark Pretest**.

1) Complete each diagram. Note time and accuracy.
2) Correct diagrams as needed.
3) Write a multiplication fact and a division fact for each. Note time and accuracy.
4) Archive this in your Fact Notebook as a record.

Name _____
Date _____
Day _____

Diagram Accuracy: _____/10 Time: _____
Sentences Accuracy: _____/20 Time: _____

⑧ × ① = ____ _____

⑧ × ⑤ = ____ _____

⑧ × ⑨ = ____ _____

⑧ × ② = ____ _____

⑧ × ⑩ = ____ _____

⑧ × ⑥ = ____ _____

⑧ × ④ = ____ _____

⑧ × ⑦ = ____ _____

⑧ × ⑧ = ____ _____

⑧ × ③ = ____ _____

© 2013 C. Woodin & Landmark School

Multiplying 8 by Magnitudes of 10: Form 8A

 Name
 Date
 Day

This fact sheet is to be done before **Multiplication Form 8A**.

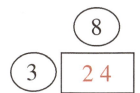

× **Fact**

7 x 8 = _____
    x 10

7 x 80 = _____
    x 100

7 x 800 = _____

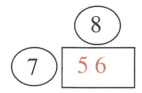

× **Fact**

7 x _____ = _____
    x 10

7 x _____ = _____
    x 100

7 x _____ = _____

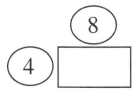

× **Fact**

7 x _____ = _____
    x 10

    = _____
    x 100

    = _____

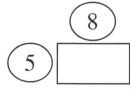

× **Fact**

7 x _____ = _____
    x 10

7 x _____ = _____
    x 100

7 x _____ = _____

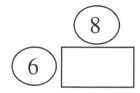

× **Fact**

7 x _____ = _____
    x 10

    = _____
    x 100

    = _____

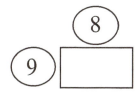

× **Fact**

7 x _____ = _____
    x 10

    = _____
    x 100

    = _____

© 2013 C. Woodin & Landmark School

8 x 3-Digit Multiplication: Form 8A

Name
Date
Day

Facts

3 × 8 ☐   4 × 8 ☐   5 × 8 ☐   6 × 8 ☐   7 × 8 ☐   9 × 8 ☐

Standard Algorithm

   5 | 3 | 2
 × | | 8

Expanded Notation

  5 0 0
     3 0
 +   2
  5 3 2

Tabular Array Diagram

⑧

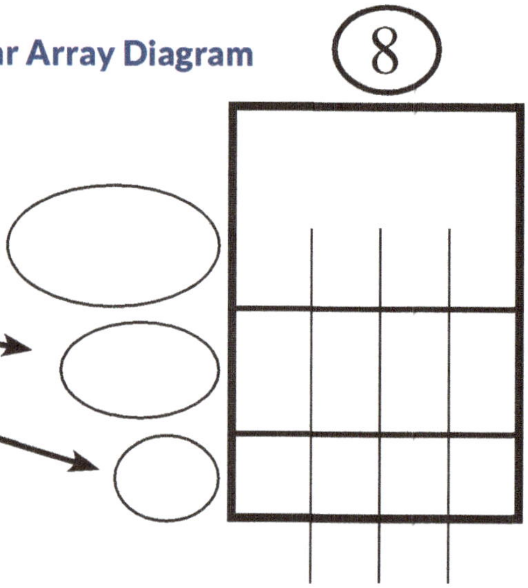

Add these partial products.

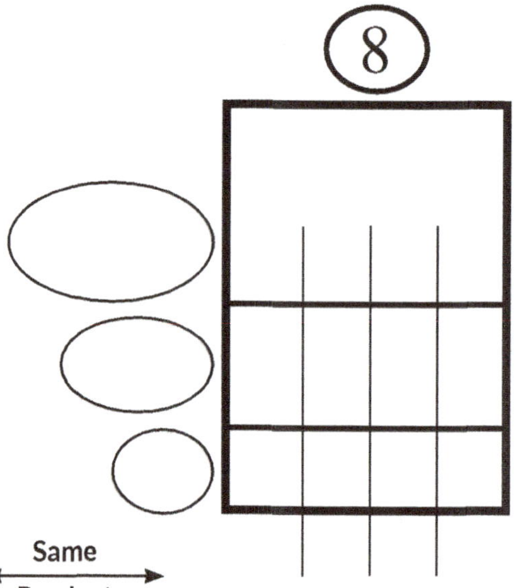

   6 | 4 | 3
 × | | 8

Same Product

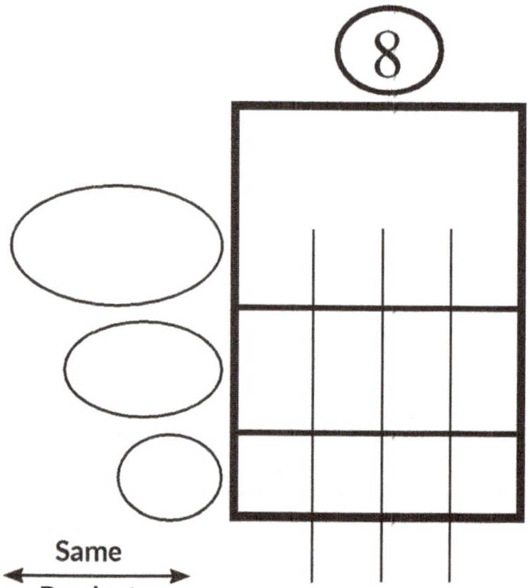

⑧

   9 | 2 | 7
 × | | 8

Same Product

⑧

360   © 2013 C. Woodin & Landmark School

Multiplying 8 by Magnitudes of 10: Form 8B

This fact sheet is to be done before **Multiplication Form 8B**.

Name
Date
Day

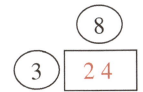

× **Fact**

$8 \times 3 =$ _____
　　x 10

$8 \times 30 =$ _____
　　x 100

$8 \times 300 =$ _____

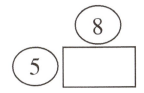

× **Fact**

$8 \times$ _____ =
　　x 10

$8 \times$ _____ =
　　x 100

$8 \times$ _____ =

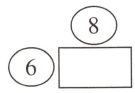

× **Fact**

$8 \times 6 =$ _____
　　x 10

$8 \times$ _____ =
　　x 100

_____ =

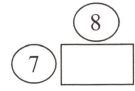

× **Fact**

$8 \times$ _____ =
　　x 10

$8 \times$ _____ =
　　x 100

$8 \times$ _____ =

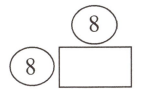

× **Fact**

$8 \times$ _____ =
　　x 10

_____ =
　　x 100

_____ =

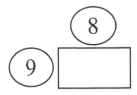

× **Fact**

$8 \times$ _____ =
　　x 10

_____ =
　　x 100

_____ =

8 x 3-Digit Multiplication Form 8B

Name
Date
Day

Facts

③ × ⑧ ☐   ⑤ × ⑧ ☐   ⑥ × ⑧ ☐   ⑦ × ⑧ ☐   ⑧ × ⑧ ☐   ⑨ × ⑧ ☐

Standard Algorithm

Tabular Array Diagram

5 | 6 | 3   →   **Expanded Notation**
×   8

500 →
 60 →
+   3
───
563

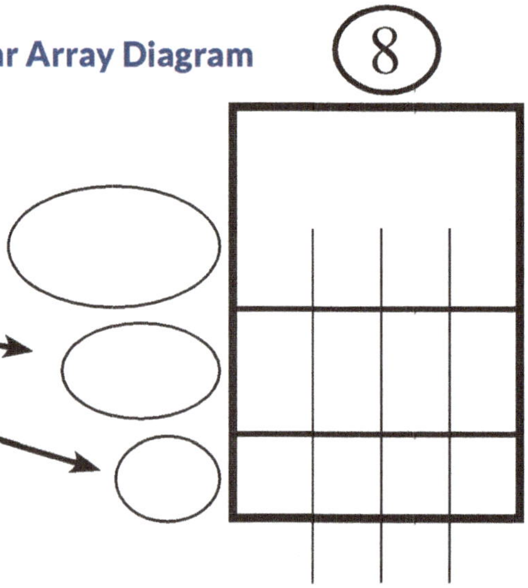

Add these partial products.

8 | 5 | 9
×   8

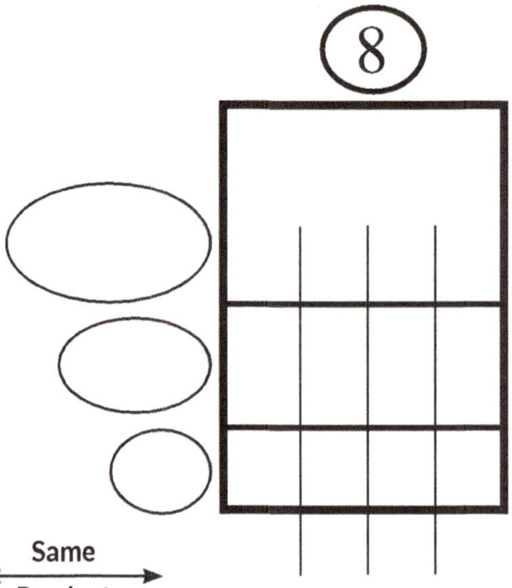

← Same Product →

9 | 3 | 7
×   8

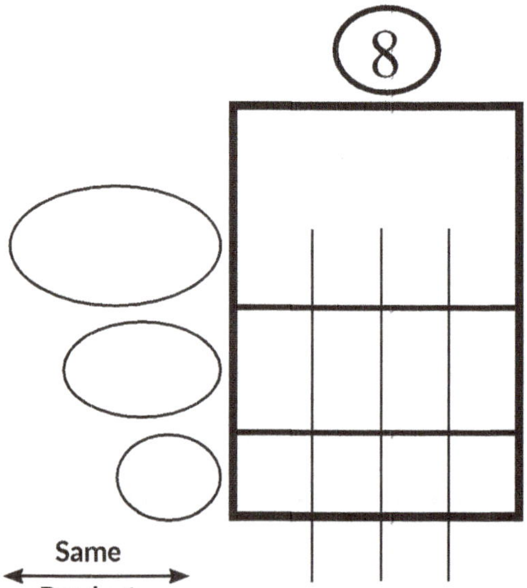

← Same Product →

362   © 2013 C. Woodin & Landmark School

The 11× and 12× Facts

TEACHING THE 11× FACTS
Gain 21 more easy facts after learning the 11x facts.

- This is an easy fact family to learn when the facts are presented whole to part. The missing factor is the same as either the ones or the tens digit in the product!
- Using the 11x flash cards, ask students to verbalize the facts in multiplication, as well as division formats.

$$\begin{aligned} 2 \times 11: \\ 2 \times 1 \text{ ten} &= 2\;0 \\ + \;2 \times 1 \text{ one} &= \underline{2} \\ &\;2\;2 \end{aligned}$$

TEACHING THE 12× FACTS
Gain some more useful facts after learning the seven most useful 12x facts..

- This is an important fact family to learn because 12s are associated with several common contexts. Time, linear measurement and common packaging units involve 12s.
- Look at the 12x flash cards to explore some 12x facts that people encounter on a daily basis.
- Using the 12x flash cards, ask students to verbalize the facts in multiplication, as well as division format.

EXAMPLES

- TWO FEET: 24 INCHES ("2 × 12 = 24").
- 1 YARDSTICK = THREE FEET : 36 INCHES ("3 × 12 = 36").
- FOUR FEET: 48 INCHES ("4 × 12 = 48").
- A CLOCK FACE SHOWS 12 GROUPS OF 5 MINUTES= 1 HOUR: 60 MINUTES.
- A SIX FOOT TALL PERSON IS 72 INCHES TALL.
- LUMBER, LIKE A COMMON "TWO BY FOUR" IS 8 FEET OR 96 INCHES LONG.
- ONE GROSS IS A BUNDLE OF 12 PACKAGES OF 12. THERE ARE 144 ITEMS IN A GROSS.

Pattern-Driven 11× Facts

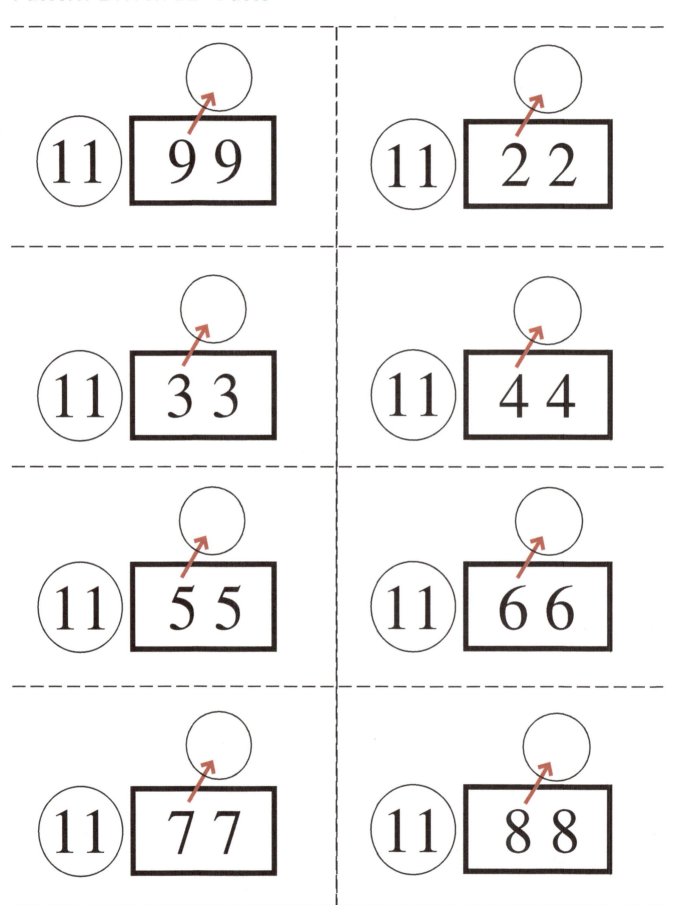

Semantic 12 x Facts

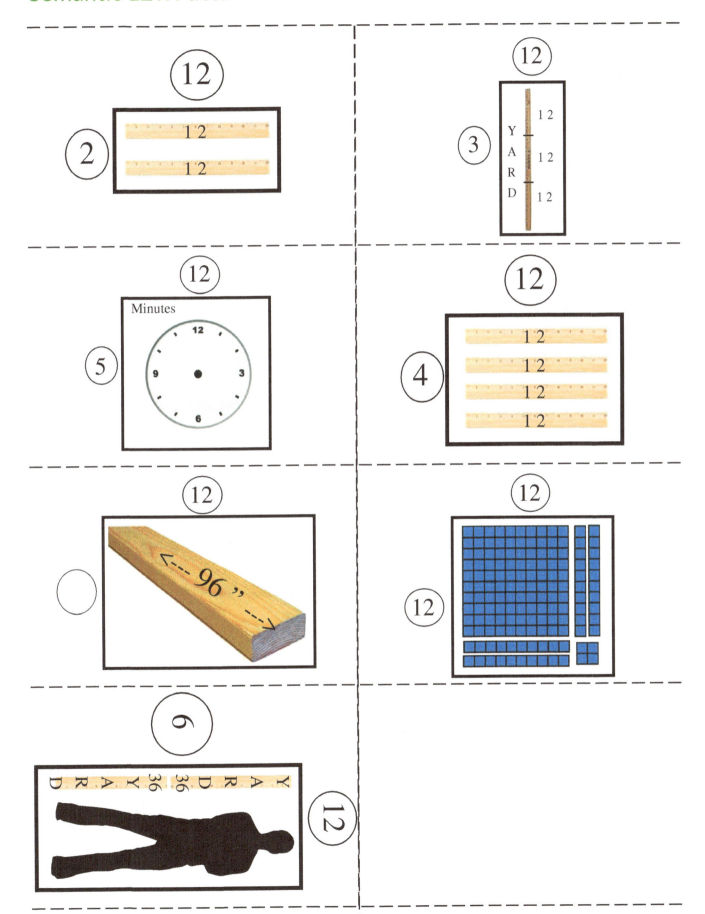

APPENDIX 1 : TEMPLATES FOR MULTIDIGIT MULTIPLICATION

Two-Digit × Two-Digit Multiplication: Composite Area Models

As with the semiconcrete area model, the tabular array should be set up so that the number in the bottom position of the multiplication problem represents the width (horizontal dimension) of the array. This will allow the vertically aligned subproducts of the tablular array to match the subproducts in the standard algorithm.

Start with one-centimeter grids with an area of 12 units × 13 units, such as the one on the following page.

Follow these steps to demonstrate how to complete each composite area model:

1) Using a red pencil, complete the right side of the area model:
The area model should be constructed so that the bottom number of the standard multiplication problem corresponds to the horizontal axis of the area model.

For example, 12 is the bottom number in the problem, so the diagram should be twelve units wide.

2) Total those subproducts (20 + 6 = 26).

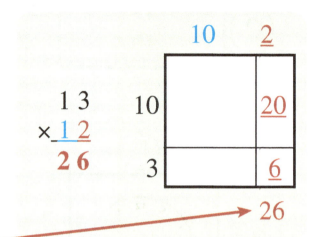

3) Now, trace the 2 with a red pencil (the ones portion of the number 12) in the standard multiplication problem.
Perform the 2 × 13 portion of the problem. The product should match the red part of the area model.

4) Put down the red pencil, pick up a blue one, and complete the left side of the area model (10 × 13).

5) Total those subproducts from the area model (100+30 = 130).

6) Perform the 10 x 13 portion of the standard problem.
The product should match the blue part of the area model.
Start by referencing the 10 × 3 portion of the area model—mention that it is 10 × 3, not 1 × 3.

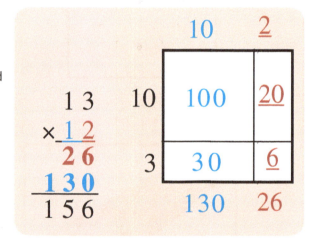

*After the place values involved with this initial blue step have been acknowledged, complete the procedural portion without reference to place values.

Too much verbalizing of relative place value labels within the procedure beyond fact expression can overwhelm students who have auditory-processing limitations. After the procedure is finished, compare the procedure-driven product with the corresponding portions of the area model. Compare the values of the digits in the procedure-driven subproducts with comparable partial products of the area model.

7) Add the red and blue subproducts to find the final product.

It is very productive to practice the standard algorithm and area model using gross motor processing. Have students hop on the successive production steps of a large complete problem while classmates identify the corresponding area on a large twelve-foot by thirteen-foot area model.

* See a movie of this process located on the Landmark School math website:
www.landmarkschool.org/resources/woodinmath.)

Two-Digit x Two-Digit Multiplication Problems

Facts

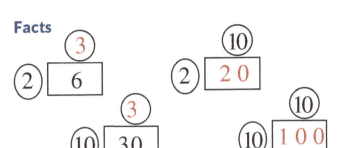

Estimate: _10 × 10 = 100_

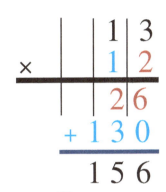

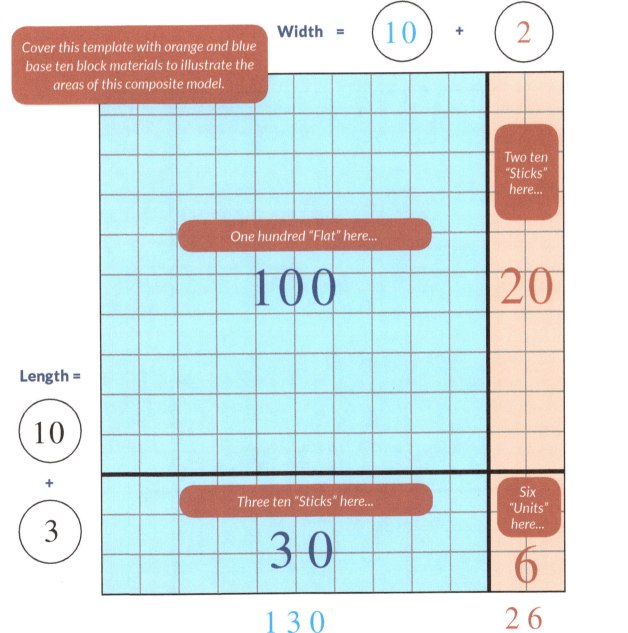

Two-Digit x Two-Digit Multiplication Problems

Facts

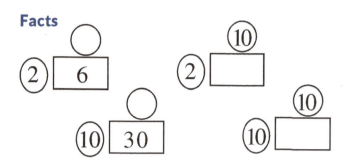

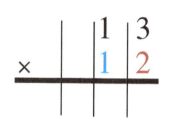

Estimate: $10 \times 10 = 100$

Width = ◯ + ◯

Length = ◯ + ◯

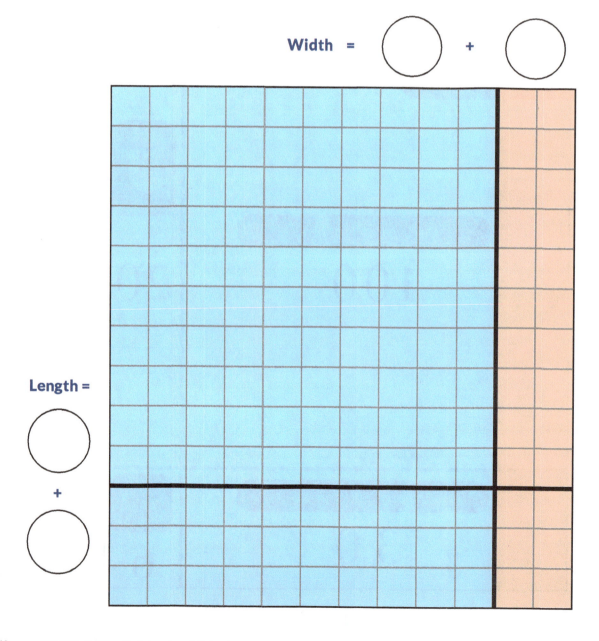

Two-Digit x Two-Digit Multiplication Problems

Name _____
Date _____
Day _____

Facts

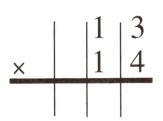

Estimate: _____

Width = ◯ + ◯

Length =
◯
+
◯

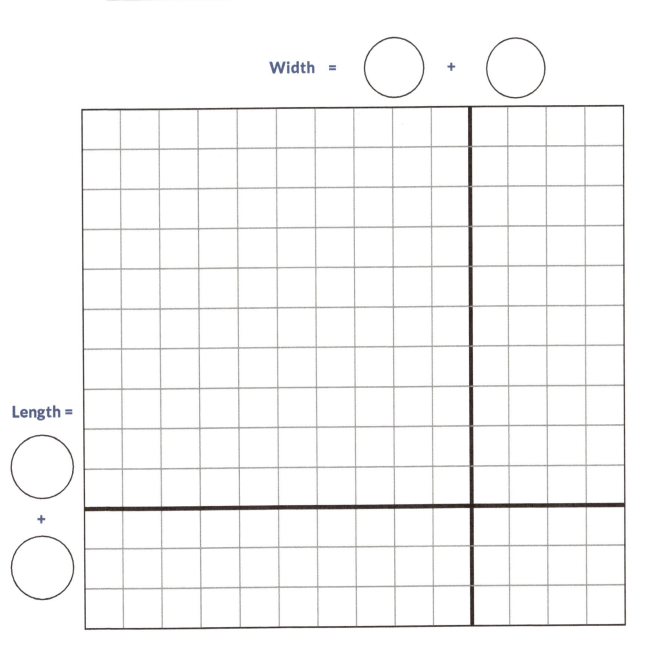

© 2013 C. Woodin & Landmark School   369

Two-Digit x Two-Digit Multiplication Problems

Name _____
Date _____
Day _____

Facts

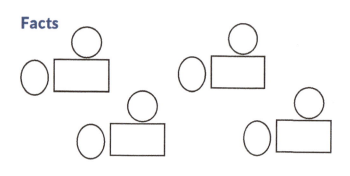

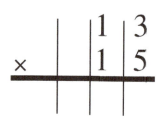

Estimate: _____

Width = ◯ + ◯

Length =
◯
+
◯

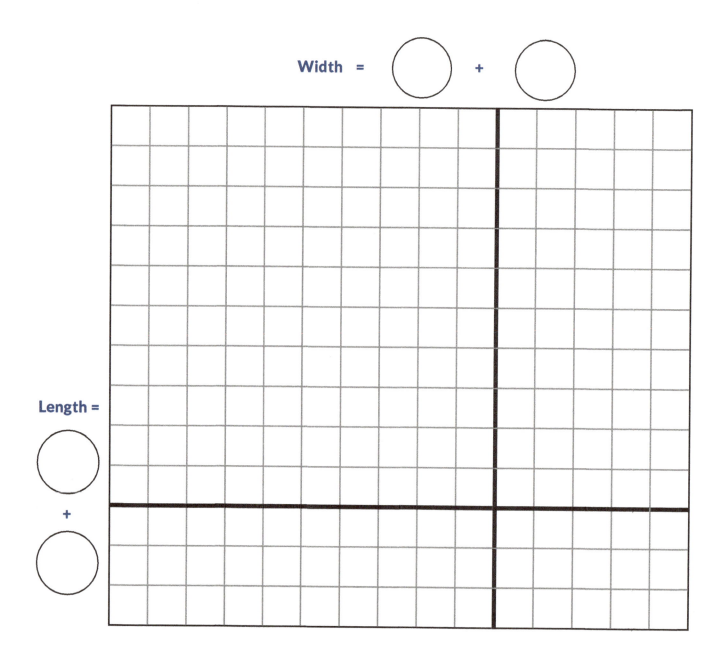

Two-Digit x Two-Digit Multiplication Problems

Name _____
Date _____
Day _____

Facts

$$\begin{array}{r} \,1\,|\,4 \\ \times\,1\,|\,2 \\ \hline \end{array}$$

Estimate: _____

Width = ◯ + ◯

Length = ◯
+
◯

© 2013 C. Woodin & Landmark School

Two-Digit × Two-Digit Problems Using Tabular Arrays

After students gain some proficiency with the semiconcrete two-digit by two-digit area-model activities, it is time to introduce the tabular array. True area models become too large to be practical. That's why base-ten models shift to the thousands cube rather than using a plastic tile that is a square meter!

The tabular array model is used in a manner similar to the base-ten-block area model described earlier, except that the diagram takes a more abstract form that is not proportional to the product. Though less didactic spatially, this model allows for the multiplication of larger factors, while continuing to afford the student a self-correcting mechanism of a secondary product and the opportunity to explore the place value inherent to larger numbers.

Tabular arrays are completed the same way as the red and blue composite area models.

As with the semiconcrete area model, the tabular array should be set up so that the number in the bottom position of the multiplication problem represents the width (horizontal dimension) of the array. This will allow the vertically aligned subproducts of the tablular array to match the subproducts in the standard algorithm.

Follow these steps to demonstrate the completion of tabular arrays:

- First, using a red pencil, fill in the red (right) portions of the diagram (tabular array), and then add them to establish the first subproduct.
- Next, use the red pencil to complete the first row (subproduct) of the problem in the standard algorithm.
- Then, compare the two products. Both red subproducts should be identical.
- After that, use a blue pencil to complete the left side of the tabular array, and then add the column of blue quantities.
- The second row (subproduct) of the standard algorithm should be identical to the blue sum from the tabular array.
- Finally, if both the red and blue pairs of subproducts check out, add them within the format of the standard algorithm to find the product of 43 x 29. It should be similar to the up-front estimate of 40 x 30 = 1200.

Estimate: 40 x 30 = 1200

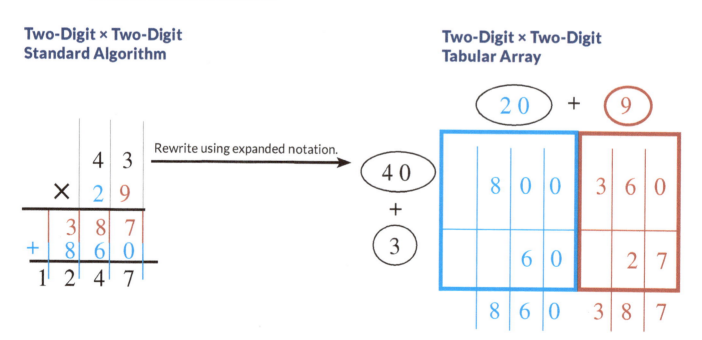

Two-Digit × Two-Digit Standard Algorithm

Two-Digit × Two-Digit Tabular Array

372   © 2013 C. Woodin & Landmark School

Multiplication and Tabular Arrays

2-Digit x 2-Digit Problems

× Facts:

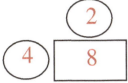

$4 \times 2 = 8$
$2 \times 4 = 8$

$3 \times 9 = 27$
$9 \times 3 = 27$

$4 \times 9 = 36$
$9 \times 4 = 36$

Two-Digit × Two-Digit Standard Algorithm

Two-Digit × Two-Digit Tabular Array

Estimate: $30 \times 40 = 1200$

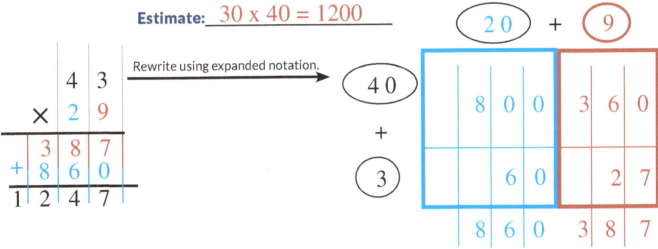

Estimate: $40 \times 30 = 1200$

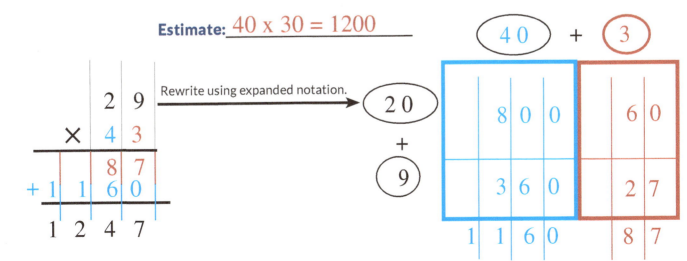

© 2013 C. Woodin & Landmark School 373

Multiplication and Tabular Arrays

2-Digit x 2-Digit Problems

Teachers: customize this template by filling in blanks with appropriate values.

Name
Date
Day

× **Facts:**

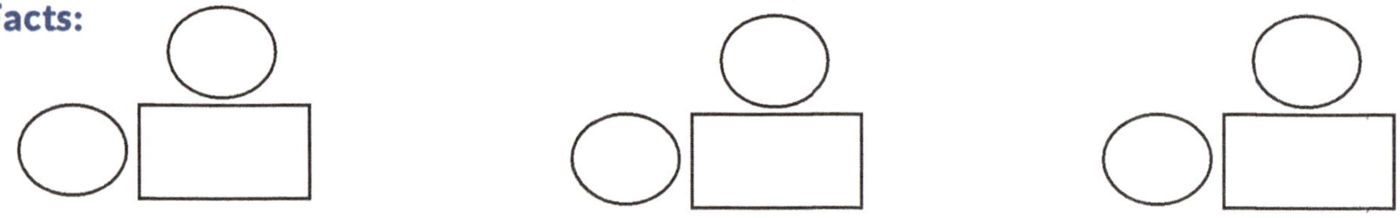

Two-Digit × Two-Digit Standard Algorithm

Estimate: _____

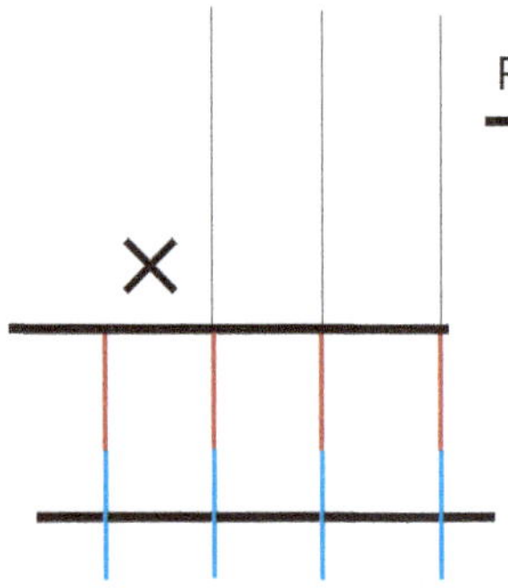

Rewrite using expanded notation.

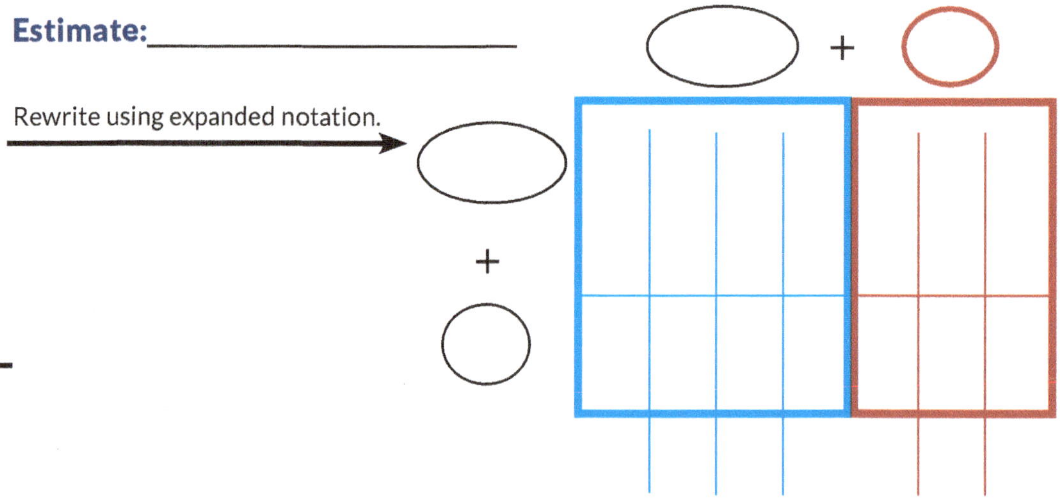

Estimate: _____

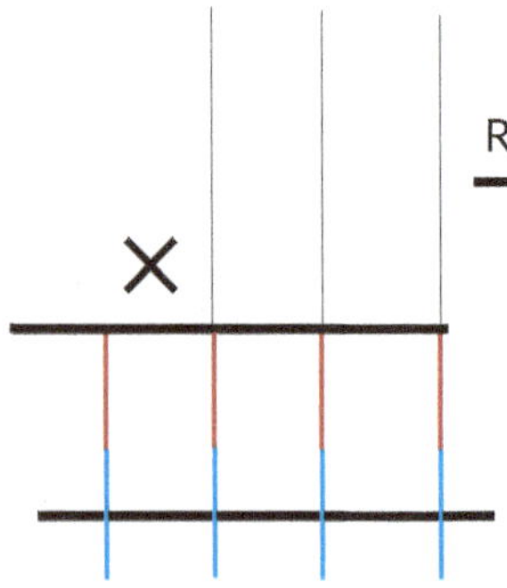

Rewrite using expanded notation.

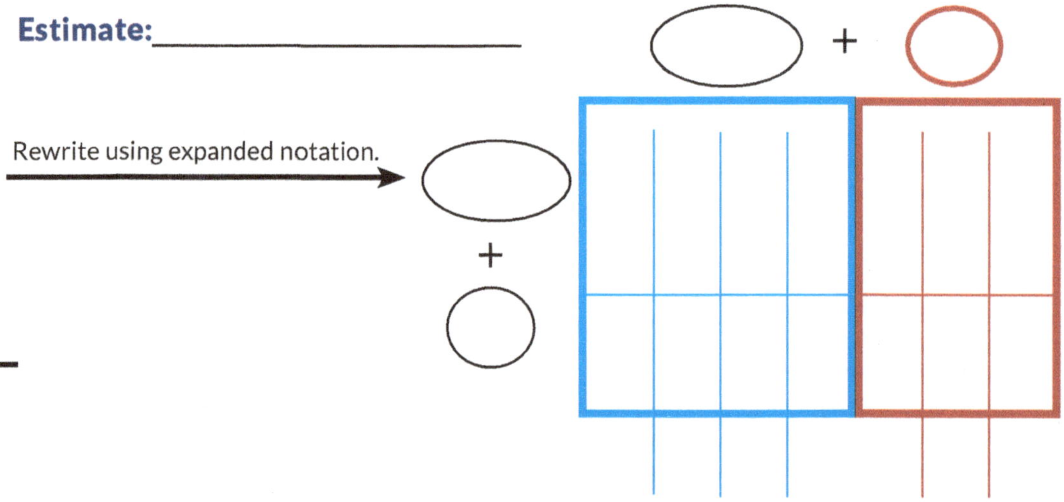

Two-Digit × Two-Digit Tabular Array

374   © 2013 C. Woodin & Landmark School

Two-Digit × Three-Digit Problems Using Tabular Arrays

In terms of the scope and sequence of curricula, it is rare to see tests that include any multiplication problems involving more than two-digit by three-digit multiplication. Two-digit by three-digit multiplication is supported by the tabular array format presented below. Follow these steps to demonstrate how to present the multidigit tabular array.

As with multidigit problems supported by area models or tabular arrays, the multiplication process should commence with an upfront estimate of the product, generated by multiplying the rounded leading digits of the problem.

For example, the problem below should be estimated as 500 × 10 = 5000.

To initiate the actual solution process, the red portion on the right side of the table should be completed and added before the same product is produced within the standard algorithm. After these two products are compared and found to be equivalent, students should complete the blue portion of the array. Then students multiply by the digit in the tens place in the standard algorithm, compare this product to the blue subproduct for accuracy, and add the red and blue subproducts to compute the final product. That final product should be compared to the upfront estimate.

Estimate: $500 \times 10 = 5000$

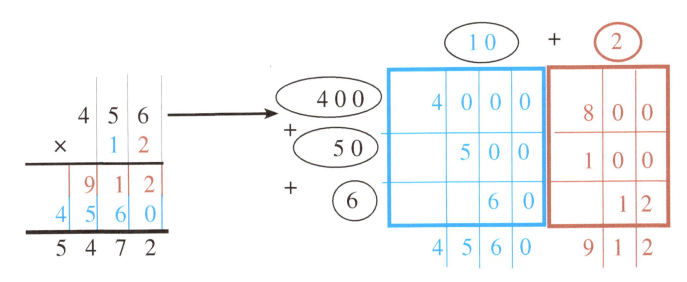

Multiplication and Place Value

2-Digit x 3-Digit Problems

Teachers: customize this template by filling in blanks with appropriate values.

Name
Date
Day

× Facts:

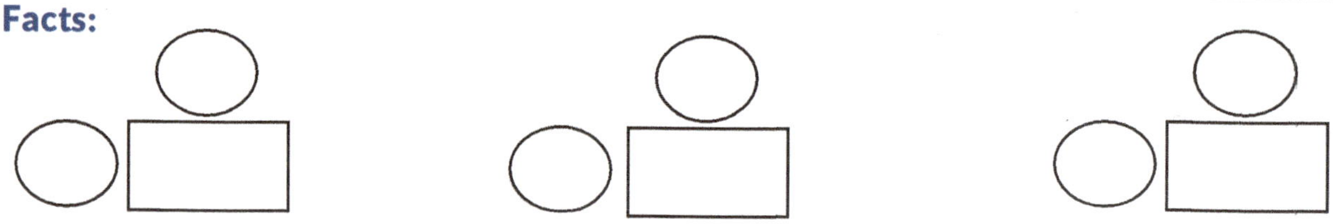

Estimate: _____

Rewrite using expanded notation.

2-Digit x 3-Digit Tabular Array

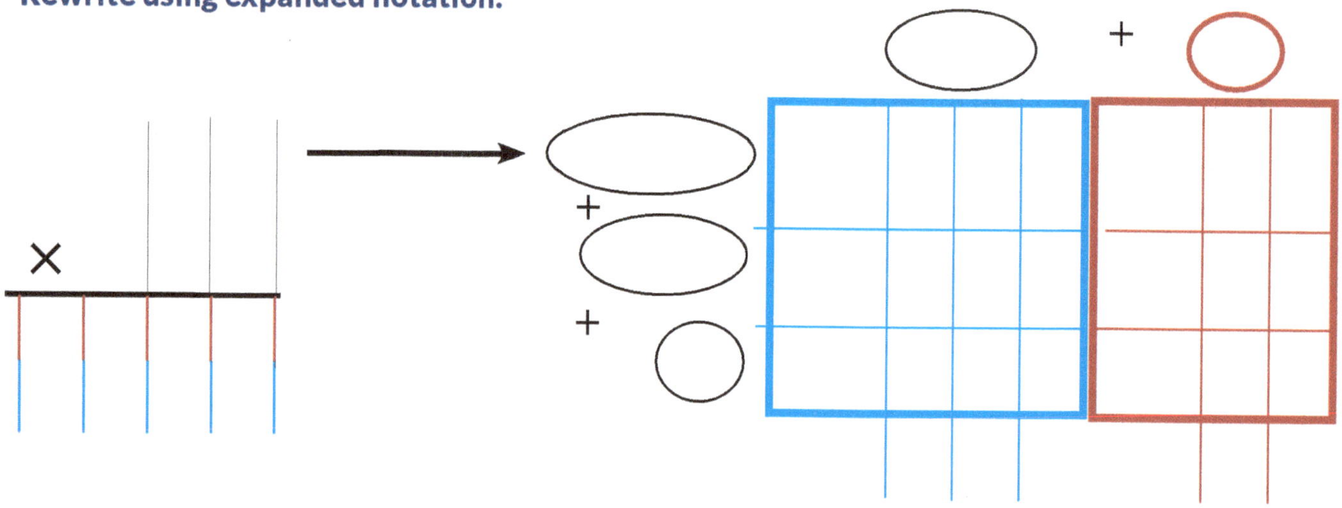

Estimate: _____

Rewrite using expanded notation.

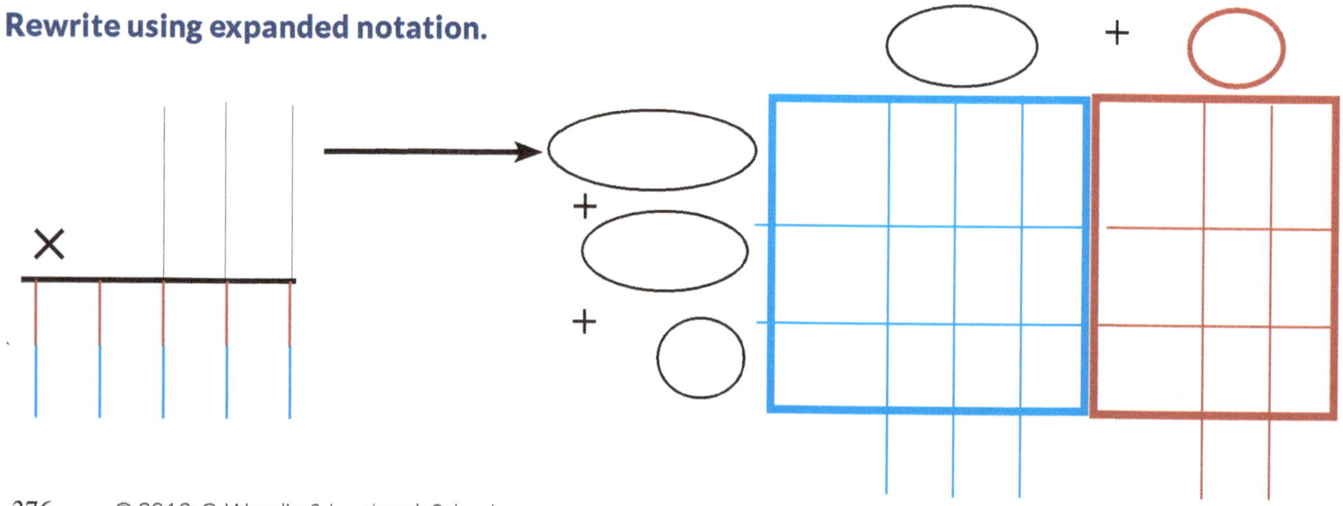

376 © 2013 C. Woodin & Landmark School

APPENDIX 2

Multiplication Grid (12 × 12)

×	1	2	③	4	5	6	7	8	9	10	11	12
1	1	2	3	4	5	6	7	8	9	10	11	12
②	2	4	6	8	10	12	14	16	18	20	22	24
3	3	6	9	12	15	18	21	24	27	30	33	36
4	4	8	12	16	20	24	28	32	36	40	44	48
5	5	10	15	20	25	30	35	40	45	50	55	60
6	6	12	18	24	30	36	42	48	54	60	66	72
7	7	14	21	28	35	42	49	56	63	70	77	84
8	8	16	24	32	40	48	56	64	72	80	88	96
9	9	18	27	36	45	54	63	72	81	90	99	108
10	10	20	30	40	50	60	70	80	90	100	110	120
11	11	22	33	44	55	66	77	88	99	110	121	132
12	12	24	36	48	60	72	84	96	108	120	132	144

© 2013 C. Woodin & Landmark School

APPENDIX 3

Instructional Video References with QR Codes

Finger-stamping 2x facts.mov:

http://www.youtube.com/watch?v=9IhjZXP44Is

Students stamp quantities of fingerprints two times to learn 2x facts within the context of base ten models.

Whole-To-Part 2x Facts and Related Word Problems:

http://www.youtube.com/watch?v=b7owGd6VpUY

Teach multiplication facts within the context of familiar whole-to-part images that drive the expression of 2x facts.

2x Multiplication Facts to Procedure

http://www.youtube.com/watch?v=MsyNRv4qSbk

Establish fact knowledge using multimodal instruction. Activate and facilitate fluent expression of these facts using kinesthetic processing of standardized graphic organizers. Apply these facts to a completed procedure using whole-to-part kinesthetic processing. Replicate the same procedure using pencil and paper.

Kinesthetic -Driven Story Problems

http://www.youtube.com/watch?v=jdoyAyRpFNQ

Use visual, semantic and kinesthetic processing to drive the production of multiplication and division story problems.

Kinesthetic 5x Facts

http://www.youtube.com/watch?v=kHZ4o1D4G3k

Teach the 5x multiplication facts using a clock as a graphic organizer with kinesthetic enrichment.

Baseball Fact Game

http://www.youtube.com/watch?v=TgIxEWPNoAc

Play this interactive baseball-inspired game to help develop fluency with multiplication and division facts.

Chris Woodin's Landmark School Math Website

http://www.landmarkschool.org/resources/woodinmath

© 2013 C. Woodin & Landmark School

References

Ayers, J. A. (2005). Sensory integration and the child: Understanding hidden sensory challenges.
Los Angeles, CA: Western Psychological Services.

Ayers, J. A. Improving academic scores through Sensory Integration.
Learning Disabilities 1972: 5: 338-343.

Bloomfield, L. and C. L. Barnhart. (1961). Let's read: A linguistic approach. Detroit, MI: Wayne State University Press.

Dehaene, Stanislas. (1997). The Number Sense: How the Mind Creates Mathematics.
New York, NY: Oxford University Press.

Fischer, B., Gebhardt, C., and Hartnegg, K.
Subitizing and Visual Counting in Children with Problems in Acquiring Basic Arithmetic Skills.
Optometry & Vision Development 2008: 39(1): 24-29.

Fischer, B., Köngeter, A., and Hartnegg, K.
Effects of Daily Practice on Subitizing, Visual Counting, and Basic Arithmetic Skills.
Optometry & Vision Development 2008: 39(1): 30-34.

Gfeller, K. E. Musical mnemonics for learning disabled children.
Teaching Exceptional Children. (1986): Fall, 28-30

Paivio, A. (2006). Mind and its evolution: A dual coding theoretical Interpretation.
Mahwah, NJ: Lawrence Erlbaum Associates, Inc.

VonGlasersfeld, Ernst.
Subitizing: The Role of Figural Patterns in the Development of Numerical Concepts.
Archives de Psychologie. 1982: 50, 191-218,.

Wender, Karl F. and Rothkegel, Rainer. Subitizing and Its Subprocesses.
Psychological Research 2000: 64: 81-92.

Williams, D. M. and Collins, B. C. Teaching multiplication facts to students with learning disabilities: teacher-selected versus student-selected material prompts within the delay procedure.
Journal of learning disabilities 1994: 27(9): 589-97.

Wolters, G., VanKempen, H., and Wijlhuizen, G. Quantification of Small Numbers of Dots: Subitizing or Pattern Recognition?
American Journal of Psychology, 1987: Vol. 100, No.2, 225-237.

Woodin, Christopher. (1995). The Landmark Method of Teaching Arithmetic.
Prides Crossing, MA: Landmark Publishing Co.

About the Author

Christopher Woodin is a specialist in the fields of mathematics and learning disabilities. A graduate of Middlebury College and Harvard Graduate School of Education, he has taught extensively at Landmark School in Massachusetts. At Landmark School, Elementary-Middle School Campus, he holds the Ammerman Chair of Mathematics. He is the author of The Landmark Method of Teaching Arithmetic (1995), in addition to several journal articles. He served on the Massachusetts Department of Education's Mathematics 2011 Curriculum Framework Panel and teaches graduate-level education courses. Christopher Woodin was the 1997 Massachusetts Learning Disabilities Association (LDA) Samuel Kirk Educator of the Year. He has presented at numerous international LDA and International Dyslexia Association (IDA) conferences and led math workshops to audiences across the country.

Multiplication and Division Facts for the Whole-to-Part, Visual Learner:

AN ACTIVITY-BASED GUIDE TO DEVELOP FLUENCY WITH MATH FACTS

Christopher L. Woodin, Ed. M.
2013

Students need multiplication facts to multiply and divide multidigit numbers and perform fraction operations. These facts need to be available in both multiplication and division format, and organized through a relational context so that they may be ordered and compared. Learn to provide students with a way to store, access, and express multiplication and division facts through multimodal activities that utilize visual and kinesthetic processing. The techniques presented support various learning styles and culminate in the ability to learn, compare, and express math facts in an accurate and fluent manner.

This program utilizes semantic reasoning strengths, and a combination of whole-to-part processing and gross motor kinesthetic therapies to compensate for deficits in working memory, expressive language mechanisms, and executive function. Multiplication concepts and facts are linked to the student's existing knowledge base across a broad spectrum of modalities. By establishing a strong conceptual base, students are able to learn, store, and retrieve facts accurately and efficiently apply them to solve problems. Graphic organizers provide a means to hold information in working memory long enough to formulate fact sentences. Gross motor activities provide students with the ability to interact with these graphic organizers without being constrained by fine motor written output issues. This program is helpful to all, and especially valuable to those students with language-based learning difficulties.

Updated materials and other resources are available online on the Landmark Outreach website at:

www.landmarkoutreach.org.

OUTREACH PUBLICATIONS

Outreach publications model evidence-based practical strategies that develop students' listening, speaking, reading, and writing skills. They provide the guidance and materials you need to enhance language-based instruction.

Join our mailing list and receive a FREE subscription to our e-resource, *Spotlight on Language-Based Teaching*! View archived issues on our website, www.landmarkoutreach.org.

While you're online, investigate our other books and booklets on language-based teaching. You can read about the authors and view sample pages of our materials.

Learn more!
Landmark Outreach Professional Development

Consulting
Summer Professional Development Institutes

WWW.LANDMARKOUTREACH.ORG